Celtic Minded 3

essays on religion, politics, society, identity . . . and football

JOSEPH M. BRADLEY

ARGYLL✠PUBLISHING

This edition first published in 2009

Previous editions in 2004, reprinted 2005;
2006

Argyll Publishing

Glendaruel

Argyll PA22 3AE

Scotland

www.argyllpublishing.com

**British Library Cataloguing-in-
Publication Data.**

**A catalogue record for this book is
available from
the British Library.**

ISBN 978 1 906134 32 7

Printing: Bell & Bain Ltd, Glasgow

ACKNOWLEDGEMENTS

The author would like to thank colleagues
and friends who have provided comments
on drafts, Ricky Fearon for providing the
memorabilia for the front cover and Bob
Lavery for his patience and kindness with
photographs. Chief thanks to the
contributors to this volume of essays who
have assisted greatly in making this series
possible. I hope that your analysis and
commentary provides knowledge and
understanding and in a small way helps
make Scotland a better place for all.

to the memory of
Tommy Burns
(1956 – 2008)

Contents

Celtic supporter and missionary priest Fr Martin Chambers of the Society of St James
working in a shanty town, Nueva Properina near Guayaquil in Ecuador in 2009,
with Celtic tops that were originally left at the temporary memorial shrine erected
by supporters at Celtic Park to Tommy Burns in the days after he died

Shirt worn by Celtic players in league match against Hibernian in May 2009,
a day earmarked as National Famine Memorial Day
amongst the Irish diaspora worldwide

(this page and over) Scenes from the life of Tommy Burns as a Celtic fan, player, manager and coach

The Great Irish Hunger, Celtic FC and Celtic Supporters

JOSEPH M BRADLEY

An Gorta Mor

One of Celtic's first and most significant of patrons, Michael Davitt, referred to the Great Hunger that devastated Ireland in the mid nineteenth century as 'the holocaust of humanity'. Professor Christine Kinealy states that the price paid by the Irish for the Famine was: 'privation, disease, emigration, mortality and an enduring legacy of disenchantment'.[1] Dr Douglas Hyde, later to become the first President of Ireland, concluded:

> The past is never dead. It's not even past. (William Faulkner)

> The Famine destroyed everything. Poetry, music and dancing stopped. Sport and pastimes disappeared. And when times improved, those things never returned as they were.[2]

It is in the history of the conquest, colonisation and plantation of Ireland that many of the explanations for, and consequences of, the Great Irish Hunger can be found. It is also in such processes that more contemporary events in Ireland and beyond (including in Scotland) find their roots.

Since the twelfth century Ireland had been increasingly subjugated by English and then, from 1603/1707, British occupation. All colonial relationships involve power struggles between dominated and dominator and in turn often by racism and prejudice. Such consequences characterised much of Britain's relationship with Ireland's indigenous population and over the centuries the Gaelic Catholic Irish lost their lands, their faith was

1 Kinealy, 1994, p.359
2 The Irish Post, 2/9/95

demeaned and punished and they faced the gradual erosion of the status of their culture, native identities and national independence. Those planted in Ireland from Britain, mainly Scots Protestants in the province of Ulster, were the Crown's favoured section of the population and to a greater or lesser extent varyingly profited from their colonial status. By 1685 British settlers had dispossessed the indigenous population of their holdings and acquired control of almost 80% of Irish land. During the eighteenth century some 1,500 absentee landlords owned 3.25 million acres of land in Ireland while they lived in London. A further 4.25 million acres of Irish land was in the hands of another 4,500 absentee landlords who chose Dublin as their home. A few years after the enforced union with Britain in 1800, only one in twenty of the Irish population were eligible to vote: Scotland had one in eight and England one in five. A series of prejudicial laws handicapped and disabled the development of industry in Ireland. One single example of this is pertinent. Wealthy native British and Ulster colonists dominated and controlled the rich linen industry of the northern half of Ireland. Gradually production became even more concentrated in the heavily colonised parts of Armagh, Tyrone and Antrim and in the process many small domestic weavers and spinners lost an important source of income. 'This forced them to depend even more on their small plots of land and, significantly, on potatoes'.[3]

In itself the potato was a very good source of food. Before the Great Hunger crops of potato in Ireland were amongst the highest in Europe, although in 1846 the potato represented only about 20% of total agricultural production in Ireland. The potato economy provided farmers with a cheap and well-fed workforce. For Kinealy however, the British perspective was that potato growing was increasingly associated with cultural backwardness and, 'when linked with "Papism", this proved to be a fatal combination'.[4]

Apart from decisive colonial explanations as the cause of the Great Famine, it is clear also that numerous other related reasons can be added. Nonetheless,

3 Kinealy, p.31

4 Ibid p.51

. . . nothing should be allowed to disguise the fact that a truly terrible tragedy occurred at the heart of the richest Empire in the world, and that much of this suffering resulted from ideological, political and commercial constraints, rather than the simple fact of a potato blight in Ireland.'[5]

Throughout the worst years of the Famine, landlords and British administrators continued to export Ireland's food. Between 10th October 1845 and 5th January 1846 alone, over 30,000 oxen, bulls and cows, over 30,000 sheep and lambs, and over 100,000 pigs left Ireland for Britain, as well as large quantities of wheat, barley and oats. The peasants who produced this abundance were unable to eat it: they had to turn it over to the landlords in payment of rent to avoid eviction. The British government refused to stop exports or to buy up and distribute the food.

A number of writers look to Britain's Free Trade Laws — essentially a process of not interfering with the supply or distribution of food — as being important to the deathly outcome of the Famine. From 1846 to 1849 grain exports increased from Britain to Europe. Not only therefore was this not used to feed the starving Irish, some of it actually originated in Ireland. In 1847 a New York newspaper noted that: 'arrivals of wheat from Ireland. . . during the last fortnight have been very considerable'.[6] At the end of 1846 goods arriving at Liverpool on at least one Irish ship from Sligo included 'pigs, calves, eggs, butter and. . . forty-seven bags of potatoes'.

One year later a Belfast-based newspaper reporting on aspects of the ensuing Famine focused on an inquest into the death of Thomas McManus:

> Both the legs, as far as the buttocks, appeared to be eaten off by the pig, is of the opinion his death was caused by hunger and cold. There was not a particle of food found in the deceased's stomach or intestines. Those who saw the body were of the opinion, from the agonised expression on McManus's countenance, that he was alive when the pig attacked him.[7]

Around the same time two Oxford students visited the Cork town of Skibbereen.

We have found every thing but too true; the accounts are not

5 Ibid p.15

6 Herald (New York) 5/7/1847

7 The Vindicator, 20/1/1847

exaggerated – they cannot be exaggerated – nothing more frightful can be conceived. The scenes we have witnessed during our short stay at Skibbereen, equal anything that has been recorded by history, or could be conceived by the imagination.[8]

In relation to starvation there is little doubt concerning the degree of suffering encountered when the human body consumes no food.

Every expenditure of energy is subservient to the greater need, to keep the brain going via the heart and liver. Metabolism is reduced, the body shuts down on unnecessary physical activity. This produces the familiar signs of lethargy. Apathy is not just a description, it is a recognised medical symptom of starvation. The onset of protein loss is quite quick. . . the guts atrophy, vital organs are reduced in size, vitamin deficiency increases, raising the apathy. Victims begins to lose any desire to move. Further, the skin stops repairing itself and immune responses are greatly weakened. Gradually, or sometimes suddenly, the human body dies.[9]

Another writer at the time of the Great Hunger in Ireland said:

A mother and some small children; the latter some of them quite naked, mere skeletons, but with that enlargement of the abdomen now so common amongst them. A thing of mere bone, of about two years old, lay on an old red petticoat, looking as near death as I could have wished it. I gave the woman a loaf of bread; in one moment she had torn a piece out of it and placed it in her own mouth; I was just about to point to her to give some to the children when, with a look I shall never forget, she placed her finger in her mouth, drew out the moistened bread and at once began to place it between the child's lips.[10]

In 1846 alone approximately 400,000 people died in Ireland, directly or indirectly from want of food. By July 1847 three million people were in receipt of free rations of soup to help keep them alive. Soup kitchens proved to be an inexpensive way to provide short-term direct relief during the Famine. They also proved that the British Government had the administrative and logistical capacity to carry out such relief: if it had the desire/ commitment to do so. However, the year after the soup kitchens closed relief was subsequently governed by the amended Poor Law. One Irish doctor described the developing scene as starving

8 From Kinealy, quoted in Patrick Hickey, 'The Famine in the Skibbereen Union' in Cathal Poirteir, The Great Irish Famine, Cork, 1995, pp.187-189.

9 Observer Sunday, 23/12/90, p.13.

10 Report of Select Committee appointd to enquire into the administration of the Poor Law in the Kilrush union since 19 September 1848 1850 [613] xi, p.xii.

in the midst of plenty, as literally as if dungeon bars separated them from the granary:

> . . . when distress has been at its height, and our poor have been dying of starvation in our streets, our corn has been going to a foreign market. It is, to our own poor, a forbidden fruit.

This might also be viewed as a comment on the distribution of food and other such resources in today's world: an earth of plenty amidst such decimation, destitution and starvation.

During the Famine suffering increased further in Ireland when tenants failed to pay their rents and landowners responded by turning the peasants out and opting to graze cattle on their farms. Troops and police evicted the destitute tenants who were unable to pay their rents whilst they demolished their houses. This is what happened to the family of Celtic patron Michael Davitt. Generally, crime rates – especially against property, but not against people – rose in Ireland as the Famine continued, as did the unhygienic living conditions of millions of poor.

Over time British Government responses were almost completely inadequate in combating the Famine. The repeal of the Corn Laws by Prime Minister Peel had no effect as it cut the price of imported food to Britain from Ireland. A scheme for public works by the government in 1846 got underway so that the destitute could earn money to buy food and survive. Corn, which Peel had bought from the USA, was stored in Ireland to help control prices. Key British official Charles Trevelyan was in charge of this and he decided to open government depots holding the corn. Very quickly the corn was finished as the starving peasantry took what they could almost immediately. Even where good will and effort to relieve the worst effects of famine occurred, incompetence in British officialdom was compounded by a growing capitalist economy driven by forces unmoved by, and disregarding of, the plight of the Irish peasant. Government representatives summed up some of the effects of the Famine stating that the starving people lived upon the carcasses of diseased cattle, upon dogs, and dead horses, but principally on the herbs of the field, nettle tops, wild mustard, and watercress: in some places dead bodies were found with grass in their mouths.

Starvation was followed by typhus, dysentery and scurvy. Panic-stricken by the spectre of famine and fever, tens of thousands rushed to emigrate: many took disease with them and thousands died on the often weeks-long journeys on so called 'coffin ships', others when they arrived at their destination or within a short time of arrival there. Some landlords took advantage of their tenant's desperation to clear them off the land, offering them a few shillings for their passage-money. Others frightened their tenants into leaving by threatening them with court action for non-payment of rent, so that thousands fled rather than risk imprisonment.

The potato blight affected numerous other countries, France, Holland, Belgium and Britain amongst them: in fact during 1845-46 the potato loss was higher in some of these other countries than it was in Ireland. However, most of the Government responses in these countries were shaped by changes to existing law, for example on the importation of foods, which meant that food shortages in those countries were much better managed. Generally, the failure of the potato did not result in social disaster because unlike Ireland, most countries were not exposed to such devastation caused by a downturn in potato production. In Ireland the blight took place in a different economic, social, cultural and political context: in other words, in a country essentially ruled from beyond its own shores.

International aid arrived to assist the desperately impoverished Irish. For example, some of the most successful fund-raising activities were carried out in the USA. From the Vatican Pope Pius sent financial aid and organised three days of prayers for Ireland while churches in Venezuala, Canada, South Africa and Australia organised collections. Numerous individuals and organisations arranged donations: in Britain assistance frequently cut across political and religious lines and aid on the part of the Quakers in Britain became amongst the most well known. The Choctaw Indians of North America who had endured their own suffering and marginalisation in 1831 when they were forced to walk from their homelands and re-settle in Oklahoma made a most remarkable donation. However, although welcome and life-saving in the short term, much of the aid diminished after the

In England such concepts as justice, liberty and objective truth are still believed in. They may be illusions, but they are very powerful illusions (George Orwell)

first few years of Famine: the British Government used the absence of potato blight for a short period to announce that the Famine was 'over' and this detrimentally affected donations.

In addition, as Irish paupers began arriving in Britain and North America and became a perceived threat to jobs, public health and as a burden on local taxation, this also affected donations. Overall during the Famine over one million pounds was raised privately for Ireland. The richest and most industrially advanced Empire in the world Great Britain, under whose jurisdiction Ireland fell, gave 'only' ten million pounds: most of which was issued as a loan and had to be repaid even as the Famine continued. This amounted to one half per cent of Britain's Gross National Product. Ten years before the same Government gave twenty-two million pounds compensation for the abolition of slavery. It was possibly with this in mind that the leader of the British parliamentary opposition said of his Government's failure to keep an accurate record of the number of deaths occurring.

> The time will come when we shall know what the amount of mortality has been, and though you may groan, and try to keep the truth down, it shall be known, and the time will come when the public and the world will be able to estimate, as its proper value, your management of the affairs of Ireland.[11]

Officially and permanently, between 1849 and 1854 approximately 250,000 persons were evicted – often with great cruelty – from their homes, to emigrate or to end up in dugout holes in the ground. The actual figure, including illegal evictions and 'voluntary' surrender of land, is almost certainly much greater. Between 1846 and 1851, at least one million died from a base population of over eight million people through starvation, disease and emigration. Around one million left Ireland, thousands dying en route. Over the following decades Ireland's population was halved from eight million, its pre-Famine total. The Famine made an impact all over Ireland although the poorer counties, particularly those in the south and west suffered the most: often in these counties whole families and communities were wiped out. Ireland's Lord Lieutenant of 1847, like a number of others, viewed as hopeful the disappearance of so many Catholics from Ireland, especially if they could be replaced with Protestant

Political language is designed to make lies sound truthful and murder respectable, and to give an appearance of solidity to pure wind (George Orwell)

11 Cormac O'Grady, Ireland Before and After the Famine, Manchester, 1993, p.104

settlers from Scotland and England. He stated that:

> The departure of thousands of papist Celts must be a blessing to the country they quit. [12]

The high population losses make the Irish Famine one of the most lethal in modern world history. Even 150 years later, Ireland has not recovered demographically from the consequences of the Famine, and within Europe, it is the only country to have a smaller population than it had in 1840.

Great is truth, but greater still, from a practical standpoint, is silence about truth (Aldous Huxley)

Celtic & The Great Hunger

In late 2009, the Museum of Religion in Glasgow held an exhibition that used the Great Irish Hunger as the context for its display. The following words formed part of a description connected to a set of paintings by famed artist Peter Howson.

> Between 1845 and 1850 one million people died in Ireland when the potato harvests failed. [13]

This description of the Great Irish Hunger as a 'potato famine' is characterised with ideological significance and understanding. Reporting on the exhibition, the Sunday Times in Scotland reinforced the Museum's view:

> The potato famine, which began in 1845, was caused by late blight, which destroyed crops. It led around 1.3m Irish people to emigrate to Scotland, England, Australia and North America. [14]

This kind of narrative can be viewed as consistent with how Britain has traditionally explained and represented Famine in mid-nineteenth century Ireland, and is problematic. Specifically, such a conceptually limited explanation and representation contributes towards the Great Hunger erroneously – even immorally – being constructed and viewed as a 'natural disaster'.

However, often even 'natural disasters' have more logical and human explanations. For example, one reason why so many poor die as a result of city located earthquakes can be due not so much to the tremor, but to the marginalised and unpopular areas they have been forced to live and the pitiable construction

12 Kinealy, p.146

13 See The Herald, 29/5/09, p.5

14 The Times (Scotland) 9/11/08, p. 5

of their crowded housing which easily collapses when such events occur. Many poor blacks lost their lives in the New Orleans floods of 2005 as a result of Hurricane Katrina. However, it is argued that the effects of the floods were exacerbated due to the absence of appropriate protection against such damage offered by authorities that in turn were accused of discriminating against this section of the population by not caring or responding quickly enough to the unfolding disaster.[15] While a single crop failure would be unlikely to incapacitate a modern capitalist country, the same might not hold for that of a Third World one. Thus financial security, access to resources, and the system of food distribution would all favour a rich as opposed to a poor country if such crisis occurred. Nevertheless, few of these eventualities happen by accident or 'nature': often the human contribution to a disaster can be decisive. The favoured or exposed condition of a country in dealing with disaster has long been predisposed by historical events and developments, including: colonised – coloniser; exploiter – exploited; defeated – victor in war; shorn of resources – a taker of the property and possessions of others. The list almost always involves degrees of power and powerlessness: elevating and favouring those with power and dehumanising and inferiorising those without.

In this light it is clear that describing the catastrophe that happened in Ireland in the mid-nineteenth century as a 'natural' disaster or 'potato famine' is amongst the most serious of deceptions.

It is clear that the Irish Famine did not take place in an economic, social, cultural and political vacuum. For example, two hundred and fifty years previously a proposal by the English Viceroy in Ireland was specific in how famine could be used to progress the colonisation of Ireland. Writing to Lord Burghly, Queen Elizabeth's chief adviser, on 22nd November 1601, Sir Arthur Chichester reflected:

> I have often said, and written, it is Famine which must consume them; our swords and other endeavours work not that speedy effect which is expected for their overthrow.

Culpability for the Famine, although not easily apportioned,

> No man is an Island, entire of itself; every man is a piece of the Continent, a part of the main. . . Any man's death diminishes me, because I am involved in Mankind. . . (John Donne)

15 See http://www.cwsworkshop.org/katrinareader/node/161

has become clearer as a result of much recent research in Ireland, Britain and the USA. What has become apparent is that Britain's 'conquest, dispossession and cultural extirpation' is in fact at the heart of the root causes and death and emigration statistics that arise from the Great Hunger.[16]

In a time of universal deceit, telling the truth is a revolutionary act. (George Orwell)

In Scotland the Irish Famine story is almost entirely omitted from formal Scottish/British education. The vast majority in Scotland have virtually no knowledge of this catastrophe or its effects on social, economic, political and cultural life to this day, and particularly as to why there are so many people of Irish descent living in Scotland's west-central belt. To a lesser extent this lack of knowledge also includes many of the descendents of Famine victims and migrants, who also attend Scottish state schools.[17]

There are countless events and people omitted from history books in Scottish schools, and debates over what should or should not be included are ever present. However, in British society it can be argued that 'amnesia' regarding the Great Irish Famine has a number of 'other' explanations regardless of matters of space, time, perceived importance or utility. It might be the case that in the past a range of elites and commentators did not want people to know the truth: of the causes, meanings or consequences of the Famine. Some may also have been unable to fully comprehend the tragedy or recognised the reality of the Famine.

A more stark assessment of British actions in the context of British colonialism in Ireland might say the attitude that dominated at the time was simply one that didn't care. For some there seems also to have been a degree of eagerness at the prospect of Ireland becoming de-populated, specifically of 'Papists'. There is evidence to substantiate all these arguments. It was the London Times of June 26th, 1845, that pointed out:

> They are suffering a real though artificial famine. Nature does her duty; the land is fruitful enough, nor can it be fairly said that man is wanting. The Irishman is disposed to work; in fact, man and nature together do produce abundantly. The island is full and overflowing with human food. But something ever intervenes between the hungry mouth and the ample banquet.

16 Kinealy, 1997, from Daltun O'Ceallaigh (ed) Reconsiderations of Irish History and Culture, Dublin, 1994, pp.12-13.

17 Amongst those of Irish ethnicity this has changed to a small extent as manifest in some of the songs of the Celtic support, the erection of a Famine monument at Carfin in Lanarkshire and in Celtic Football Club joining with other parts of the Irish diaspora to commemorate Ireland's National Famine Day during May 2009. It is also worth noting that academics and others interested in the teaching and knowledge of Scottish history in Scottish schools is also of great concern.

In the USA the New Jersey State curriculum includes the Great Famine under the category of 'genocide and holocaust' studies. At Drew University in the same state the study of the Irish Famine is part of a course on 'Irish History and Literature' that is shaped by the question, 'whether or not this horrible event can be properly classified as genocide as defined in the modern period'.

For many years traditional orthodoxies meant that the Famine has been given no significance in Irish or British history: first, the Famine was not a watershed but was merely an accelerator of existing trends in Ireland; second, that in view of Ireland's large population and underdeveloped agricultural sector, a subsistence crisis was inevitable; and third, that, judged by the standards of the 1840s-1850s, the British government did all that reasonably could be expected of it. Further, in Ireland and amongst the Irish abroad many were so decimated and dispirited that the memory of the horrors of the Famine were best forgotten.

The Great Hunger represented as a 'potato famine' is also ideologically consistent and congruent with 'it was their own fault' type of argument. In this sense the racist and British-centric discourses over many centuries that inferiorised the Irish by portraying them as indolent, violent, stupid, etc, can be utilised to lessen the reality of mass suffering and death – because these people were seen as less than human and were thus authors of their own misfortune.[18] The use of the description 'potato famine' ignores or conceals the torment and mortality of the Great Hunger (as also can mind-numbing statistics) while the role of British cultural stereotyping and racist attitudes as contributory factors of the Famine, reactions to it, and reporting of it, are neutralised and marginalised. A similar process occurs in relation to suffering in many Third World countries today (former colonies) where the victims are not white skinned and who live in countries that are former colonies of white European powers.

In the relevant British discourses of the nineteenth and twentieth centuries, over-dependence on the potato was not and is not portrayed as a product of being rendered landless; being a small landowner or being enslaved like a serf to a wealthy landlord as a result of British colonisation; or, as a people making

18 In relation to ideas of the Irish as being violent, and despite statistics that would suggest otherwise in the years immediately prior to the outbreak, the same line of thinking was often promulgated to partly justify a significant British military presence in the north of Ireland as 'peace keepers' during the recent Troubles. See Curtis 1988 for references.

the best use of limited resources; especially in using as good quality a food as the potato. In a context of the centuries-long portrayal of the Irish as 'unintelligent', racial inferiorisation can be portrayed as an Irish 'decision' to live on the potato: a decision that can be seen as 'stupid' resulting in a way of living that would inevitably bring desolation sooner or later. In this sense the Famine can be seen as a natural disaster whose consequences were even worse due to the fault of the Irish themselves. Therefore, use of the description 'potato famine' reduces a catastrophic six years (and more) of wretchedness to a single factor, thus ignoring that the blight triggered food shortages but the Famine was caused by a complex combination of political, religious, racial and economic factors. As already noted, the potato blight affected numerous countries but nowhere else was the population required to endure anything resembling that of the Irish famine. Additionally potatoes only accounted for 20% of agricultural output on the eve of the famine, and the Irish economy was far more complex than that single phrase 'potato famine' suggests. Most significantly, Ireland was a conquered island, had been planted with British Protestant colonists who held most land, influence and power, while the indigenous population had virtually no say in the economic and political life and direction of the country and almost all important relevant decisions were made in Britain.

The emergence of Celtic Football Club

Although there was a significant Irish presence in Scotland prior to the Famine, it was the Great Hunger that initiated the mass migration that continued apace for several decades, thus making Scotland, particularly the Glasgow and Lanarkshire areas, amongst the major recipients of Irish immigrants in the late nineteenth and early twentieth centuries. It is in the narrative of Irish migration to Scotland that the seeds of Celtic Football Club and its supporting community are found. The men that founded Celtic, played for the club or built the first ground and supported it had in the main either survived the Famine or were the offspring of refugees who escaped to Scotland. Again, many if not most would have lost family and friends in the great catastrophe. They knew oppression and recognised and experienced an environment in Scotland that, although for most represented progress, was often a re-cycling of the mass suffering with which they were familiar. In a revived and recovering sense of spirit, strength, charity, friendship and community, some decided to challenge the despair, distress, torment, racism and religious prejudice that surrounded them. It is in this context that Celtic Football Club was founded and sustained. In a documentary former captain and manager Billy McNeill stated that Celtic Park was itself a monument to the Irish in Scotland.[19] In this volume of essays Aidan Donaldson says:

> Celtic Football Club is a Catholic and Christian response to the conditions of the poor. Celtic is an answer to cultural, social, political and religious oppression, domination, racism, bigotry and exclusion. These are the reasons and rationale as to why Brother Walfrid, John Glass, Pat Welsh, John O'Hara, Thomas Flood, William McKillop, Hugh and Arthur Murphy and Dr. John Conway – gave birth to a unique and special Irish community focus in the shape of a football club.

The Great Famine in Scottish Football

Various factors might preclude or at least dissuade a person from ridiculing and belittling an event such as the Great Irish Famine, among them moral rectitude and integrity, knowledge and understanding of the catastrophe, respect for other peoples' cultures, experiences and sufferings, consideration too for the dead, those that barely survived as well as for their offspring. Other things might predispose or influence someone to do the opposite; immorality, deceitfulness, deficiency and ignorance, with regards such a holocaust, contempt regarding other peoples' cultures, experiences and sufferings, giving little or no thought to those that died, barely survived or their descendents. In this vein other related features might characterise, amplify or exacerbate these; racism, bigotry, prejudice, negative discrimination, detestation and revulsion. Respect, commemoration and meaning for the Great Hunger can become evident or marked by way of silence, prayer, song, or a spiritual or physical memorial, singular or repeated in nature. Disrespect, marginalisation and a lack of feeling or emotion sympathetic to the event might emerge,

19 Celtic: The Irish Connection, Produced/Directed by Brian O'Flaherty for rmgchart entertainment, Dublin, Ireland, 2006

manifest as disregard, obstruction, damage, interference or distortion: sometimes 'silence' can be demanded by those that hold hegemony and power and would prefer that such events were 'not' remembered.

On 23rd November 2006 a question was asked in the Scottish Parliament of the Scottish Executive by Denis Canavan MSP.

> It is a national scandal that the Scottish football authorities turned a blind eye to anti-Irish racism in Scottish football for many years. It was not until UEFA took action that certain people were brought to their senses. As well as using the law to prosecute those who are guilty, will the Lord Advocate urge the Scottish football authorities to take strict disciplinary action against any guilty players, supporters or, if necessary, clubs, to stamp out all forms of racism and sectarianism, which should not be tolerated in a multicultural, multi-ethnic Scotland?

Despite football being Scotland's national team sport, dominating the national sports pages and often beyond, watched by hundreds of thousands of people in stadia and on television weekly throughout the football season, notwithstanding racism being an extremely topical and ongoing issue, and even though those of Irish descent in Scotland make up the country's biggest single and oldest immigrant and ethnic community, virtually no one – if anyone – in the media reflected or reported on Canavan's question.

In 2001, the erection at Carfin in Lanarkshire of a national monument to the victims and refugees to Scotland of the Great Famine in Ireland caused a furore. The unveiling of the monument by Taoiseach Bertie Ahern, was originally cancelled because of fears of a sectarian reaction against the erection of the monument. Generally, the Scottish media reflected a certain embarrassment as an aspect of the country's history and character became evident for people throughout Britain, Ireland as well as internationally.[20] Around the world where the Irish had settled Famine monuments had previously been raised, often elaborately and at great expense, particularly around 1995-2002, the years marking 150 years since the calamity. The erection of monuments in towns and cities in North America and Australia in particular, as well as Wales and England, did not cause any untoward social,

20 See for example, articles in The Scotsman 10/2/01 and The Herald 9/2/01

cultural or national commentary, never mind furore.

As the Carfin debacle unfolded, amidst much distorted, erroneous and sensationalist reporting, most of the subsequent media comment stated that the uproar should not have occurred and Ahern should have been made welcome. Nonetheless, the proposed memorial provoked widespread hostile statements and observations that reflected upon several aspects of the commemoration, including Irishness in Scotland, an Irish Premier visiting Scotland, the relevance of the 'potato' Famine to Scotland, the Catholic dimensions of the ceremony, why 'Scots' would be interested in such an event anyway, etc. For example one letter to a newspaper stated:

> How kind of the Scottish people to erect a memorial to remind us of the Irish potato famine. I'm assuming this has been done because Ireland has erected memorials for Bannockburn, Culloden and the Highland Clearances. Quite what the Irish potato famine has to do with Scotland (apart from the Irish coming over here) is beyond me. I can only think that part of Lanarkshire is full of Irish-Scots who want to re-create Ireland in Scotland. I am not bigoted in any way – I am from the Highlands – and think that Irish history should be remembered there, just as Scottish history should be remembered here.[21]

> It has always been a mystery to me how men can feel themselves honoured by the humiliation of their fellow beings. (Mohandas K Gandhi)

At the Celtic versus Glasgow Rangers league match played at Celtic Park in May 2004, Rangers fans threw potatoes onto the trackside of Celtic's stadium. Hardly anyone in the media raised or discussed this while the few that did made only a brief reference. The Daily Record used the headline, 'Spuds and Duds: Gers can't handle it when the chips are down'.[22] The article continued saying that Rangers 'provided the mince' (a Scottish slang description for something that is not good, is rubbish, but is also a food traditionally aligned with potatoes) although 'they tiptoed their way':

> . . . through the distasteful debris of King Edwards and Maris Pipers hurled onto the park by their supporters, Rangers once again could offer no bite. . . For the record, those potatoes were a dubious reference to the great Irish famine of 1846 by a group of fans whose racial abuse of Bobo Balde [a black player in the Celtic team – this abuse was also aimed at Didier Agathe another of Celtic's black players] was more sinister and objectionable.

21 Evening Times, letters, 16/2/01

22 Daily Record, sport, 10/5/04, pp.4-5

An Express reporter continued in a similar vein advising that anyone who thought the actions of Rangers fans was anything more than untoward recommended that:

> There are some handwringers who found the act of throwing potatoes onto Parkhead before kick-off distasteful, but it was nothing more than a wind-up between rival fans and should be treated that way.[23]

The Sunday Herald match correspondent also briefly mentioned the scenes.

> Rangers. . . Their supporters threw beach balls and potatoes to taunt the Celtic fans but it could not be said their players threw in the towel.[24]

In November 2007 few in the media reported a similar occurrence at Celtic Park. Akin to an infamous incident involving former football manager and pundit Ron Atkinson making comments against black footballers, when he thought the microphone was off (calling Chelsea's Marcel Desailly a 'f****** lazy thick nigger'), Sky presenter Jim White was 'caught' on air making a jibe towards Celtic fans singing a club anthem, The Fields of Athenry. White was heard to say: 'Oh here we go again, the tottie famine'. His co-presenter Charlie Nicholas replied, 'Aye, and they're all eating chips singing this'. Initially the comments were heard by some people watching Sky TV outside of Britain. Subsequently, Sky Television said it was 'investigating' while Celtic FC said it was also looking at the matter.[25] The day afterwards the Daily Record's Tam Cowan congratulated both commentators for how they celebrated Celtic's winning goal the previous evening in the Champions League.[26] Neither Cowan nor any other public commentator mentioned the jibe. Subsequently nothing else was publicly heard about it either. Alluding to the Irishness of the club and its fanbase Celtic supporters are regularly referred to as 'tattie munchers' in a variety of football fanzines and websites in Scotland, and on established radio and television 'comedy' shows such as BBC Scotland's 'Off the Ball' and 'Only an Excuse': thus demonstrating the widespread popularity and acceptability of such a depiction and narrative.

23 Gary Keown, The Express, Sport Football, 10/5/04, p.5

24 Sunday Herald, Sport, 9/5/04, p.3

25 The Irish Post, 19/1/08, p.57 and the Daily Record, website, 30/11/07

26 Daily Record, 1/12/07, p.61

'The Famine is over, why don't you go home'?

Why don't you go home?

I often wonder where they would have been
If we hadn't have taken them in
Fed them and washed them
Thousands in Glasgow alone
From Ireland they came
Brought us nothing but trouble and shame
Well the famine is over
Why don't you go home?

Now Athenry Mike was a thief
And Large John he was fully briefed
And that wee traitor from Castlemilk
Turned his back on his own
They've all their Papists in Rome
They have U2 and Bono
Well the famine is over
Why don't you go home?

Now they raped and fondled their kids
That's what those perverts from the darkside did
And they swept it under the carpet
And Large John he hid
Their evil's seeds have been sown
Cause they're not of our own
Well the famine is over
Why don't you go home?

Now Timmy don't take it from me
Cause if you know your history
You've persecuted thousands of people
In Ireland alone
You turned on the lights
Fuelled U boats by night
That's how you repay us
It's time to go home.

On 16th April 2008 a song was publicly aired for the first time by Rangers fans again at Celtic Park. Like many football songs, only its chorus was aired: to the tune of 'Sloop John B' by the Beach Boys.

'Why don't you go home, Why don't you go home,
The Famine is over, why don't you go home'

In the following days Celtic supporters began to discuss the words as well as the chorus of the song and air their shame, anger and feelings of belittlement: the overwhelming consensus was that its singing constituted anti-Irish racism and anti-Catholicism of a most unambiguous and unashamed nature. In May of 2008 a small delegation representing several Irish community groups and Celtic Supporters held a meeting with Show Racism the Red Card (Scotland). The organisation confirmed with the delegation that the song was indeed racist and it would pursue the matter with the Scottish Premier League, the Scottish Football Association and Glasgow Rangers Football Club. The organisation's representatives said they would also consider addressing the issue of general anti-Irish racism in Scottish football and putting something appropriate on its website. SRRCS also said that it would be better to leave the matter until after the UEFA Cup Final which Rangers were playing in the following week: all at the meeting agreed. Subsequently, the song was aired by Rangers fans and heard live on radio and TV during the UEFA Final in Manchester. Despite this, by June Show Racism the Red Card in Scotland had yet to mention the song or anti-Irish racism in Scottish football in its communications and the delegation was not contacted further. In late August 2007 a communication was forwarded to SRRCS from one of the delegates at the May meeting.

> We find your lack of correspondence on this issue deplorable, your lack of interest shocking and your general attitude to be on the side of the offender and not the offended. Can you please make some contact with any one of the organisations you met and inform us of what is happening regarding the singing of anti-Irish songs at Scottish football matches?[27]

In the following weeks the singing of the Famine Song was generally either ignored or casually or flippantly remarked upon by some commentators. However, a few in the media did begin to pick up on its meanings and thought it worthy of comment. A few days after the Manchester final and the riots involving Rangers fans, a Sunday Mail columnist said:

27 Copy of letter provided by delegate from May 2008

Then there's the singing. They've controlled themselves all season in grounds but it was a different story on the streets. And this latest favourite of theirs: 'The famine's over, why don't you go home'? It has to go. If it was 'Go back to Africa' to a black player would we accept it? [28]

Despite a growing awareness of the song – and its full repertoire – and despite repeated airings by Rangers fans, including again at Celtic Park in August and being played on 'YouTube' thousands of times, it was September 2008 before its singing became an issue of extensive media reporting. This was due to the matter being raised by a Celtic supporter in communication with Ireland's Consul General in Scotland, Cliona Managhan, who in turn raised concerns about the singing of the song at one of her regular meetings with Scottish Government officials.[29] More voices were subsequently heard and opinions offered on the issue. In the Sun newspaper Professor Patrick Reilly repeated the sentiments of the Sunday Mail columnist of four months before:

> Can you imagine such a song as the Famine Song being directed at any other ethnic group? Consider what would happen if it was Jews or West Indians who were being singled out for such vile treatment. There would be an outcry.[30]

However, clearly Reilly's argument was not shared by the Sun as one of its main sports writers and columnists demonstrated.

> All this guff over this Famine Song. . . include all those who try to intellectualise bigotry, like Glasgow University Professor Patrick Reilly. . . In yesterday's paper he said of The Famine Song: 'can you imagine it being directed towards any other ethnic group'. . . he can't see that it wasn't directly towards 'an ethnic group'. That's the point of the song. It's Rangers fans telling Celtic fans they're Scottish, not Irish and it's time to stop pretending otherwise. That's not me justifying the song. That's just how it is.[31]

A few days later the Sun re-iterated this stance on the matter when another columnist said:

> What a mind-numbing waste of time, space and energy. . . Like many songs belted out by fans, The Famine Song is a total wind-up. It is also not bigoted. . . If we become that picky and PC

28 Gordon Waddell, Sunday Mail, 185/08, p.80

29 BBC News Channel, 15/9/08, The Irish Times, 16/9/08, p.24

30 The Sun (Scotland), 17/9/08, p.5

31 Bill Leckie, The Sun, 18/9/08, p.11

than all singing and chanting should be banned as someone somewhere is bound to take offence. Let's have some common sense and stop being so touchy. . . we should be able to spot a wind-up, a daft bit of banter and be able to take it squarely on the chin.[32]

The Rangers Supporters Trust agreed with the Sun:

The 'Famine's Over' chant is quite clearly a typical football chant mocking the myths rival fans perpetuate about themselves and should be treated as such.[33]

A Daily Record columnist who has an image built upon a perception of 'humour' decided not to discuss the issue directly or publicly, apart from mentioning its political ramifications:

Considering it's developed into a diplomatic incident I'll leave the debate about The Famine Song to the politicians.[34]

A Mirror reporter also mentioned the furore over the Famine Song saying that it was one of Rangers' fans songs of hate. Nevertheless, the focus of comment on this occasion was not on the chant as a 'song of hate', but the journalist introduced a new element to comment saying that the 'song about the Irish potato famine' was a slight on Rangers fans because the Famine wasn't about Catholics or Protestants.

There might however, have been some confusion given that the memorial in Scotland to those who perished in that 'natural disaster' [editor's emphasis] is housed in Carfin Grotto, not a known haunt for Rangers fans, but helping perpetuate the myth that only Roman Catholics were wiped out by the blight.

The same journalist condemned the Celtic supporter for lodging his complaint at an Irish political level and introduced yet another religious dimension saying:

What next. A visit to the Italian Consul the next time you're served a dodgy pizza at Parkhead?. . . For those who haven't picked up on that song, it was a parody of a Beach Boys number from a few years back. There is no truth in the rumour that Brian Wilson's tune was based on the previous Pope falling in the shower. So for the paranoid, it isn't called 'Slip John P'.[35]

32 Donald MacLeod, The Sun, 20/9/08, p.25

33 Reported in The Scotsman, 18/9/08, p. 26

34 Tam Cowan, Daily Record, 20/9/08, p.60

35 Stewart Weir, The Mirror, 19/9/08, p.65

As a result of the furore and complaints regarding the song, Rangers 'approached Strathclyde Police for guidance'. The club subsequently gave out 50,000 leaflets requesting that fans stop singing the Famine Song and issued a statement. [36]

> Clearly the Famine Song has provoked such a response in certain quarters. It is the club's view that the interest of our supporters and the club will be best served by supporters refraining from singing the Famine Song.[37]

Later the club stated that:

> We as a club do not wish to see any of our supporters leaving themselves open to arrest and believed, that by putting the messages [against singing the song] on the screens and scoreboards last night, we were only fulfilling our obligations to you, our supporters. . . we have another match at Ibrox on Saturday and the same applies to that fixture.[38]

Graham Spiers at the Times (Scotland) called the Rangers statement timid saying:

> I'm sorry? Unfairly 'singled out' and a mere 'wind-up'? Given the recent tradition of the bigotry problem at Rangers, I fear this latest dirge about 'Irish' or Fenians' being sent back to Ireland deserves something slightly more withering than Bain's [Rangers' Chairman] folksy 'wind-up' claim. The song is trash, it is racist, and he should find the guts to say it. . . neither bigotry or racism is funny.[39]

The song continued to be sung publicly by Glasgow Rangers fans and also on occasion by supporters of several other football clubs in Scotland. Rangers supporters Bill and Will (The Dirty Blighters) recorded the full version of the Famine Song, their YouTube recording received several hundred thousand hits and they cut a CD of the song which was made available for fans. Despite this, little substantial and critical social, cultural or political commentary followed in the Scottish media.

However, Rangers fans singing a personalised version of the song aimed at Scots-born Irish internationalist eighteen year old James McCarthy – at a Hamilton versus Rangers match during October 2008 – did prompt some media commentary, although most continued to ignore the ongoing issue of general anti-Irish racism in Scottish football. Some newspapers mentioned the abuse of McCarthy while a Herald sports writer called the continued singing of the song 'a source of embarrassment to an exasperated club. . . their crassness knows no bounds'.[40] A Daily Record sports columnist said the singing of the song shouldn't be 'allowed to pass without disapproval'.[41] Strong condemnation came from the Daily Mail's reporter who stated:

> If they had begun chanting about black players being shipped back to Africa or the Caribbean, they would have been arrested.[42]

When asked about the hounding of McCarthy, Hamilton manager Billy Reid asserted a view that Irish players like McCarthy can expect this kind of abuse and have 'to get on with it'. He said:

> I didn't hear the full extent of the abuse as I was concentrating on the game. He [James McCarthy] is just concentrating on playing for Hamilton Accies. He is an Irish player and he just has to get on with it. [43]

In trying to make sense of the ill-treatment as well as protect his young player Reid asserted a view that Irish players like McCarthy have to expect this kind of abuse and just have 'to get on with it'. As the media's attention began to look towards the singing fans, Glasgow Rangers also warned supporters again regarding what might occur if they were caught singing the song. When Rangers played Hamilton again a few days later two huge screens at Ibrox Stadium carried the following warning:

> The club, in consultation with Strathclyde Police, have to advise supporters that the singing of The Famine Song will result in those responsible being arrested.[44]

McCarthy was booed as he left the field at Ibrox after being substituted that evening.

The relevance of the Famine Song and the personalised version sung to James McCarthy of Hamilton again became notable in November when Hamilton travelled to play Motherwell. On the same day as 'Show Racism the Red Card' publicly campaigned at numerous football matches in Scotland, including

40 Sunday Mirror, Stuart Darroch, match report on Hamilton v Rangers, 26/10/08, p.62,
David Leggat, The People, 26/10/08, p.53,
Stephen Halliday, The Scotsman, 27/10/08, p.6 (sports). For comment see Darryl Broadfoot, The Herald, sports section, 27/10/08, p.4

41 Hugh Keevins, sport, 27/10/08, p.4

42 John Greechan, Daily Mail, 27/10/08, p.69.

43 The Express, 28/10/08, sport, p.64.

44 The Times, Sport (Scotland), 29/10/08, p.76.

45 Daily Record, Gavin Berry, 2/11/08, p.87.

at the Motherwell match, McCarthy was booed and the Mother-well fans sang to him, 'You're in the wrong f****** country' to be followed by the Scottish anthem, 'Flower of Scotland'.[45] Scotland on Sunday's match correspondent wrote with regards Scottish football: 'Red-carding racism obviously doesn't apply when the subject is Irish'.[46]

After hearing Rangers fans sing the song in a match at Hamilton in late 2008, six months after the song began to be popularised and after the issue was raised, SFA President George Peat commented on 'offensive chanting' generally and said that:

> At the minute we've left it in the hands of the SPL to look into things and try to eradicate it. . . Rangers have contacted Strathclyde Police about the 'Famine Song' and we will be in touch with both parties to consider what, if any, action is needed.[47]

By October 2008 the Celtic Chairman strongly condemned the song as 'vile, vicious and racist':[48]

> We should condemn racism and sectarianism wherever they arise. . . Both Rangers and Strathclyde Police have acknowledged that the content of The Famine Song, which is directed against the community of Irish descent living in Scotland, is in breach of race relations legislation.[49]

The growing publicity, as well as its continued singing, meant the song was by now difficult to ignore. One journalist in an English-based Irish community newspaper said:

> But the Famine Song is only the most recent manifestation of Scotland's oldest racism – moreover it is tolerated by the leaders of Scottish society.[50]

In the same article Piara Power of the National Director of 'Kick it Out', an English-based organisation, welcomed the intervention of the Irish Government official:

> This is a matter of ethnic and national identity and it is appropriate that the Irish Government should have become involved on behalf of its citizens.[51]

After a number of communications, eventually the Chair of the Scotland Committee for Equality and Human Rights

46 Martin Hannan, 2/11/08, Sport, p.4

47 BBC Scotland website 27/10/08

48 John Reid quoted in The Herald, 18/10/08, pp.4-5

49 The Times, 6/10/08 (Scotland), Sport, p.4

50 Irish Post, 4/10/08, pp.16-17

51 Ibid.

Commission, Morag Alexander, stated that:

> The behaviour in question is both racially and religiously motivated, feeding on a broader legacy of community tensions that have been part of Scottish society since the nineteenth century. . . the singing of this song is clearly intended to inflame both racial and religious prejudices and as such it is a criminal matter.[52]

In its annual review for 2008/09 SRRCS said:

> The campaign is very aware that racism is not dependent on skin colour. . . Racism towards Irish communities manifested itself in football through the singing of 'The Famine Song' and racism directed towards players who were born in Scotland and who elected to play for the Republic of Ireland. Our concerns were discussed with Rangers FC, the Scottish Premier League and the Scottish Football Association. Rangers proactively asked their fans to refrain from singing 'The Famine Song' through a leaflet distribution and stadium announcements. Court judges have declared the song to be racist. The campaign will continue to speak to all football clubs, the footballing authorities and the police to eradicate this type of behaviour.

In November 2008 a Rangers fan was found 'guilty of religious and racially aggravated breach of the peace for singing the Famine Song' at a match at Kilmarnock.[53] In December stickers began to appear around parts of Glasgow that proclaimed: 'The Famine's Over P&O Takes You Home'. The same sticker formed the visual aspect of a YouTube recording of the song.[54] In 2009 the fan found guilty for singing the Famine Song in public at a football match appealed his conviction. His counsel, Donald Findlay QC, said:

> 'The famine's over why don't you go home'. . . there is nothing at all that could in any way be said to be racist or racially motivated about those words. It is, in my submission, an expression of political opinion. . . in a free society, subject always to the operation of the rules of law, we are entitled to express our opinion and to do it forcibly if we wish.[55]

Despite Findlay's arguments to support the offender's case that he had done nothing against the law, appeal judges ruled that the song was indeed racist.[56]

52 Letter to Tom Minogue after a period of communications (beginning on 15th September) in which he did not perceive himself to have been satisfactorily answered in previous letters to Alexander. This correspondence, 7/10/09

53 The Sun (England) 17/12/08, p. 27

54 http://www.youtube.com/watch?v=xbsZTX2DLHA&feature=related

55 The Herald, 16/5/09, p.2

56 The Irish Post, 4/7/09, p.10

Reflecting on Famine Song discourses

Celtic and Irish organisations in Scotland alerted 'authorities' to the Famine Song during the first days and weeks it was publicly aired. At the same time, Celtic supporters also made contact with numerous people working in the sports media and requested that they begin to speak out on the issue. However, while a small handful of sports commentators referred to it during that time, it took until a Celtic supporter prompted the Irish Consul in Edinburgh to raise the issue at Scottish Government level before more substantial comment and debate ensued: although even then as the evidence reflects, many in the media still did not mention it. The first reaction by many in the Scottish media and elsewhere, including Scottish politicians, was 'silence'. Indeed, as early as May 16th MP George Galloway, stated on a radio talk show that he had tried to refer to the singing of the song in his regular Daily Record column, 'but it didn't make the cut'.[57] Nevertheless, eventually a most significant and critical exposé did emerge via the narratives that permeated the Scottish media over the next eighteen months.

It is not those who inflict the most, but those who suffer the most who will conquer (Terence MacSwiney)

One factor exposed publicly during the song's debate was not only the lack of knowledge and understanding that contributed to the mass singing of the song, but also the degree of ignorance that prevails in Scotland about the Great Irish Hunger (and Irish-British history generally) and the Irish as a multi-generational Irish community in 'multi-cultural' Scotland. This ignorance manifested itself in media and public body responses that signalled the beginning of inappropriate, inadequate ineffectual comment paralleling a lack of recognition over the depth of hate and prejudice involved in such chanting. Comprehension of the significance and meaning of the Famine and the song being sung publicly at Scottish football stadia might have been expected to draw widespread attention and apposite comment and action on the part of politicians, law and order agencies, the media, football authorities, etc. For people with knowledge of the Famine, for those of the Irish-descended community in Scotland (and elsewhere) whose families and communities were decimated by it, for many Irish-descended who were born and lived in Scotland partly or entirely because of it, and for people with a moral standpoint that perceives such

57 TalkSport, 16/5/08

abuse as 'vile, vicious and racist', it can be difficult to understand why it has not been dealt with radically differently. After all, this was a national trauma visited upon Ireland (then a part of the British Empire/United Kingdom) and the Irish and that resulted in so much death, emigration, family and community rupturing, destitution and poverty and, with a legacy still felt to this day.

Although it arguably took the Irish Consul's involvement before the matter became difficult to ignore, several comment-ators in the Scottish media criticised this intervention.[58] Others addressed it in stereotypical fashion by applying the 'shame on both your houses' mantra beloved by many in the Scottish sports media, and characterised by the technique of mentioning 'both' Rangers and Celtic whenever controversial issues require comment, even if one club or the other is not is 'involved'.[59] This custom is not only used to portray apparent objectivity with regards such matters, but it can also reflect lack of knowledge and understanding as well as a prejudicial attitude and identity around the topic. Critically, it means that roots, origins, manifest-ations and blame are rarely if ever informed by substantive knowledge or motivated by the goal of finding as much 'truth' as is possible with a view to understanding, admission of guilt, forgiveness and reconciliation.

Nevertheless, two other features of the discourses surround-ing the song are conspicuous and remain the most significant and revealing. The first can be signified by remaining silent about the issue, overlooking it as an important concern, saying that other things were more important, and disregarding it as a matter of racism in Scotland: all of which have been manifest in the Scottish media during the most vocal periods of the singing of the Famine Song. This is the point made by Professor Reilly who stresses that if this song was directed at Jews or West Indians 'there would be an outcry': so why has there not been an outcry with regards those of Irish descent, Scotland's largest ethnic minority? Writing in the Sunday Mirror Auua Suith is critical of those who ignore the issue and others who have been lacking in detail when 'mentioning' it. She is especially critical of people in positions of power – in the Scottish media, Scottish Parliament and at Glasgow Rangers – 'who lost an opportunity to be absol-utely clear on why this song was immoral and wicked'. Suith

58 Daily Star, 17/9/08, p.15, Stewart Weir, The Mirror (Scotland), 19/9/08, p.65

59 Chick Young, The Express (Scotland), sport football, 11/10/08, p.98 & 1/11/08, p96

states that 'Pakistanis, Chinese and Jamaicans' can have their diasporas without requiring to face "racist chants". . . but not the Irish. They have to listen to this bile'.[60]

Suith points towards the notion of hierarchies of ethnic recognition as well as racism. 'Colour racism' (against non-whites) in Scottish society has a long history – indeed, it partly defines the existence of the British Empire – although its recognition and acknowledgement as a problem is a relatively recent occurrence. Nevertheless, racism is an ongoing issue in Scotland infusing the law, politics, employment, education and the media. In recent decades numerous laws have emerged making it illegal to be racist and more difficult to be publicly 'racist'. Although manifestations of 'coloured racism' (the term is being used on the understanding that 'coloured' is itself often a racist description – as 'all' persons are 'coloured') have diminished greatly in Scottish and British football in recent decades, numerous examples remain. In Scotland, racist abuse of Trinadad and Tobago striker Jason Scotland by some Motherwell fans in a match against St Johnstone in February 2007 received wide-spread media coverage.[61] In the lower divisions of Scottish football in May 2009 a white player was suspended by the SFA for abusing a black opponent on the basis of his skin colour.[62] An ongoing issue in Scottish football is the considerable under-representation of non-white footballers born in Scotland: especially from Pakistani, Indian and Chinese backgrounds, despite their significant presence in Scotland for the past half-century.[63]

Widespread reporting and condemnation of racism against people who are not white-skinned in Scottish football has become the norm after years of relative silence. This silence existed because such racism, linked as it was to the wider social, political and cultural habitus, was simply seen by many people as normal – it was/is what happens when people who view themselves as superior talk about or interact with people constructed as inferior. This was/is a consequence of the power relations involved in the British colonisation of much of the world – where in fact the majority of people are 'not' white. Evidence, stories, academic and journalistic analysis of 'normalised' and 'embedded' racisms abound, especially in relation to countries that have traditionally built significant aspects of their identities on notions of white

60 21/9/08, p.14

61 BBC Scotland Sport 1/3/07

62 Football for all website, http://www.footballforall.org.uk/, 2/10/09

63 Ibid.

superiority, like USA, South Africa and Australia. Such racisms have their roots in the colonialism of white Europeans and this history requires to be utilised to explicate contemporary re-cycled forms and manifestations of the same.

However, as evidenced here, what numerous commentators are suggesting regarding the racism of the Famine Song, is that the previous non-recognition – or lethargy in relation to its condemnation – of widespread, normalised and embedded white versus non-white prejudice and bigotry, remains for the ethnic Irish in Scotland: something that would be less likely to occur if the targets were ethnic Jews or black/brown-skinned people. In late 2008 Respect MP George Galloway tabled a question asking Secretary of State for Scotland Jim Murphy if he would hold discussions with Holyrood ministers on: 'instances of anti-Irish racism at football matches involving Scottish clubs'.[64] Galloway was repeating Denis Canavan's question to the Scottish Executive in 2006. Nonetheless, as before the issue was largely ignored by the relevant politicians but more significantly, by the Scottish media. Again the wider society refused to acknowledge this racism, but also to explore (eg, question why it exists, why it's so widespread and normalised and why is it largely ignored) the issue of anti-Irish racism in Scotland.

For its Irish-descended targets a lack of acknowledgement of the presence or significance of anti-Irish racism in Scottish football and beyond can have a double effect in relation to the Famine Song – in the way that its targets not only experience the song as victims, and also how this is exacerbated by its lack of recognition on the part of the rest of society. The experience of being subjected to anti-Irish racism is largely marginalised and ignored while others in society intentionally and unintentionally collude in this, particularly within politics, law and the media. As this text demonstrates, the sports media in Scotland is crucial to the operation and effectiveness of such collusion.

This ignoring and marginalisation – akin to how bullies perform – takes on a further dimension. Defenders of the song such as some Rangers groups state that its singing is aimed at the 'plastic paddies' that support Celtic: a reference to those they are telling to 'go home', who in the main are 2nd, 3rd and

64 Press
Association,
11/11/08

4th generation Irish. For example, when a discussion was aired on BBC Radio 4 in December 2008, a Rangers fan interviewed stated that in relation to 'The Famine Song':[65]

> The song is about people who are British but who wish to be Irish and would prefer to be Irish and we're saying ok, go to Ireland and be Irish or be British.

Another said:

> There's almost this plastic Paddyism that happens over here. . . but at every opportunity they keep telling us they're Irish. . . if you don't like it here then leave, it's the old when-in-Rome scenario, they're in our country now.

A different interviewee stated:

> They're clinging to this link to Ireland. This is a small country that can't incorporate a lot of ethnic minorities. . . this is about people purporting to be Irish when in fact they're not, they're Scottish.

Apart from references to Celtic and its support, views forwarded in relation to national and ethnic authenticities, and the denial of the legitimacy of Irish ethnicity in such comments, a discourse of rejection, mocking, discrimination against, and the bullying of people of Irish ethnicity in Scotland is a dominant theme throughout football fandom at club and international level. Dundee United fans sing to Celtic supporters 'can you sing a Scottish song' while Aberdeen fans taunt Celtic supporters with 'You're in the wrong country'.[66] Motherwell supporters chanted this towards Celtic's Aiden McGeady in February 2009 and to Hamilton's James McCarthy at a Scottish Premier League match the previous week. The month before, Dundee United fans sang 'The Famine is over, why don't you go home' to James McCarthy. In November 2008 Hearts fans joined in by singing the Famine Song at their game versus Celtic.[67] In 2006 at a match in Glasgow, Rangers fans held up a banner to Celtic supporters with the slogan, 'This is our city, where in Ireland is Glasgow'? Late in 2008 in a match against Celtic at Ibrox, another banner was unfolded by the Club's 'Blue Order' fan group.[68] The banner pictured a red, white and blue bus with an arrow next to it pointing to Stranraer, the main ferry port in Scotland for travel

65 The World Tonight, BBC Radio Four, documentary presented by Graham Spiers reflecting upon Rangers fans' identification with anti-Catholic bigotry, 29/12/08

66 Celtic v Dundee United, 28/1/06

67 The Mirror, 5/11/08, p.55

68 Glasgow Rangers v Celtic, Ibrox Stadium, Glasgow, 17/12/06

to Ireland. The bus, which had a Celtic hooped figure boarding it, was pictured with writing stating 'all aboard. . . o'ffended bus',[69] thus expressing similar sentiments to those contained in the Famine Song and reflecting the inter-textual nature of such bigotry and prejudice. Consequently before the Famine Song was made popular the discourse of a rejection of the Irish diaspora in Scotland on the part of many football fans was already popular. The longevity of this private and public discourse was also evidenced in a Channel Four TV production in 1995 when 'Sam', a Rangers fan talking about Celtic supporters, tells his interviewer, 'this is our country, we didn't ask them to be here'.[70]

Attitudes and identities such as these have long pervaded the Scottish sports media. A popular TV, radio, newspaper pundit and columnist discounted the possibility of any racist connotations or intentions in the singing of 'The Famine Song'. Making light of the song and referring to Celtic supporters' Irishness he derisively and mockingly added that having recently played Motherwell he would congratulate them for 'at last' having 'sung a Scottish song at the match'. This was because Celtic supporters had sung 'Go home ya huns go home' to the tune of 'Auld Lang Syne', a well known Scottish song.[71] In 2001 another Scottish tabloid newspaper columnist and radio commentator aligned himself with the sentiments that underpin the Famine song chorus when he stated to those of Irish descent in Scotland who are Celtic supporters.

> Plastic Irishmen and women who drink in plastic Irish pubs and don't know their Athenry from their Antrim. . . perhaps they could do us all a favour and relocate to Dublin.[72]

Talking about Irish ethnicity and Celtic supporters, a broadsheet journalist agreed:

> No inconsistency in packing their ground to wave the flag of another country. They flap the Irish tricolour and sing sad Irish songs and roar of the Irish struggle. There's a country called Ireland for goodness sake, why don't they go and live there?[73]

Yet another sports columnist re-iterated these sentiments:

> . . . there is a section of the Celtic support, in particular, who

69 http:// img357.imageshack. us/i/ img62881wh7.jpg/

70 Football, Faith and Flutes

71 Tam Cowan, BBC Radio Scotland, Sportsound, 13/9/08

72 Gerry McNee, News of the World, 6/5/01 & 7/10/01

73 John MacLeod, The Herald, 18/2/02

turn my stomach with their allegiance to the Republic of Ireland in preference to the nation of their birth.[74]

A well-known personality in Scottish football circles wrote specifically about the 'Famine song'. Critical of those who complained about the song and 'their' perceptions of bigotry and racism, he went on to restate the song's main theme:

> Go find a better place to live and leave us to get on with the job of making something good of this country.[75]

As was discussed in the previous book, Celtic Minded 2, Celtic's 3rd generation Irish player Aiden McGeady has been a recipient of many such sentiments from fans throughout Scottish football as well as in the media.

> . . . that wee traitor Aiden McGeady, who turned his back on the land of his birth to play international football for a foreign country. . . [76]

> McGeady got shirracked by Hearts fans at the weekend and will get booed wherever he goes because of his decision and I don't really see how he can expect anything else.[77]

Such remarks constitute one of the most important discourses contained within the Famine Song as well as accompanying media commentary: that is, the denial of the Irish ethnicity of those of Irish descent in Scotland. The focus here might be on the Famine Song, but such anti-Irish references are recurrent in Scottish society and the 'choices' that Scotland's multi-generational Irish community is faced with are clear: Celtic supporters, as well as Celtic Football Club, are compelled to forget and eradicate their Irish ethnicity and identities, become British and/or Scottish or, 'go home to Ireland'.

One lead writer in the Sunday Times in an article entitled, 'Forget the famine', refused to accept or tolerate Irish ethnicity and identity in Scotland when she argued that Celtic supporters were 'as Scottish as mince 'n' tatties'. Subsequently, this columnist blamed the Celtic supporters for inviting such 'racism' in the first place saying that the term 'plastic paddy' described a:

> . . . real phenomenon in which some modern Scots construct

74 Raymond Travers, Scotland on Sunday Sport, 9/11/97

75 Jim Traynor, Daily Record, Sports Section, p.24, 22/9/08

76 Follow Follow, Glasgow Rangers supporter website fanzine, http://www.followfollow.com/ 26/4/05

77 Daily Star, Scottish Edition, p.27, 31/12/04

their own myths and so play into the hands of bigots like The Fans of the Famine Song.[78]

A tabloid columnist mocked the Celtic supporters for complaining about the song, reduced its significance to that of a 'wind-up' on the part of the singers, and argued that criticism of its sentiments could not be classed alongside abuse of any other ethnic group in Scotland because:

> . . . it wasn't directly towards 'an ethnic group'. That's the point of the song. . . It's Rangers fans telling Celtic fans that they're Scottish, not Irish, and that it's time to stop pretending otherwise. That's not me justifying the song. That's just how it is.[79]

In a similar vein, in 2002 the same columnist criticised Celtic and its fans' Irishness and questioned the authenticity of their ethnic background and identity, demonstrating both the widespread nature of this criticism and its embeddedness and acceptability in Scottish culture. This journalist referred to the diaspora in Scotland as the 'pseudo-Irish' who support Celtic as well as their penchant for 'diddly-dee music'.[80] The prejudice involved in denying the heritage, origins, cultural background and identities of the Irish-descended in Scotland – and their right to perform Irishness in the same way as people perform Scottishness and Britishness or other national identities – mean that such a strategy in effect works to de-ethnicise this community. This strategy in turn not only denies and rejects Irish ethnicity, but also signifies that the ethnic Irish in Scotland cannot be seen as targets of racist sentiment. Simultaneously, this also reduces and condenses such issues to a straightforward and stereotypical 'each side is as bad as the other' type of contest where additionally, a simplistic construction of 'sectarianism' is catch-all in effect. Such a strategy also disguises and re-constructs many of the reasons why such problems exist in the first place. Whether it is the Famine Song, chants and abuse of fans from other football clubs, from Scotland's Tartan Army[81] or, commentary from a range of people involved in the sports media, Irish ethnicity in Scotland is constantly disparaged, diminished and denied: Irishness in Scotland is a decidedly problematised concept and identity for many Scots.

78 Joan McAlpine, 23/11/08, Review, p.8

79 Bill Leckie, The Sun, 18/9/08

80 Bill Leckie, The Sun, 8/4/02

81 See forthcoming research

The Famine Song has acquired a wider currency since first aired in April 2008. Partly reflecting this, the Sunday Times reported how a Scottish Labour candidate was allegedly sent a text message by a political lobbyist saying: 'The famine is over. Why don't you go home? FTP' (an abbreviation for f*** the Pope).[82] On a Radio Scotland show one caller said: 'a Ryanair flight will get them back to Ireland quicker than they can get to Celtic Park'.[83] When discussing the song in his Daily Record column MP George Galloway recounted how, when campaigning for Labour's Helen Liddell during the fractious Monkland's by-election of 1993, he was told to get 'back on the boat to your own country, you Fenian b******', thus reflecting that the attitudes conveyed by the song are not new, but simply a collective public expression of long-held views.[84]

The second most significant discursive strategy used by commentators regarding the song and its critics has been utilised in an attempt to trivialise the song's origins, meanings, sentiments and significance. Humour and comedy have in recent decades become part of the staple diet of football discourses in the media, with both radio and TV shows significantly using this medium. Contemporary football events and individual actions have been utilised to project a particular brand of humour that might occasionally be termed 'risky'. The nature of interpreting, receiving and consuming such humour can be determined and shaped by knowledge, understanding, morality, circumstances, environment, experience, timing and context: meanings, both hidden and apparent, are also important. Nonetheless, despite these, and regardless of the disclaimers, ambivalence, hilarity and jocular nature of much of the media commentary surrounding the Famine Song, it can be seen that bigotry, prejudice, racism and hatred are not humourless activities.

One popular football journalist at the Daily Record and BBC radio said:

> So when did the gallows humour of the terracing, which for decades has made us all smile by cutting right through pomposity and politically-correct boundaries become such a terrible thing?[85]

Postings on Rangers fan websites and fanzines concurred

82 Scotland, 9/809, p.1
83 16/10/09
84 17/11/08, p.13
85 James Traynor, Radio Scotland BBC Monday 22/9/08

by significantly promoting the 'banter' explanation whenever the song was publicly aired and some in the media discussed it. With no sense of self-irony, one fanzine editor utilised an aspect of prevalent 'thick paddy' discourses by referring to the song as a 'bit of mickey taking', a phrase culturally specific to British society whereby Irishness has traditionally equated with racist connotations of thickness, stupidity and laziness.[86]

> It is, quite simply, football rivalry and a bit of mickey taking and they should get used to it.[87]

A further paradox arises from this statement when one considers that the Irish being 'thick, stupid and lazy' was also utilised as one of a number of British understandings as to why the Great Hunger occurred in the first place.

Celtic Football Club's Irishness is occasionally the object of the 'thick Paddy' sub-culture in the Scottish media. For example, a Herald columnist stated that after going through sound checks on the public address system, came the following words from the stadium supervisor: 'if this announcement cannot be heard in your part of the stadium, please contact control'. A humorous story, and of course, just as well for Celtic's 'continuing links with Irish ways' added the Herald.[88]

The apparent humour contained in the Famine Song and the attention it had received was alluded to by one sports commentator who said:

> I feel this is going too far, and there's a freedom of speech issue coming in here and I think the line in there I think, 'the Famine's over why don't you go home'. . . I don't think it's racist, I think it's gallows humour. People will say you shouldn't laugh about something where a million people died and so many people were displaced but I don't think they're inciting violence at all. . . I think we've got more things to worry about than a silly line in a silly song.[89]

On his show a week later, the same commentator repeated these sentiments, laughing the issue off saying that football fans always poke fun at each other, wind each other up and that 'there are plenty of songs worse than this one'.[90] Such comment is imbued with numerous ideological components. In this sense,

86 See references by Joe Horgan, The Irish Post, 8/11/08, p.17. Horgan speaks of 'a new knowledge now about the relationship between humour and power. . . and humour and social disregard'.

87 Follow Follow Rangers' Fanzine editor, Reported by the Press Association, 11/11/08

88 The Herald 9/2/96, p. 21

89 James Traynor, Radio Scotland BBC Monday 22/9/08

90 Radio Scotland BBC Monday 29/9/08

the Scottish sports media can reproduce and perpetuate these notions and the ideological components that reflect, construct, and serve to create and reinforce, rather than challenge, racism, sectarianism, prejudice and discriminatory behaviour and attitudes.

In the same month on Radio Clyde's Superscoreboard programme presenters and guests included retired footballers Andy Walker and Derek Johnstone and Sunday Mail columnist, Mark Guidi. At the end of a show that discussed various relevant 'football' matters from the previous weekend the following exchange took place when the last caller mentioned the Famine Song.[91]

> Caller, 'I was just laughing at this latest Rangers song. I'm a Rangers fan and I think its getting ridiculous (the Famine Song). . . it's not a sectarian song, is that what we're saying now, is it no' tongue in cheek, know what I mean?'
> Johnstone, letting out a sigh, 'Is there no fun involved in football these days Andy? We know all about the sectarian thing and we're not talking about that.'
> Walker, contradicting himself, 'There's certainly a bit of fun. I don't think that's a bit of fun. I don't think that's offensive. I think some of the other chants are offensive. But, it's been going on for some time hasn't it Derek?'
> Johnstone, 'What about tonight Andy bhoy. Carlos Cuellar, a wee chance he'll be making his debut for Aston Villa away at Tottenham. . . ?'
> Guidi, interrupting, 'I think its going to be a belter. . . I'll certainly tune into that one tonight.'
> Walker, 'I fancy Tottenham to get off the bottom of the table, I fancy them for a win.'
> End of show

Thus again, in rendering the song 'humorous', by ignoring it and rapidly moving onto other matters, the sum total of analysis and serious commentary in this sports media broadcast is reduced to 'a bit of fun' and 'banter'.

It is possible that assertions that trivialise and make light of the singing of this song as 'fun' and 'banter', among other things, actually act as disclaimers in relation to the seriousness of the sentiments, ideologies and identities declared. The assertion of banter therefore is a rhetorical construction that cuts off, or at least does not invite serious discussion, consideration or under- 91 15/9/08 standing, at least in relation to those targeted by the song. Indeed, a question is raised about how much the sentiments are actually shared – wholly or partly – by some or many in the sports media? Reflection on the meanings being constructed – in this case as 'banter' – by people in the media in relation to the Famine Song, also points to aspects of social and cultural power and the popularity and normalisation of not recognising Irish ethnicity, but also in its Scottish context, its corollary of anti-Irish prejudice. In addition, this also offers insight into how such sports media personalities typically utilise a limited, inadequate and uninformed construction of 'sectarianism' in Scottish football and beyond when discussing that specific issue.

The meta-discourse surrounding the so-called humour of the Famine Song is particularly revealing, not least in relation to the sports media. Painfully, for those who live or work at creating as much of a non or anti-racist culture in Scotland as is possible, the variety of justifications concerning the song as well as the general denial of it as a serious issue, does not reflect a society that can acknowledge its anti-Irishness and the damage this does to positive ethnic as well as religious relations in society. Ethnic or racial jokes cannot be considered in the abstract and certain discursive constructions around the Famine Song reflect a less innocent and disturbing side of humour than is portrayed by either its defenders or those that trivialise its meanings. The Famine Song cannot be looked at in isolation and there is much evidence beyond its renditions regarding the hostility, prejudice and hatred of Irish ethnicity in Scotland: in fact, in some ways the Famine Song is a celebration of this hostility, prejudice and hatred. Much of the meta discourse around the song reveals attitudes as well as identities that conspire in targeting Irish ethnicity in Scotland as an unacceptable and problematic 'other'.

Sartre suggests that bigots take pleasure in the 'joy of hating' while 'freeing themselves from the demands of logic and reasonableness'.[92] Freud argued that 'the joke format provides a socially accepted means of breaking taboos': the taboos being the fact that otherwise many kinds of racism are largely outlawed in British society.[93] Billig says that in the USA survey evidence notes that:

92 Billig, 2001
93 Ibid.

. . . blacks and whites differ in their evaluation of utterances about race. Whites are more likely to defend remarks as being 'just a joke that blacks will be likely to criticise as racist and therefore not something to be found funny'.

Underlining the connections between hatred and humour, Billig describes a situation that can be applied to the singing and treatment of the Famine Song in Scotland – a song claimed by many as 'banter', thus allowing its perpetuators and supporters to say the unsayable: that which is usually rendered in private and that constitutes a part of the identity of various individuals and communities. On analysing Ku Klux Klan sites in the USA Billig found racism that is portrayed by its purveyors as 'humour' often functioning as legal disclaimers. For example:

. . . this site is meant as a Joke. . . and is not to be taken seriously. . . we are not real life racists. . . YOU MUST HAVE A SENSE OF HUMOR. IF YOU ARE OFFENDED, THEN F*** OFF!!!

And again:

. . . none of the above sites promote feeding niggers to dogs and are listed for informational purposes only. None are associated with our website. This site is a parody, and meant only as a JOKE! Do not take it seriously.[94]

In this way we can see that not only its singing, but that relevant comment with regards the Famine Song can demonstrate that bigotry, prejudice, racism and hatred 'are not humourless activities'. Social, moral, cultural and political positions are assumed and adopted in relation to the Famine Song; in terms of its singing, its reception, ignoring, reactions, reporting and representations. The Famine Song represents a discourse around which social and cultural power is constituted and operates.

Recognising ethnicity: recognising racism

Although it took a long time for appropriate responses to emerge and evolve with regards the song's presence in Scottish football, the song has been confirmed and agreed as a public display of anti-Irish racism by the football authorities, anti-racist bodies and the law in Scotland. However, even though there exists some

94 Ibid.

agreement on the discrimination and bigotry invoked by the song, the discourses around its life are significantly revealing in relation to Scottish society. It is clear that utterances and identities of anti-Irish ethnicity in Scottish football and society are vibrant and have a history that predates the singing of the Famine Song. Further, this racism is generally ignored, even at a time when 'racism' is highly topical in the media, education and in terms of law and order. It appears that anti-Irish racism in Scotland is one that many Scots find the most difficult to deal with. Media and other public discourses around the Famine Song demonstrate that there is a lack of knowledge and understanding not only concerning the Great Hunger in Ireland, but also in terms of Irish ethnicity in Scotland.

Two other factors are important. Similarly there appears to be a general lack of knowledge and understanding as well as acknowledgement in relation to Scotland as the junior partner in the conquest and colonisation of Ireland and its incorporation into the British Empire. Further, as the Great Hunger and the Famine Song are a consequence of this colonial relationship then ideologically so also is its singing, its ignoring, the denial of its significance or its social and cultural acceptance, even as 'banter'. Indeed, its singing can be seen as a celebration of Britain's conquest and colonisation of Ireland over several centuries and in this way power is validated and asserted, as it also is in the Glasgow Rangers fan song 'we are the people': a refrain that links with the sentiments of the Famine Song. In this sense the song corresponds to the historical ideological anti-Irish racism that has provided one of the foundation stones for Britain's centuries-long relationship with the island of Ireland, amongst whose consequences have been mass hunger and emigration.

The Famine Song is but one micro manifestation of that relationship. It is also a reminder that colonialism signifies modes of domination that do not simply disappear once colonisation is reduced or ended. Mac an Ghaill believes that for Britain: the dominant black-white colour paradigm, the selective forgetting of Empire (and its consequences) and the assimilation that develops from a myth of cultural homogeneity and questions of difference/sameness, are at the core of Britain's problematising of the Irish in Britain.[95] In Scotland, problematising the Irish and their offspring, and of course Irishness itself, is further exacerbated by the religious questions commonly referred to as 'sectarian' issues.

This work has reflected upon the short refrain of the song, 'The Famine is over, why don't you go home'. It has not reviewed the full version that reflects upon a 'welcoming' Scotland for ungrateful Irish immigrants and their offspring who in turn are perceived as an embarrassment to indigenous Scots, includes further disparaging references to the Great Hunger, Scots-born Irishman Aiden McGeady and ex-Celtic manager Jock Stein, child abuse, accusations towards Catholics and the Catholic Church, the Irish supposedly 'betraying' Britain during the Second World War while continually asserting the sentiment, 'The Famine is over, why don't you go home'. The lyrics of the song constitute an even greater ideological significance than does the refrain which is repeated by football fans who often reduce many songs to refrains and 'easier to sing' aspects rather than sing full versions. It might be argued that Glasgow Rangers fans that share in the attitudes and identities expressed through the Famine Song by singing or listening to it at games or on supporters buses, pubs and clubs, or who refuse to recognise the song's racist lyrics and sentiments, defend it is as 'a wind-up' and as something not to be taken seriously, can also be considered as victims of the consequences of a history of British colonialism in Ireland. It might also be the case that moral rectitude and integrity, knowledge and understanding of the catastrophe, respect for other peoples' cultures, experiences and sufferings, consideration too for the dead, those that barely survived as well as for their offspring and, a general recognition and acceptance in a spirit of toleration and reconciliation of Irish ethnicity and differentiation in Scotland, can help cease such racist renderings.

Within the Scottish sports media the construction of a particular kind of Scottishness as well as specific Irish-Celtic (and frequently Catholic) otherness, invokes questions regarding the presence or otherwise of social and cultural spaces in Scotland that accept or/and allow for the acknowledgement, represent-ation and expression of social and cultural distinctiveness not

95 Mac an Ghaill, 2001

based on popular or dominant notions of Scottishness or Britishness. In relation to a wide spectrum of fans in Scottish football at both club and national levels, and the sports media, it is evident that there are various levels of resentment and opposition towards manifestations of Irish ethnicity in Scotland: so much so that Irishness and Irish ethnicity are not only frequently attacked, demeaned, decried and rendered unacceptable, but are mocked and diminished as illegitimate and inauthentic. Further, that those who recognise and esteem their Irish ethnic identities are informed that they are in error and are instead, Scottish or/and British. If such people don't accept this then they can 'go home to Ireland'.

The evidence shows that Irish ethnicity in Scotland brings many people from within and beyond football together in mutual hostility and antagonism. In this light, seemingly contradicting the ideal of religious, national and ethnic distinctiveness rightfully existing in Scottish society, at an 'anti-sectarian' conference held in Glasgow in 2006 a Church of Scotland spokesperson repeated the maxim of numerous Scottish football fans and sports media persons in Scotland stating: 'as the basis of challenging these prejudices we should be pushing our identities as Scots'.[96] At the same conference a Lanarkshire-based school teacher ignored the ironic content of her own discourse when she stated:

'One Scotland Many Cultures and then our children go to different schools. . . how can that be'?

For this teacher, and for many others who are passionate about their Scottishness and/or Britishness, especially pursued and manifest through football, when it comes to specific 'other' (Irish) ethnic, national and religious distinctions in Scotland that are not Scottish, not sufficiently Scottish, seen as distorting a Scottishness that ought to be shared by all, or that are constructed by malevolent authorities, organisations and individuals as oppositional to Scottishness, then there is little room for differentiation. This is especially so with regards ethnic Irishness that requires to be forgotten, concealed or erased.

Much of the media discourses reflected here, as well as other commentary, and the Famine Song in particular, shows that people

96 Nil By Mouth and Museum of Religion joint seminar, Glasgow, 13/11/06

of Irish ethnicity are being partly encouraged, compelled and forced to conform, to de-culturalise or/and assimilate. Through particular discourses, stated or implied, Scottishness is utilised as a rhetorical testing instrument, and through a process of negative labelling and marginalisation, silencing or rendering perceived outsiders as 'negative others', Irishness can be correspondingly disempowered and rendered illegitimate in a Scottish context. In this sense we can see how Van Dijk's notion of privileged access to a socially valued resource, like the sports media, allows for the exercise of cultural power.[97] In this way also a consensus about and acceptance of Scottishness and Britishness are manufactured while a corresponding disparaging of specific other identities that have relevance for Scotland's socio-cultural, religious and political history and contemporary multi-ethnic society – specifically Irishness – takes place.

Like other national and ethnic identities, Scottishness is continually constructed partly in the context of, or in opposition to, other important ethnic, national and cultural identities and communities. In this way, the dominant notion of Scottishness – and Britishness – in the Scottish football environment and beyond, is one that frequently both reveals and obscures 'historical conflicts, social tensions and unequal power relations'.[98]

For Stone, football does not exist in a social and cultural vacuum and can be seen as varyingly connected to, and as an extension of, everyday living.[99] Sugden and Tomlinson regard the world's most popular team sport as a critical site and source 'for the expression of forms of collective belonging, affiliation, and identity'.[100] The Scottish football environment is a location and space for the collection of shared social, cultural, national, religious as well as political ideas, emotions, allegiances and identities. As a place for concomitant collective antagonisms, hostilities, resentments, rivalries and prejudices, the Scottish football environment is also an arena for the contestation of numerous other identities that help constitute not only football in Scotland, but modern Scottish society.

97 Noted in Ricento p.615 from Van Dijk T 'Principles of Critical Discourse Analysis', in Discourse & Society, 4, pp.249-283, 1998

98 Ricento 2003, p.625

99 Stone 2007, pp.169-184

100 Sugden & Tomlinson 1998, p.171

For the hundreds and millions of lives
You destroyed and terrorised
Or have you never realised
Did you never feel shame
For what was done in your country's name
And find out who's to blame and why they were so inhumane
And still they teach you in your school
About those glorious days of rule
And how it's your destiny to be
Superior to me
But if you've any kind of mind
You'll see that all human kind
Are the children of this earth
And your hate for them will chew you up and spit you out
    (Excerpt from singer/songwriter Damien Dempsey, 'Colony')

FROM DEATH AND DESOLATION
TO DREAMS AND SONGS TO SING

'The Famine Killed Everything': Ireland's Great Hunger

CHRISTINE KINEALY

The event that commenced in 1845 as a result of a crop failure in Ireland is referred to as 'The Great Famine' or, in its Irish rendition, 'An Gorta Mhór'. Its ending is harder to date, because although the potato crop of 1852 was free from disease, the impact of the Famine continued to be felt for decades. This was especially evident in terms of population, with Ireland's population dropping to over four million by 1901 – half of its eight million pre-famine level – while even in 2009, despite the changes wrought by the 'Celtic Tiger economy' the population of Ireland remains smaller than it had been in 1845. The Famine affected Irish people in other ways that are harder to quantify, but which ensured that it lived on in popular memory – both by those who remained in Ireland and sometimes, more intensely, by those who emigrated. Furthermore, the Famine changed not only the subsequent development of Ireland, but also that of the various destinations of the millions of emigrants, including those who arrived in the west of Scotland.

The Irish Famine occurred at the heart of the largest and wealthiest empire in the world. Ireland's colonial relationship with Britain had its roots in small invasions during the twelfth century and subsequent conquests (for example by Elizabethan and Cromwellian forces) and plantations of Scottish and English settlers into Ireland. However, in the wake of a defeated democratic, republican revolution in 1798, the constitutional relationship between Britain and Ireland changed. Rather than winning independence after 1798, Ireland had been coerced into a closer political relationship with Britain, in which she was rendered a subjugate 'partner'.

On 1st January 1801 centuries of colonialism in Ireland resulted in Ireland, England, Scotland and Wales becoming part of a unitary state known as the United Kingdom. This union had entailed the demise of the Irish parliament in Dublin with a smaller number of MPs (still Protestant only as Catholics were excluded under the Penal Laws) being sent to the Westminster parliament in London. It was not until 1829, largely due to Daniel O'Connell's masterful campaign, that Catholics would be able to sit in the British parliament.

In the decades that followed the Act of Union, the condition of the Irish economy was a source of concern to both British politicians and economists. Generally, Ireland was regarded as underdeveloped; the economic stagnation was due to the twin problems of a large peasantry relying largely on potatoes for subsistence, and a landowner class, a large section of whom were absentee (living in Britain), indebted, or unwilling or unable to invest in their properties. Ireland's poor were regarded as a potential burden on British taxpayers and so various commissions were convened to try to solve the perceived problems of Ireland.[1] These concerns disguised the fact that the potato economy underpinned and sustained a highly productive commercial sector, in which vast amounts of other foods were produced, largely for export. Potatoes, in fact, accounted for only 20% of Ireland's agricultural output. By the 1840s, Ireland was exporting sufficient corn (that is, wheat, barley, corn and oats) to Britain to feed two million people, and this had earned it the title 'the bread basket of Britain'. Significantly though, Ireland was far from being a country where famine appeared inevitable; it was producing a large agricultural surplus each year and, for much of the year, its population was healthy and well fed. However, the workers of Britain, rather than the workers of Ireland, were the key beneficiaries of the cheap and plentiful production of corn in Ireland.[2]

Following the passing of the Act of Union in 1800, the British government intervened frequently in the affairs of Ireland,

[1] For example, The Poor Enquiry Commission, which sat between 1833-36, and the Devon Commission, looking at landholding in Ireland, which reported in early 1845

[2] This is not to imply that there was no poverty in Britain – see Frederich Engels, The Condition of the Working Class in England (first pub. in 1844)

especially in the areas of policing, education and poor relief. In each of these areas, Ireland was treated differently from the rest of the United Kingdom.[3] This was particularly evident in regard to poor relief. In 1833, the government appointed a commission to report on Irish poverty. After three years' exhaustive enquiry, the Commissioners suggested that Irish poverty could be ameliorated and the economy improved if state-funded public works and state-assisted emigration were introduced. They were unequivocal in believing that the English or Scottish Poor Law systems, based on local taxation, were not suited to conditions in Ireland. The recommendations – which would have necessitated government expenditure – were rejected. Instead, an English Poor Law Commissioner was sent to Ireland. Following a six week stay, he reported that a Poor Law should be extended into Ireland. His report found favour with the government and, in 1838, the Irish Poor Law was introduced. The Irish legislation, however, differed from both the English and Scottish Poor Laws in a number of significant ways, namely, the 'right to relief' was not given to the Irish poor, and relief could only be given within a specially-built workhouse, not in the home of the poor. Moreover, paupers, as the poor were to be designated, could only enter a workhouse if they did so as a family unit. These provisions meant that in Ireland, poor relief was to be more stringently provided than elsewhere in the United Kingdom. It was based on a general perception that the Irish poor were lazy and feckless, and needed to be forced from their high dependence on potatoes. By 1845, 118 of the planned 130 workhouses were operational. For the most part, they had few inmates. However, the extension of a Poor law to Ireland meant that at the time of the Famine, Ireland possessed a relief system, which was overseen by officials in Dublin and London, and a national network of workhouses.

In 1843 a new strain of blight appeared on the potato crop in the Americas. Two years later, the disease crossed the ocean and destroyed some of the potato crops in Belgium, France, Switzerland and England. By September 1845 it had appeared in Ireland. The fact that the Irish poor had a high dependence on potatoes as their main form of subsistence was a source of concern. In the same month that the disease appeared in the country, the Gardner's Chronicle posed the question 'Where will

[3] Christine Kinealy, A Disunited Kingdom. England, Ireland, Scotland and Wales, 1800-1949 (Cambridge University Press, 1999)

Ireland be in the event of a universal potato rot?'[4] Fortunately, because the blight had appeared relatively late in the harvest season, the destruction was partial, with the loss of approximately 50% of the crop.

The government, led by Sir Robert Peel, responded quickly to the news. It put in place a programme of measures that would become effective the following Spring, when the shortages would start to be felt. These measures included the import of food – Indian corn – into the country by the government, the establishment of public works in the distressed areas, and matching grants to any local relief committee. Peel also used the subsistence crisis to further his own political ends: repealing the Corn Laws in the summer of 1846. This measure, which allowed the cheap import of corn into the United Kingdom, earned him the gratitude of the British poor, but the opprobrium of his own Tory Party. Despite assertions to the contrary, it did nothing to alleviate the situation in Ireland.

The failure of the potato crop was not seen as being a totally bad thing by some government officials, who regarded dependence on it as perpetuating the perceived backwardness of the Irish economy and people. In the words of Sir Randolph Routh, who had overall responsibility for the relief operations:

> The little industry called for to rear the potato, and its prolific growth, leave the people to indolence and all kinds of vice, which habitual labour and a higher order of food would prevent. I think it very probable that we may derive much advantage from this present calamity.[5]

Overall, the policies introduced in the first year of shortages reflected the government's longer-term aspirations for Ireland.

In the first year of shortages, nobody died of famine in Ireland. This lack of excess mortality was attributed to Peel's quick and comprehensive response. He himself, however, was a political casualty of the Famine as many in his party abhorred his action in repealing the Corns Laws. As a consequence, a minority Whig government headed by Lord John Russell assumed power in the summer of 1846, just as news of the reappearance of the blight was emerging. Moreover, the fact that it appeared earlier

[4] Gardner's Chronicle and Horticultural Gazette, 16th September 1845

[5] Sir Randolph Routh to Sir Charles Trevelyan, 1st April 1846, BPP, Correspondence Explanatory of the Measures Adopted by Her Majesty's Government for the Relief of Distress arising from the Failure of the Potato Crop in Ireland, 1846 [735], p.139

in the harvest season than in the previous years had ominous implications for the potato crop.

In 1846, almost the entire potato crop was destroyed: moreover, the corn harvest was smaller than usual. A second, and more extensive, year of food shortages was inevitable. Yet, regardless of this, the programme of relief introduced by Russell's administration was more restrictive than that of the previous year. Public works were the primary form of relief, but the way in which this form of relief was provided made it unsuitable to provide effective support to a hungry people. Numerous bureaucratic checks were imposed, which meant the works were slow to be established; wages were based on 'piece work', which disadvantaged people who were already weakened by hunger; a wages ceiling was imposed despite spiralling food prices; and the works undertaken were to be of no value to the community but were simply to act as a test of genuine destitution. Consequently, the people who did manage to get employment on the public works (and not everybody did) were engaged in hard physical labour, for twelve hours a day, building roads that led nowhere and walls that surrounded nothing. The fact that the winter of 1846-1847 was one of the coldest on record, with snow falling as late as April, added to the misery of those so employed.

Despite the greater food shortfall in 1846, the government decided to import a smaller amount of Indian Corn to Ireland than in the previous year, preferring to leave food imports to market forces. Moreover, demands for the ports to be closed to allow food supplies to remain within the country, were rejected. Consequently, the fate of the poor lay in the hands of Irish and British merchants who inevitably were motivated by profit margins rather than the welfare of the people. In contrast, many European governments were intervening in the market place in order to protect the food supplies of their people. The failure of the British policy was admitted privately by some of the highest ranking figures in government. The Earl of Bessborough, who was Lord Lieutenant of Ireland, wrote to the Prime Minister complaining that the merchants had 'done their best to keep up prices'. He went on to say:

I cannot make my mind up entirely about the merchants. I know all the difficulties that arise when you begin to interfere with trade, but it is difficult to persuade a starving population that one class should be permitted to make a fifty per cent profit by the sale of provisions, while they are dying in want of these.[6]

By the end of 1846, Irish doctors were recording a sharp increase in mortality. However, as in any famine, hunger-induced disease rather than starvation itself was the main source of death. For the victims, the end was slow, painful and undignified. One of the main causes of death was dysentery, which caused aching in the legs, arms and head, a swelling of the limbs, and an inability to keep anything in the stomach. A doctor in Skibbereen in County Cork, which was to achieve notoriety for the suffering of its population, recorded that:

all talk of exaggeration is at an end. The people are dying – not in twos or threes – but by dozens; the ordinary forms of burial are dispensed with.[7]

In the winter of 1846-47 excess mortality increased throughout Ireland, from Skibbereen to Belfast.[8]

The British parliament was fully aware of this situation. At the beginning of 1847, Lord George Bentinck, leader of the Protectionist part of the divided Tory Party, led a sustained attack on the policies and attitudes of the Whig Party and many others to the deteriorating situation in Ireland. Bentinck, supported by Benjamin Disraeli, condemned many aspects of the Whig government's relief polices, including the fact that they had reduced the size of rations to the Irish poor, they had left food importation to private traders and speculators, and they had exaggerated the quantity of foodstuffs imported into Ireland.[9] Apart from censuring the government for allowing such high mortality, he criticised the fact that records of famine deaths were not being kept. He repeatedly protested that it was within the capability of the British government to do so.[10]

At the beginning of 1847, the British government decided to close the public works; not because they were failing to save lives, but because they were expensive and cumbersome to administer. At this stage, 15,978 people had been employed, at

[6] Earl of Bessborough to Lord John Russell, Russell Papers (National Archives, England), 23rd January 1847

[7] Freeman's Journal, 5th December 1846

[8] For more on the impact of the Famine in Belfast, especially on the Protestant population, see C. Kinealy and G. MacAtasney, The Hidden Famine: Hunger, poverty and sectarianism in Belfast, 1840-50 (London: Pluto Press, 2000)

[9] Hansard, cxi, 29th March 1847, pp.570-74

[10] Lord George Bentinck in Hansard, xciii, 28th June 1847, pp.302-310, 1014

a cost of £410,000; meanwhile, the cost of providing relief for less than six months had reached £4.5million, most of which was provided as a loan to the Irish tax-payers.[11] Yet, despite this high expenditure, the public works had not only failed to save lives, but had exacerbated existing problems; the works had diverted people from their normal agricultural pursuits, while requiring vast amounts of energy from an exhausted and hungry population.

To replace the public works, a Temporary Relief Act, popularly known as 'the soup kitchen act' was introduced. As its name suggested, it was viewed as an interim measure, until the Poor Law could be modified to enable it to provide for both ordinary and famine relief. The introduction of the soup kitchen act marked an ideological break with earlier relief provision, which had generally viewed the giving of gratuitous relief to be both flawed and dangerous. As one government advisor reminded the Prime Minister, 'a continuous and indiscriminate almsgiving by the state tends more to deteriorate than elevate the people'.[12] Nonetheless, this legislation was the most successful of all introduced by the Whig government, both in terms of saving lives and regarding value for money. At the beginning of July 1847, over three million people were receiving free rations of food from the soup kitchens, and thousands more were buying food from them at affordable rates. The Act demonstrated that, logistically and financially, it was possible to save the lives of the Irish poor, if the political will existed.

Although it had been intended for the Temporary Relief Act to terminate on 30th September, the Treasury – which was increasingly intervening in the day-to-day provision of relief – ordered that the soup kitchens should close in the first two weeks of August to coincide with the early harvest.[13] Although much of the potato crop was blight free in 1847, lack of seed potatoes and employment of public works at the time of sowing meant that the crop was small. Ominously also, the government announced that the Famine was over, which meant that the private donations that had been sent to Ireland in 1847 started to dry up.[14] The closure of the soup kitchens meant that all relief and medical assistance was now the responsibility of the Poor

[11] Hansard, xciii, 28th June 1847, p.1005

[12] Earl of Bandon to Russell, Russell Papers, (National Archives, England), 30 22 5C, 7th September 1846

[13] Treasury Circular to Inspecting Officer of each Poor Law Union, Freeman's Journal, 3rd July 1847

[14] For more on private donations, see Christine Kinealy, The Great Irish Famine. Impact, Ideology and Rebellion (Lomon, Palgrave-Macmillan, 2001)

Law and Irish tax-payers. Not only was this opposed to the spirit of having a united kingdom, it meant that the fate of the Famine poor – now re-designated as paupers – lay in the hands of Irish, rather than British, taxation. This decision flew against the original purpose of the Poor Law. George Nichols, an English Poor Law Commissioner who was the man responsible for introducing the Poor Law to Ireland, had warned that it could not provide relief during a famine. He regarded this decision as misguided on the grounds that, 'where land has ceased to be productive, the necessary means of relief cannot be obtained from it, and a Poor Law will no longer be operative to the extent adequate to meet such an emergency as then existed in Ireland'.[15] He went to say that in subsistence crises on this scale, it was the duty of the Empire to provide the relief needed.[16]

The decision to make Irish taxation responsible for the famine relief after 1847 was clearly motivated by political rather than practical considerations. In the summer of 1847, there was a General Election in the United Kingdom and Russell's Whig party hoped to turn their parliamentary minority into a majority. Their electoral promises included lower taxation and less government intervention. Not surprisingly, the Whigs were victorious in the election, helped by the continuing divisions within the Tory Party.

The Famine was far from over after 1847, but the transfer to Poor Law relief had an immediate and negative impact on the poor, as they entered their third year of shortages. In October 1847, the new Lord Lieutenant, the Earl of Clarendon, who had arrived in Ireland only a few weeks earlier, expressed his alarm to the Prime Minister:

> There is one thing I must beg of you to take into serious and immediate consideration which is, that whatever may be the anger of the people or the parliament in England, or whatever may be the state of trade or credit, Ireland cannot **be left to her own resources**. They are manifestly insufficient. We are not to let the people die of starvation.[17]

His plea to the Chancellor of the Exchequer, Charles Wood, was even less unequivocal:

> I hope Lord John Russell will not persist in his notion that Irish

[15] George Nicholls, The Irish Poor Law (London, 1856), p. 3

[16] Ibid., p. 357

[17] Earl of Clarendon to Russell, Clarendon Irish Papers, Bodleian Library, 23rd October 1847

evils must find Irish remedies only, for it is **impossible** that this country will get through the next eight months without aid in some shape or another from England – it may be very difficult – very disagreeable. Irish ingratitude may have extinguished English sympathy, and the poverty of England may be urged against further succour to Ireland, but none of these reasons will be valid against helpless starvation.[18]

Significantly, Clarendon's comments revealed the deep-rooted resistance of some people in Britain to come to the rescue of the Irish poor, regardless of their suffering, and the existence of the United Kingdom. Clarendon's pleas fell on deaf years, with many politicians in London continuing to justify minimal intervention by laying the blame for the situation on the poor themselves, their laziness and their ingratitude. Clearly, the Irish people were not regarded as equal partners with the Union.

The Poor Law, which had been extended through the building of thirty-three additional workhouses and the permitting of outdoor relief, was granting relief to over one million people in 1848. The fact that this was paid for by local taxation put pressure on the poorest districts, and some workhouses faced closure because they could not pay their own debts. Reluctantly, the government intervened and designated twenty-two unions, mostly along the west coast, as distressed and therefore entitled to limited government assistance. This assistance was minimal and insufficient to save lives or stop the haemorrhaging of people from Ireland. Moreover, evictions had increased massively, facilitated by the 1843 legislation, which had placed a higher tax burden on property that was much sub-divided, together with a provision in the amended 1847 legislation that deemed that anybody who occupied more than a quarter acre of land was not eligible to receive Poor Law relief. The consequence was an increase in both evictions and the voluntary surrender of property. After 1848, therefore, homelessness aggravated the problems caused an on-going hunger.

The appearance of blight on the potato crop in 1848, in many parts of Ireland, was as devastating as it had been in 1846. However, a good corn crop and an improvement in the industrial sector contributed to a geographical shift in the impact of the

[18] Ibid., Clarendon to Wood, 26 October 1847

food shortages, with some areas on the east coast beginning a slow recovery from famine. Nonetheless, mortality, emigration and evictions were all proportionately higher than they had been in 1847 – frequently remembered as 'Black '47'. Clearly, what was happening was no ordinary subsistence crisis, in terms of either impact or longevity. However, in Britain the influential Times newspaper, traditionally an opponent of placating Irish opinion, suggested that it was no longer to 'conciliate Paddy', but that even harsher measures were required to resolve the Irish problem.[19] The continuation of distress in 1849 exposed differences within the Whig Party as to how the government should respond to the continuing crisis. Lord John Russell and Lord Clarendon both favoured a more liberal response to the palpable continuation of famine in Ireland, but they were outnumbered and outvoted. A small but powerful group of evangelicals that included Charles Wood (the Chancellor of the Exchequer), George Grey (the Home Secretary) and Charles Trevelyan (the Permanent Secretary at the Treasury), were determined that the Famine should be used to bring about much-desired changes in Ireland. When cholera appeared in the port towns of Ireland, the disease had a short-term, but significant, impact on local mortality. Clarendon's suggestion that special government funding should be made available to meet this fresh emergency was ignored. He warned that the likely consequence would be 'wholesale starvation' that would not only be 'shocking, but bring deep disgrace on the government'.[20] He blamed the intransigence and parsimony of the government on the fact that decisions lay in the hands of three men, writing despairingly that,

> C. Wood, backed by Grey and relying on arguments (or rather Trevelyanisms) that are no more applicable to Ireland than to Loo Choo, affirmed that the right thing to do was to do nothing – they have prevailed and you see what a fix we are in.[21]

Tellingly, each of these officials was evangelical, who viewed the Famine through providentialist eyes, as a punishment from God.

The ongoing crisis resulted in a small, but unpopular, grant of £50,000 being made to help alleviate distress in Ireland. It

[19] The Times, 4th October 1848

[20] Clarendon to George Grey (Home Secretary), Clarendon Papers, 7th December 1848

[21] Ibid., Clarendon to the Duke of Bedford, 16th February 1849

was only passed because Russell threatened to resign unless it was provided. Both parliament and the press, however, made it clear that this had to be the final grant made to relieve Irish distress.[22] This was followed by another policy change. In 1849, a 'Rate-in-Aid' tax was introduced, which provided for external assistance to be diverted to the most distressed unions, but from Irish, not imperial, taxation. The new tax was unpopular throughout Ireland, but was especially disliked in the north east of the country, which was recovering from the Famine, helped by a revival in industry. The arguments put forward, however, took on a sectarian dimension that set the tone for later divisions, by suggesting that the people of Ulster were both different, and superior to those in the rest of the island. One northern newspaper averred that:

> It is true that the potato has failed in Connaught and Munster,
> but it has failed just as much in Ulster; therefore, if the failure of
> the potato has produced all of the distress in the South and
> West, why has it not caused the same misery here? It is because
> we are a painstaking and industrious people who desire to work
> and pay our just debts, and the blessing of the Almighty is upon
> our labour. If the people of the South had been equally
> industrious with those of the North, they would not have had so
> much misery among them. [23]

These and other similar arguments were well received amongst the Protestant tax-payers of Ulster, but they had little basis in reality. During the Famine, population loss in Ulster (nine counties) averaged 17%, which was higher than that in the province of Leinster. In parts of County Cavan, it was high as 40%. When members of the Society of Friends visited the north in 1847, they likened the conditions in Belfast, Lurgan and Newtownards (all predominantly Protestant areas) to those in Skibbereen.[24]

The Rate-in-Aid was disliked by some politicians who felt that it contradicted both the letter and the spirit of the Act of Union. Clarendon believed that it undermined the idea of a **United** Kingdom, and would increase support for separation from Britain.[25] The tax was also unpopular with many administrators of relief who had witnessed the impact of the various policies introduced by politicians in London. Edward Twistleton, an

[22] The Times, 1st February 1849

[23] Newry Telegraph, 6th March 1849

[24] For more, see Kinealy and MacAtasney, Hidden Famine, chapter 2

[25] Clarendon to Duke of Bedford, Clarendon Papers, 29th March 1849

Englishman who had been the Irish Poor Law Commissioner since 1847, resigned in 1849 on the grounds that the tax was an unfair imposition on the people of Ireland and he could not implement it 'with honour'. Over the previous two years he had disagreed frequently with the policies he was overseeing, and had had many angry encounters with Charles Trevelyan over the parsimony with which the Treasury had released funds. Before leaving office, he informed Trevelyan that as he and his colleagues had repeatedly been denied sufficient funding, they were 'absolved from any responsibility on account of deaths which may take place on account of those privations'.[26] A few weeks later, he told a parliamentary committee that deaths, even in the poorest unions, could have been prevented 'by the advance of a few hundred pounds'.[27]

The 1849 harvest was blight-free in many parts of Ireland, and industry, especially the linen trade, was continuing to revive. But in many parts of the country the recovery was slow and partial. In some parts of the south and west, evictions, emigrations and mortality were all higher than they had been in the previous four years. The reduction in the number seeking Poor Law assistance took place against a backdrop of an increasing number of people emigrating, peaking in 1854 when an estimated one million people left Ireland. Because emigration was largely unregulated precise numbers of those who left are not known, although it is possible as many as two million left between 1845 and 1854. Lack of regulation and the scale of the departure meant that conditions on many of the ships were appalling, although most of the emigrants reached their destination. The fact that so many emigrants were Catholics was welcomed by British politicians who hoped that their leaving would help to facilitate the regeneration of the country. Even Clarendon, an increasingly sympathetic commentator, opined that 'the depart-ure of thousands of papists Celts must be a blessing to the country they quit'.[28] This sentiment was echoed by the London Times, which prophesised that:

> in a few years more, a Celtic Irishman will be as rare in Connemara as is the Red Indian on the shores of Manhattan.[29]

Overwhelmingly, famine emigrants chose to go to North

[26] Evidence of Edward Twistleton, Select Committee on Irish Poor Law, BPP, 1849, xvi, pp. 711-14

[27] Ibid., p. 717

[28] The Times, quoted in The Freeman's Journal, 4th January 1847

[29] Quoted in Donal Kerr, A Nation of Beggars (Oxford, 1994), p. 297

America, despite the length of the journey and the higher cost of getting there. A smaller though still significantly high number came to Britain, notably the western cities of Liverpool, Manchester and Glasgow. Despite Ireland being part of the United Kingdom, the poor who travelled to Britain had no right to receive relief under the provisions of the English and Scottish Poor Laws, and so had to be returned back home. Thousands were deported under the terms of this legislation. The existence of these Laws of Removal meant that many new immigrants did not apply for any form of relief when they arrived in Britain. However, those who did reach their destination often encountered hostility and antagonism: they had escaped from famine only to find themselves exchanging poverty in Ireland for poverty and prejudice elsewhere. The emigration of so many people meant that the horrors of the Famine, and its legacy, were not simply confined to the island of Ireland but extended to the land of settlement.

After 1849, the regional impact of the Famine became more marked. Whilst recovery was evident, particularly in the north and east, the poorest groups in some of the western districts were facing a fifth year of suffering. In parts of counties Clare and Kerry, the demand for poor relief continued to rise throughout 1849 and 1850. Deteriorating conditions in the Kilrush Union resulted in an official enquiry, with the Commissioners reporting that the Union had lost approximately 50% of its population since 1846. They believed that the local poor had been doubly abandoned – by their landlords and by the British government. They concluded the report by saying:

> Whether as regards the plain principles of humanity, or the literal text and admitted principle of the Poor Law of 1847, a neglect of public opinion has occurred and has occasioned a state of things disgraceful to a civilised age and country, for which some authority ought to be held responsible, and would long since have been held responsible had these things occurred in any union in England.[30]

The 1852 potato crop was free from blight, although dependence on poor relief, disease, emigration and mortality all remained proportionately higher than they had been prior to 1845. Recovery from the Famine proved to be slow and painful

[30] Report of Select Committee appointed to enquire into the administration of the Kilrush Union since 19th September 1848, BPP, 1850, xi

in other ways. The impact of years of malnutrition was trans-generational, and those who were descended from Famine survivors were shorter in stature, and suffered from more poor health and mental illness than had their pre-Famine ancestors. In Scotland, statistics continue to show that many Catholics of Irish descent remain in the most deprived and poorest areas of Glasgow and Lanarkshire and the west-central belt generally where many of them settled. In Ireland, the continued and dramatic fall in population – which was unique amongst European countries – was a further testimony to the long-term impact of the catastrophe that was the Famine.

Nonetheless, the impact of the Famine was viewed positively by some commentators in both Britain and Ireland, who believed that the changes wrought in Ireland between 1845 and 1851 were ultimately beneficial. The first post-Famine Census concluded by saying:

> We feel it will be gratifying to Your Excellency to find that although the population has been diminished in so remarkable a manner by famine, disease and emigration between 1841 and 1851, and has since been decreasing, the results of the Irish census of 1851 are, on the whole, satisfactory, demonstrating as they do, the general advancement of the country.[31]

However 'general advancement of the country' might be taken to mean, such interpretations took no account of the human cost of the Famine – not only in terms of lives lost, but on the lives of those who had survived, and who had lost loved ones. A different explanation of the impact and legacy of the Famine was provided by one of the survivors, an Irish speaker, who came from the Rosses in County Donegal. Writing in the 1870s, she said:

> The years of the Famine, of the bad life and of the hunger, arrived and broke the spirit and the strength of the community. People simply wanted to survive. Their spirit of comradeship was lost. It didn't matter what ties or relations you had, you considered that person to be your friend who gave you food to put in your mouth. Recreation and leisure ceased. Poetry, music and dancing died. These things were lost and completely forgotten. When life improved in other ways, these pursuits never returned as they had been. The Famine killed everything.[32]

[31] General Report of Census Commissioners for 1851 (Dublin, 1854), p. lviii

[32] Recollections of Máire Ní Grianna, Rannafast, the Rosses, County Donegal. Quoted in S. Deane (ed.) The Field Day Anthology of Irish Writing (Derry, 1991), pp. 203-4

Look Back in Hunger: From the Famine to 'The Famine Song'

WILLY MALEY

Starter

I'd like to open with an anecdote. I was in a kebab shop in Partick with some friends of mine a couple of years ago. Div and Jamie are Celtic supporters like me, but Shug, from Musselburgh, is a Hearts fan. As we sat waiting for our orders, this skinny, highly-strung guy started asking about Shug's accent, where was he from, and when he heard he said, 'So, you're a Jambo'. Shug said that's right. The guy obviously assumed the rest of us were out-of-towners too, and soon revealed, in so many words, that he was a Celtic supporter, except he didn't come right out and say it, he just said something favourable about Martin O'Neill. He was as cagey as he was curious, and he was cheeky with it, but at his back, standing slightly off to his right, were two big guys in leather jackets who were listening in. I couldn't work out if they were with him or not, but guessed that they were, because usually when stick insects get lippy like that there's a couple of wasps hovering about as minders. When I said, 'Look, mate, we're Celtic supporters', he took a step back in mock amazement and said, 'Did I say what team I supported?' This verbal jousting continued for a few minutes till the highly-strung closet Celtic supporter left with his order. The two big guys shook their heads, and one of them looked at me and said, 'It was better when we were all bigots'.

I realised three things at that moment. First, that these guys were spectators, not henchmen. Second, that they were Rangers supporters, and comfortable in their own skins. And thirdly, that the big guy had a point. It was one of those moments when you think, 'I hear what you're saying, but I know what you mean'. It's not that it really was better when we were all bigots, but it was better when self-righteousness, cynicism, high-horse-ism, paranoia, and persecution complexes weren't the order of the day. I actually breathed a sigh of relief, and all the tension went out of the air, once the balloon had left the building.

Now, some might say that the edgy, cagey guy was typical of a certain kind of supporter who hedges his bets till he knows what company he's keeping, and that his strange behaviour is a direct result of his being a victim of prejudice who only raises his head above the parapet to make the odd gnomic remark, like those people who talk behind their hands so they can't be lip-read. Fair play. It's well known that the victim of bullying often displays odd behaviour while the bully appears at ease. But I think there is a risk of becoming a victim of your own success in being a victim. This anecdote is aimed at puncturing the pious and po-faced nature of a lot of the debate about 'sectarianism'. Anyway, it's just a story, skewered to my memory, and one that I place here in order for it to stand sentry over what follows.

Mains

Hunger is at the heart of the Irish experience, and since the Irish experience lies behind the foundation of Celtic Football Club, hunger is also at the heart of the Celtic experience. The club was set up in the wake of the waves of mass Irish emigration that followed on from Famine. But is the Famine over, as the song says? And was it really a nineteenth century phenomenon? Even before the Great Hunger of the 1840s there was forced starvation or shortages caused by exploitation or economic mismanagement by the British. 'Hungry man is an angry man', wrote James Joyce in his great novel Ulysses (1922), but fatigue and melancholy were also the results of slow starvation in what was potentially a land of plenty.[1] For another writer, the myths and poetry of the

[1] James Joyce, Ulysses, edited and introduced by Jeri Johnson (Oxford: Oxford University Press, 1993; 1998), p. 161

late nineteenth century had their origins in physical hunger: 'The Celtic Twilight had its origins not in mysticism but in starvation'.[2]

In an essay published twenty years ago the Irish historian Brendan Bradshaw examined sixteenth century English atrocities in order to argue that the Cromwellian massacres in seventeenth century Ireland were not aberrations but were rather 'part of a pattern of violence which was central to the historical experience of the inhabitants of the island in the early modern period'.

Bradshaw detected in recent revisionist historiography a failure to engage with what he called 'the phenomenon of catastrophic violence as a central aspect of the history of the (English/British) conquest'.[3] He accused revisionists of 'cerebralising and, thereby, desensitising the trauma'. The consequences of 'their reticence has been to marginalise a central dimension of the Irish historical experience and, indeed, in some cases virtually to write it out of the record'.[4] Bradshaw says that revisionists were first of all reacting against nationalist historical orthodoxy of the early twentieth century, and later against 'the recrudescence of radical militant nationalism in Northern Ireland'.[5]

The writings of Edmund Spenser and Jonathan Swift show that famine in Ireland was widespread long before the nineteenth century, and that colonial rule was largely responsible. The account of the victims of the Munster famine of the early 1580s is the most visited passage in Spenser's prose dialogue, A View of the State of Ireland (1633). This was a catastrophic event that emptied out a populous area of Ireland, killing 30,000 natives – one for every line of Spenser's epic poem 'The Faerie Queene' – to make way for 3,000 settlers, including Spenser, a lot of collateral damage for a little cultural gain. Spenser's notorious description of the starving Irish may be the View's most frequently cited passage, but critics remain divided as to whether Spenser is lamenting a human disaster, advocating ethnic cleansing, or merely worried about how such a tragic spectacle will affect Queen Elizabeth I's continuing commitment to conquest:

> The end will (I assure me) bee very short and much sooner then can be in so great a trouble, as it seemeth hoped for, although there should none of them fall by the sword, nor bee slaine by the souldiour, yet thus being kept from manurance, and their

[2] Denis Ireland, Eamon De Valera Doesn't See It Through (Cork: Forum Press, 1941), p. 28, cited in Kevin Whelan, 'The Memories of "The Dead" ', The Yale Journal of Criticism 15, 1 (2002), p. 59

[3] Brendan Bradshaw, 'Nationalism and Historical Scholarship in Modern Ireland', Irish Historical Studies 26, 104 (1989), p. 339

[4] Bradshaw, 'Nationalism and Historical Scholarship in Modern Ireland', p. 341

[5] Bradshaw, 'Nationalism and Historical Scholarship in Modern Ireland', p. 342

cattle from running abroad, by this hard restraint they would quickly consume themselves, and devoure one another. The proofe whereof, I saw sufficiently exampled in these late warres of Mounster; for not withstanding that the same was a most rich and plentifull countrey, full of corne and cattle, that you would have thought they should have beene able to stand long, yet ere one yeare and a halfe they were brought to such wretchednesse, as that any stony heart would have rued the same. Out of every corner of the woods and glynnes they came creeping forth upon their hands, for their legs could not beare them; they looked like anatomies of death, they spake like ghosts cryinge out of their graves; they did eate the dead carrions, happy where they could finde them, yea, and one another soone after, insomuch as the very carcasses they spared not to scrape out of their graves; and, if they found a plot of water-cresses or shamrocks, there they flocked as to a feast for the time, yet not able long to continue therewithall; that in short space there were none almost left, and a most populous and plentifull country suddainely left voyde of man and beast; yet sure in all that warre, there perished not many by the sword, but all by the extremitie of famine, which they themselves had wroughte.[6]

The narrative seems torn between the suffering arising from starvation and morbid fascination with survivors resorting to cannibalism. In the course of the account, agency and responsibility shift from the English to the Irish. The Irish were 'kept from manurance', and 'by this hard restraint they would quickly consume themselves and devoure one another', before being finally 'brought to such wretchednesse, as that any stony heart would have rued the same'. But by the end Irenius can claim that the Irish themselves have sown the seeds of their own destruction. Any compassion is cancelled out by this closing assertion. They wrought it, so they bought it.

Spenser's View was published in Dublin in 1633. In 1728, Jonathan Swift completed A Short View of the State of Ireland, a treatise whose title echoes closely that of Spenser's tract. Swift also echoes Spenser's description of lack and hunger in a land of plenty:

But my heart is too heavy to continue this journey longer, for it is manifest that whatever stranger took such a journey, would be apt to think himself travelling in Lapland or Iceland, rather than in a country so favoured by Nature as ours, both in fruitfulness

[6] Andrew Hadfield and Willy Maley (eds.), Edmund Spenser, A View of the State of Ireland (1633): from the first printed edition (Oxford: Blackwell, 1997), pp. 101-2

of soil, and temperature of climate. The miserable dress, and diet, and dwelling of the people. The general desolation in most parts of the Kingdom. The old seats of the nobility and gentry all in ruins, and no new ones in their stead. The families of farmers who pay great rents, living in filth and nastiness upon butter-milk and potatoes, without a shoe or stocking to their feet, or a house so convenient as an English hog-sty to receive them. These indeed may be comfortable sights to an English spectator, who comes for a short time only to learn the language, and returns back to his own country, whither he finds all our wealth transmitted.[7]

Swift's biting satire, A Modest Proposal (1729), appeared in Dublin the following year. It makes it clear that the outrageous idea of eating the Irish is actually already a reality for they are at that very moment being consumed by the English:

Some Persons of a desponding Spirit are in great Concern about that vast Number of poor People who are Aged, Diseased, or Maimed, and I have been desired to employ my Thoughts what Course may be taken, to ease the Nation of so grievous an Incumbrance. But I am not in the least Pain upon that Matter, because it is very well known that they are every Day dying and rotting by Cold and Famine, and Filth, and Vermin, as fast as can be reasonably expected. And as to the young Laborers, they are now in almost as hopeful a Condition. They cannot get Work, and consequently pine away for Want of Nourishment, to a Degree, that if at any Time they are accidentally hired to common Labour, they have not Strength to perform it; and thus the Country, and themselves, are in a fair Way of being soon delivered from the Evils to come.[8]

Swift argues by implication in A Modest Proposal that the real cannibals are the English, and that in advocating that Irish children be cooked and seasoned for English tables he is turning the tables on the English, insofar as he is merely proposing a more extreme version of a state of affairs that already exists. This is a crucial point, because for satire to be successful there has to be a strong element of truth in it, a measure of accuracy. Having recognised that children are dying from poverty, Swift next establishes that they are already being sold like slaves into servitude at this time. The dreadful has already happened – the rich are eating the children of the poor – and Swift's satire is not a proposal at all, but an exposure of the way things really are.

[7] Jonathan Swift, A Short View of the State of Ireland in The prose works of Jonathan Swift D. D. (Vol. 7: Historical and political tracts – Irish), Ed. Temple Scott (London, George Bell & Sons, 1905), pp. 83–91, http://www.ucc.ie/celt/published/E700001-015.html, accessed 16th March 2009

[8] Jonathan Swift, A Modest Proposal. FOR PREVENTING THE CHILDREN OF POOR PEOPLE IN IRELAND, FROM BEING A BURDEN TO THEIR PARENTS OR COUNTRY; AND FOR MAKING THEM BENEFICIAL TO THE PUBLICK (Dublin, 1729), in Seamus Deane (ed.),The Field Day Anthology of Irish Writing (Derry: Field Day, 1991) I, p. 389

The children's flesh is dear, but the landlords can afford it, and after all, since they have already devoured the parents, why not finish the job?

By the time of the Great Hunger of the 1840s, then, Ireland had long been a country where famine was a familiar feature of the landscape. When Celtic Football Club was founded in 1887/88, its establishment came as a consequence of a lengthy period of Irish immigration, and with hunger came a hunger for success. But although football was soon front and centre for many Irish immigrants in Scotland, history and politics were in the wind at their backs. In the old country, the effects of famine and conflict were still being felt. W.B. Yeats wrote a play for the great love of his life, Maud Gonne, The Countess Cathleen (1892), which depicted a starving countryside in which people were reduced to theft in order to survive – yes, they even stole Trevelyan's corn. But the Countess Cathleen sees no sin in stealing from those who stole the land, for 'starving men may take what's necessary/ And yet be sinless.'[9] Crime and a craving for food went hand-in-hand.

In April 1900, copies of The United Irishman, containing an article by Maud Gonne entitled 'The Famine Queen', were seized by the police in Dublin. 'The Famine Queen' is a passionate attack on Queen Victoria's proposed visit to Ireland:

> And in truth, for Victoria, in the decrepitude of her eighty-one years, to have decided after an absence of half-a-century to revisit the country she hates and whose inhabitants are the victims of the criminal policy of her reign, the survivors of sixty years of organised famine, the political necessity must have been terribly strong; for after all she is a woman, and however vile and selfish and pitiless her soul may be, she must sometimes tremble as death approaches when she thinks of the countless Irish mothers who, sheltering under the cloudy Irish sky, watching their starving little ones, have cursed her before they died.[10]

Maud Gonne, though of English birth, became a passionate and vociferous opponent of British colonialism, and converted to Catholicism in 1903 when she married John MacBride, one of those later executed after the Easter Rising.

[9] W. B. Yeats, The Countess Cathleen (1892), scene 2, in W. B. Yeats: Collected Plays (Basingstoke: Macmillan, 1934; 1992), pp. 20-21

[10] Maud Gonne, The Famine Queen (1900)

Irish drama at the turn of the century was preoccupied with images of hunger. In George Bernard Shaw's play, Man and Superman (1903), first performed in its entirety in Edinburgh in 1915, the wealthy Irish-American Hector Malone says:

> MALONE: . . . Me father died of starvation in Ireland in the black 47. Maybe you've heard of it.
>
> VIOLET. The Famine?
>
> MALONE [**with smouldering passion**]: No, the starvation. When a country is full o food, and exporting it, there can be no famine. Me father was starved dead; and I was starved out to America in me mother's arms. English rule drove me and mine out of Ireland.[11]

For Malone, Blighty's blight is the cause of Paddy's plight. There was certainly an outpouring of grief and sympathy on the part of Irish writers for the crisis in the country.

Famine and forced starvation went hand-in-hand with images of hunger as protest. In Yeats's powerful play, The King's Threshold (1904), the King explains the protest of the Seanchan:

> He has chosen death:
> Refusing to eat or drink, that he may bring
> Disgrace upon me; for there is a custom,
> An old and foolish custom, that if a man
> Be wronged, or think that he is wronged, and starve
> Upon another's threshold till he die,
> The common people, for all time to come,
> Will raise a heavy cry against that threshold,
> Even though it be the King's.[12]

When his oldest pupil tries to persuade him to give up his fast, the Seanchan replies:

> There's nothing that can tether the wild mind
> That, being moonstruck and fantastical,
> Goes where it fancies. I had even thought
> I knew your voice and face, but now the words
> Are so unlikely that I needs must ask
> Who is it that bids me put my hunger by.[13]

In James Joyce's Ulysses (1922), the citizen speaks of the

[11] George Bernard Shaw, 'Man and Superman: A Comedy and a Philosophy', ed. Dan H. Laurence with an Introduction by Stanley Weintraub (1903; Harmondsworth: Penguin, 2000), p. 184

[12] W. B. Yeats, The King's Threshold (1904), in W. B. Yeats: Collected Plays (Basingstoke: Macmillan, 1934; 1992), p. 109

[13] W. B. Yeats, The King's Threshold (1904), in W. B. Yeats: Collected Plays, p. 111

lasting legacy of famine, a human catastrophe that gave rise to the 'coffin ships' and fed the gothic imagination, including the mind of the Irish writer, Bram Stoker, who wrote Dracula (1897). There was a vampire sucking Ireland's lifeblood in the shape of the spectre of famine. Joyce's Cyclopean Citizen, extreme in his views, nonetheless captures some of the rage against the Great Hunger:

> We'll put force against force, says the citizen. We have our greater Ireland beyond the sea. They were driven out of house and home in the black 47. Their mudcabins and their shielings by the roadside were laid low by the batteringram and the Times rubbed its hands and told the whitelivered Saxons there would soon be as few Irish in Ireland as redskins in America. Even the Grand Turk sent us his piastres. But the Sassenach tried to starve the nation at home while the land was full of crops that the British hyenas bought and sold in Rio de Janeiro. Ay, they drove out the peasants in hordes. Twenty thousand of them died in the coffinships. But those that came to the land of the free remember the land of bondage. And they will come again and with a vengeance, no cravens, the sons of Granuaile, the champions of Kathleen ni Houlihan.[14]

In Heathcliff and The Great Hunger (1995), Terry Eagleton underlined the significance of the famine for the language and identity of modern Ireland:

> During the Famine, starving families boarded themselves into their cabins, so that their deaths might go decently unviewed. After the event, there were villages which could still speak Irish but didn't; it was considered bad luck.[15]

Declan Kiberd, in Inventing Ireland (1995), goes so far as to argue that 'Ireland after the famines of the mid-nineteenth century was a sort of nowhere, waiting for its appropriate images and symbols to be inscribed in it'. Kiberd claims that Ireland was almost obliterated by the Great Hunger: 'For, after the famines and emigration of the 1840s, "Ireland" had almost ceased to exist in the old Gaelic way: what was left – the remaining voices confirmed this – was a terrifyingly open space, in places and in persons'.[16] It was out of this desolation that the Celtic Revival came, and Celtic Football Club was part of that revival.

In 1995, the same year that the studies by Eagleton and

[14] James Joyce, Ulysses, ed. and intro. by Jeri Johnson (Oxford: Oxford University Press, 1993; 1998), p. 316

[15] Terry Eagleton, Heathcliff and the Great Hunger: Studies in Irish Culture (London: Verso, 1995), p. 12

[16] Declan Kiberd, Inventing Ireland: The Literature of the Modern Nation (London: Jonathan Cape, 1995), p. 115

Kiberd appeared, Professor Amartya Kumar Sen, winner of the 1998 Nobel Prize in Economics, and Master of Trinity College, Cambridge, published a short essay in Granta Magazine, entitled 'Nobody Need Starve'. Professor Sen wrote: 'The question that arises is this: why was Ireland, with so little food, exporting food to England, which had so much?' Sen argues:

> The British government did not set out deliberately to starve the Irish. Britain did not blockade Ireland, or foment the potato blights, or undertake public policies aimed at weakening the Irish economy. But we know from studies of famines and averted famines across the world that they are easy to prevent when the government decides to act. . . So the real question is: why were these steps not taken in Ireland? . . . This is where political alienation – of the governors from the governed – is important. The direct penalties of a famine are borne by one group of people and political decisions are taken by another. The rulers never starve. . . It is not surprising that in the gruesome history of famines there is hardly any case in which a famine has occurred in a country that is independent and democratic, regardless of whether it is rich or poor. . . The estrangement of the rulers from the ruled did, of course, take a very special form in the case of the Irish famines, given the long tradition of English scepticism towards the Irish, Ireland paid the penalty of being governed by a not particularly sympathetic ruling class, and cultural depreciation added force to political asymmetry. . . The Irish taste for the potato was added to the list of calamities which the natives had, in the English view, brought on themselves. Charles Edward Trevelyan, the head of the Treasury during the famines, who saw not much wrong with British policies in Ireland, of which he was a major architect, took the opportunity to remark:–'There is scarcely a woman of the peasant class in the West of Ireland whose culinary art exceeds the boiling of a potato.' The remark is interesting not just because it is rare for an Englishman to find a suitable opportunity for an international criticism of culinary art, but also because pointing the accusing finger at the Irish peasant diet vividly illustrates the inclination to fault some characteristic of the victim, rather than the conduct of the rulers.[17]

In The Irish Crisis (1848), Trevelyan asked, 'what hope is there for a nation which lives on potatoes?' This is the same Trevelyan who saw famine as a 'mechanism for reducing surplus population'. For this British colonial governor, the catastrophe

[17] Amartya Sen, 'Nobody need starve', Granta, 52 (1995), pp. 213-20, http://www.misu.ait.ac.th/NewsAndEvents/newsletterData/HTMLFormat/iss2no2/starve.htm, accessed 16th March 2009

that annihilated a generation (and had effects for generations thereafter) was a judgment on its victims: 'The judgement of God sent the calamity to teach the Irish a lesson, that calamity must not be too much mitigated. . . The real evil with which we have to contend is not the physical evil of the Famine, but the moral evil of the selfish, perverse and turbulent character of the people'. Trevelyan saw the famine as a godsend that had cleared the colonists of a major obstacle to their rule – the Irish people themselves:

> Now, thank God, we are in a different position; and although many waves of disturbance must pass over us before that troubled sea can entirely subside, and time must be allowed for morbid habits to give place to a more healthy action, England and Ireland are, with one great exception, subject to equal laws; and, so far as the maladies of Ireland are traceable to political causes, nearly every practicable remedy has been applied. The deep and inveterate root of social evil remained, and this has been laid bare by a direct stroke of an all-wise and all-merciful Providence, as if this part of the case were beyond the unassisted power of man. Innumerable had been the specifics which the wit of man had devised; but even the idea of the sharp but effectual remedy by which the cure is likely to be effected had never occurred to any one. God grant that the generation to which this great opportunity has been offered, may rightly perform its part, and that we may not relax our efforts until Ireland fully participates in the social health and physical prosperity of Great Britain, which will be the true consummation of their union.[18]

From Trevelyan's perspective, a nation consumed by hunger was a consummation devoutly to be wished. That's how slavemasters run plantations.

Terry Eagleton had likened the impact of the Great Hunger, its human devastation, to the Holocaust, and on September 10th 1996, the New Jersey Commission on Holocaust Education approved for inclusion in the Holocaust and Genocide Curriculum at the secondary level a new curriculum on 'The Great Irish Famine':

> This curriculum is dedicated to the millions of Irish who suffered and perished in the Great Starvation. It is also dedicated to those who escaped by emigration, and to the great Irish Diaspora worldwide.[19]

[18] Charles Edward Trevelyan, The Irish Crisis (London: Longman, 1848), p. 201

[19] 'The Great Irish Famine', http://www.nde.state.ne.us/SS/irish/irish_pf.html, accessed 15th March 2009

The 150th anniversary of the Irish Famine/Great Hunger/ Mass Starvation saw the publication of a great deal of history addressing a considerable catastrophe. Two years ago, William H. Mulligan, writing a retrospective piece on Cecil Woodham-Smith's The Great Hunger (1962), spoke of 'The Case for Emotion':

> As I see it, the great strength of [Woodham-Smith's] book, however, is not its research base, but precisely its emotional intensity. There are few shades of gray in Woodham-Smith's view of the Famine. Even the title makes a clear interpretive statement. There are villains, victims, and people who merit praise for their relief efforts. They all are well developed; they emerge as real people. Even the villains have some good qualities, but they remain villains. The character and motivation of people involved at every level is analysed in detail. There are no easy labels attached to people or policies or straw men set up as easy targets to demolish. This makes Woodham-Smith's argument harder to dismiss or discount; she has weighed the evidence and not jumped to conclusions.[20]

The Famine Song

In 2008, the Irish Famine was back on the back page. On 16th September 2008, Graham Spiers reported in The Times on 'The Famine Song', sung by some supporters of Glasgow Rangers Football Club:

> Rangers have again been left with no option but to ask their supporters to stop singing an offensive song after fresh political pressure was brought to bear on the club yesterday. A section of Ibrox fans has recently taken to singing a particular chant about the Irish-Catholic community in Scotland. The song was given fresh volume and expression at last month's Old Firm match at Celtic Park. Yesterday Rangers admitted that they have been working behind the scenes in conjunction with Strathclyde Police to try to have the song – unofficially known as 'The Famine Song' – stamped out. The club even warned that supporters could be arrested if caught indulging in the chant. The song refers to the Irish Famine of the 1840s which killed an estimated one million people and triggered mass migration to Scotland, and includes the line: 'The famine's over . . . why don't you go home?'[21]

[20] William H. Mulligan, 'The Case for Emotion: Looking Back at The Great Hunger', New Hibernia Review 11, 4 (2007), p. 152

[21] Graham Spiers, 'Rangers urge supporters to stop singing "Famine Song" ', The Times (16th September 2008), http://www.timesonline.co.uk/tol/sport/football/scotland/article4762091.ece, accessed 15th March 2009

One of the Famine Song's verses urges Scotland's Irish community to return to the old country now that the Famine is over:

I often wonder where they would have been
If we hadn't have taken them in
Fed them and washed them
Thousands in Glasgow alone
From Ireland they came
Brought us nothing but trouble and shame
Well the famine is over
Why don't they go home?[22]

The song implies a welcome overstayed, but in truth the welcome wasn't always a warm one and the contribution that the Irish in Scotland have made at all levels has often gone unappreciated, not least the contribution to Scottish and world soccer made by Celtic Football Club.

I started with Edmund Spenser, where my academic work in Irish studies began twenty-five years ago, but the real beginning of my Irish connection goes back to the aftermath of the Great Hunger that drove my grandfather and his brothers and sisters to leave Mayo, three brothers to Glasgow, three sisters to Ohio. They were among the thousands who left Ireland in the Famine's wake, pushed away by the after-effects of a tidal wave of trauma that broke on distant shores and rippled down the generations. I don't know the exact date in the late 1880s or early 1890s that my grandfather came over from Castlebar, but I came across this reference recently in Hansard, the official record of the House of Commons, that says something about the state of things in Mayo at that time:

DISTRESS (IRELAND) – FAMINE FEVER IN MAYO.
MR. A. M. SULLIVAN I wish to ask the right hon. Gentleman, Whether the Government have received in London any confirmation of the serious news from Ireland which I see reported in The Evening Standard in reference to the outbreak of famine fever in Ireland? It is contained in a report from the hon. secretary of the Charleston, county Mayo, Relief Committee, and he says – 'The famine fever (and a most dangerous [typhoid]) is now very prevalent, and making such progress that I fear there will not be ere long a village in all the parish free from it. Of course the destitute were the first to be

22 'The Famine Song',
http://
www.totalfootball
forums.com/
forums/index.php/
showtopic=35490,
accessed 16th
March 2009

visited by this awful disease; but, like death itself, it respects no persons, and very shortly makes its unwelcome visit to the well-to-do and independent. I have seen three pass by me this week to the workhouse from the little village in which I reside. Only the week before I saw the widow borne to the grave from her orphans, and only the wall separates me from the room where the wife of a respected member of our committee lies dangerously ill.' I should like to ask the right hon. Gentleman, Whether, having the experience of 1847 before him, he has any information on this sad subject? [21st June 1880][23]

'The Famine Song', that song sung by Rangers supporters urging the Irish in Scotland to go home, is sung to the tune of The Beach Boys' 'Sloop John B', a wonderful old folk song – actually a pirate song from the West Indies – recorded by The Weavers and The Kingston Trio, among others. The 1966 Beach Boys version goes:

We come on the Sloop John B
My grandfather and me
Around Nassau town we did roam
Drinking all night
Got into a fight
Well I feel so broke up
I want to go home.[24]

What goes around comes around. Six years before The Beach Boys released 'Sloop John B' as a single, Lonnie Donegan had a UK Top 10 hit with a version entitled 'I Wanna Go Home'. This was 1960, the year of my birth. Lonnie Donegan was born Anthony James Donegan in Bridgeton, Glasgow, a part of the city with strong links to Glasgow Rangers. Lonnie Donegan, as his name suggests, had many Irish connections. His Scottish-born father, Peter John Donegan, bore an Irish surname, and his Irish-born mother, Mary Josephine Deighan, completed the picture. Chris Pendergast the Gaelic Footballer was a relative, and in 2000 Donegan played on Van Morrison's album, The Skiffle Sessions – Live in Belfast 1998. He was awarded the MBE in 2000. What would this Irish-Scottish Glaswegian from Bridgeton and Member of the British Empire have made of the song he charted with in 1960 being used as a stick to beat the Irish in Scotland? Donegan died in 2002, so it's too late to ask him.

[23] http://hansard.millbank systems.com/commons/1880/jun/21/distress-ireland-famine-fever-in-mayo, accessed 16th March 2009

[24] The Beach Boys, 'Sloop John B', Pet Sounds (Capitol, 1966)

Personally, I'm against censorship when it comes to singing. The terraces are policed now in a way they never were before and the right to free speech, which will always come into conflict with the principle of no platform for racism and hate speech, is under threat in our surveillance society, with its obsession with political correctness. And while I'm against the 'curse on both your houses mentality' when it comes to the so-called 'Old Firm', I don't think Celtic supporters should get on too high a horse after the bananas and the gorilla suit at Mark Walters' debut, or the individual Celtic fan who did the post-9:11 plane-impersonation for the benefit of Claudio Reyna. We want to think of these people as a small minority — just as I would want to think of the fascist Franco supporters who wrote to me after I did a piece on the Spanish Civil War in The Celtic View as an anomaly. But all football clubs are broad churches, with quite a few non-believers standing outside. Nobody can iron out all the differences and difficulties in ninety minutes. Amid all the politics and prejudice, the banter and the bigotry, there's a pantomime element. When they get out the flute, we get out the violin.

I don't sing myself, barring an occasional rendition of 'The Willie Maley Song' and 'You'll Never Walk Alone'. I'm aware that 'The Famine Song', with its disparaging allusion to 'Athenry Mike', is clearly in part a response to 'The Fields of Athenry', a haunting air that touches on the nineteenth century realities of famine, landlordism, eviction and transportation. It is a 'rebel song' of sorts, insofar as many Irish songs are about resistance and the spirit of freedom. But then so are many national anthems. The national anthem of the United States, 'The Star-Spangled Banner', is a much more explicit rebel song that cries out in defiance in the face of the age-old strategies of British imperialism: bombing, besieging, invasion and occupation. At this point in history, when journalism urges us to forget the past, I think popular song — including the national anthem of the United States of America — has an especially important role to play in reminding us of the crimes and cruelties of empire, and of the value of resistance in the face of tyranny. 'The Star-Spangled Banner' should actually have been blazoned on the front pages given what was happening in Gaza at the end of 2008:

And the rocket's red glare, the bombs bursting in air,
Gave proof thro' the night that our flag was still there.
Oh! say, does that star-spangled banner yet wave,
O'er the land of the free and the home of the brave?

But nobody's talking about banning anti-British/English songs at all, nor even banning protest songs or rebel songs. 'Flower of Scotland' is safe. The anxiety is about any song that has an Irish theme and might be sung by Celtic supporters. I'm waiting to hear that Dana's 'All Kinds of Everything' is on the hit list. What next? Ronan Keating? Songs can be spoiled by cover versions though. As a kid, I loved Lee Marvin singing 'Wandering Star' in Paint Your Wagon (1969), but they hijacked it with their Union Jack and a song about a migrant spirit becomes a hymn to her Britannic majesty. 'Do you know where hell is? Hell is in hello, hello'. If you're still feeling 'Lee Marvin', there's a sweet to follow.

A little bit of afters

Ironically, 'The Famine Song' has raised the spectre of the famine again, in the act of declaring it over, just as Trevelyan declared it over, even in the face of mass starvation. The Irish in Scotland know different. We still walk in famine's wake, in the footsteps of our grandfathers, grandmothers, great grandfathers and great grandmothers. Nietzsche says somewhere that mob memory – popular memory – doesn't stretch back much further than the grandparents, but even that can be quite a stretch. In my case it goes all the way back to 1871. There is a collective memory, passed down within families, of the experience of dislocation and distress. Although the stories of the Irish in Scotland are as diverse as the thousands of individuals who carry those tales in their heads, there is a common root. Speaking of the African-American experience, Toni Morrison has said: 'My single solitary and individual life is like the lives of the tribe; it differs in these specific ways, but it is a balanced life because it is both solitary and representative'.[25]

Those of us who've made our home in Scotland, whose Irish families fled famine fever and the many other consequences of

[25] Toni Morrison, 'Rootedness: The Ancestor as Foundation', in Dennis Walder (ed.), Literature in the Modern World: Critical Essays and Documents (Oxford: Oxford University Press, 1990), p. 327

81

British rule, aren't going anywhere. We are entitled to call Coatbridge, Glasgow, Greenock, etc, home now. This land is our land. Irish labour helped build Scotland's infrastructure, its canals, bridges, houses, roads and railways. And in the East End of Glasgow a shrine was built to the Irish experience in Scotland, a Cathedral of Football. There was always more than one forge at Parkhead. Celtic Park was a forge where a community bruised by history took refuge.

Hopefully Celtic fans would never find it within themselves to sing 'The Plantation's over, Why don't you go home'. I know that for Ulster Scots the sacrifice at the Somme is a major event. In 1916 the Easter rising and the Ulster Scots sacrifice at the Somme will be marked. The Somme Heritage Centre, which opened near Newtownards, Co. Down, in 1994, is one measure of the continuing impact of that event on political consciousness in the North. I teach texts that treat the trauma of the Somme from a Northern Irish perspective, in drama and poetry, including Michael Longley's powerful verse 'Wounds' (1985) and Frank McGuinness's moving play, Observe The Sons of Ulster Marching to the Somme (1986).

When I hear some Celtic fans add that line to the wonderful 'On the One Road' that says 'Soon there'll be no Protestants at all', I'm angry, not just as a Celtic fan, but as a bridge-building, border-crossing, Irish-Scottish Bhoy with an Irish-born grand-father, a Catholic father, and a Protestant schooling. I don't like 'The Famine Song' but like the Murphy's, I'm not bitter. How could I be? The great Irish writers I've cited above – Swift and Yeats and Shaw – were all Protestants. Finally, it's sacrilege for a Celtic supporter to confess, but last year's guilty pleasure was It's Rangers For Me? (Fort Publishing, 2008), edited by Ronnie Esplin and Graham Walker. If you can't join them you've got to read them. Besides, my wee mammy's a bluenose, and provided I can keep her flute hidden I can live with that.

Celtic is about more than football. It is about faith and family, and yes, the Famine's there too, as part of the history of Irish immigration that brought the club into being. History's never over, which is no reason to assume that the same old story has to be told over and over. We can look back in hunger, yes, and around us in bewilderment at times, but forward too in hope. I wrote these lines after my father died. I never knew his Irish-born father, my grandfather, Edward Malley, who died in 1929, or my great grandfather, Michael Malley, whose children left Ireland haunted and hungry and scarred by scarcity:

> We walk in famine's wake
> In the footsteps of families
> Driven out of homesteads at hunger's hands
> Into the often unwelcoming arms of strangers
> My grandfather slept in a doorway
> Three nights
> Coming to Glasgow
> To work in famine's wake
> Now, up to our knees in knee-jerk reactions
> Watching grown men in shorts
> Leathering leather, white on emerald
> We're told it's over, time to go home
> But home is where we put down roots
> Where we watched the first green shoots
> Of recovery from trauma
> This is where we'll line the loam
> In Paradise, the place we call home.

CELTIC STORIES

'They Gave Us James McGrory. . .'

Gerard McDade

On the 29th January 1977, Celtic drew 1-1 with Airdrie at Broomfield in the third round of the Scottish Cup. Johnny Doyle popped up with a crucial equaliser that day to take the tie back to Glasgow and keep Jock Stein on course for a League and Cup double in the Master's last meaningful season at the helm. It was also the day Neil Coll died. . . and he was my grandfather.

Granda Coll had taught me many things in my, as then, twelve years. Pale Ale was best served cold, John Wayne had never made a bad 'picter', Red Rum was a National 'cert' and above all, the greatest player who ever kicked a ball in Celtic colours was **James McGrory**. When I poured his beer, glass tilted at 45 degrees to afford the slightest head, he would let me sip the delicious foam. Saturday nights were re-scheduled if one of the 'Duke's' westerns was on the box so that we could pay homage together and when Red Rum crossed the line at Aintree two years in a row, we cheered as though we owned the damn horse!

But. . . McGrory!. . . who was he when we had Dalglish? Big 'Neilly' was aye adamant.

Look 'im up in yer history books. . . James McGrory, the Celtic's greatest ever goal-scorer.

In the 1970s, of course, there was no Google . There was no Ask Jeeves.com. Thankfully, there was the Scorcher! Annual 1975 which, that year, had an item called The Celtic Story.

True to its claim, this was an illustrated, albeit abbreviated version of the Hoops history. Packed full with the legends, the goals and the games, it was a treat for any Celtic-minded individual and there, amongst the glitterati, Stein, McNeill, Johnstone, Dalglish et al was one 'Jimmy McGrory'. He even had a panel to himself highlighting his achievements. The 50 goal season of 1935-36, the astonishing 8 goals in one game record versus Dunfermline in 1928 and the outstanding career total of over **five hundred** competitive goals: these and more marked McGrory out as one of the true greats. No wonder he was my Granda's favourite.

Yet Neilly had another reason for touting McGrory as the most revered of all Celts. . . he was his cousin! Or so he said for, true to his roots, he was a man fierce with the craic. Those roots had him born in the hilly, Creaghdoes area of St Johnston, Co. Donegal in May 1905. It would be decades later, on one of my infrequent trips to that windswept, relatively unchanging hinterland that I would learn that Neilly's mother, shortly after giving birth to him, had died and as a result, he had been farmed out to his mother's sister to be reared. She lived a short distance from Creaghdoes in a cottage at the edge of what was, with brilliantly observed Irish wit, referred to as the Five Roads End. So called because it sat at the convergence of, yup, you guessed it, five roads. Only in Ireland, could a crossroads have five points as opposed to the traditional four!

Like so many of his compatriots, he left his birth-land in search of employment on a journey that took him across the Irish Sea to a gasworks in Greenock on the River Clyde. By that time, Neilly was in his early 30s, married to Annie-Jane, also late of St Johnston and was on his way to raising seven children. The west of Scotland wasn't exactly Shangri-la but it did have work, a certain amount of job security and of course, it had 'the Celtic'. At that time, the club was approaching its fiftieth birthday and apart from being an established success story on the field, it had also proved a rallying point for those displaced Irishmen, such as Neill Coll, who discovered that Celtic was more than just a football club. To the Celtic-minded, it was a way of life.

This would be the legacy that he would pass on to me, coming along as I did, at the outset of the glorious Stein era. By the time I was 10, Celtic had achieved the 9-in-a-row, been crowned

European champions and I had been steeped in the tradition and heritage of, as my granda would say, the **only** club. When you've just reached double figures and filled your scrapbooks on all things Celtic, then anything no matter how implausible, that could link you to the Bhoys, would be regarded as life-defining! Under normal circumstances, I would have grabbed the McGrory legend and held onto it for all of its value yet, I knew my granda . . . I knew his way with the craic! On any number of occasions, I'd been well hung out to dry by his Donegal tales recounting horse-drawn hearses with no drivers or the story of the colleen who'd gone to the forbidden Sunday dancing only to discover that her jive partner had the cloven hooves of the devil!

But this was McGrory!

This was Celtic!

At school, once, there was a girl who swore blind that her father worked with the sister-in-law of Jim Brogan and although, clearly, she could never actually claim to be related to the stylish Hoops defender, this information was enough to have us all following her around like lovesick puppies for a week. I guess we always thought that Brogan might just appear one day and pick her up because her father had to work late with the famous sister-in-law!

In the midst of all this high-pitched Celtic fever, I casually slipped into a classroom conversation one day that Jimmy McGrory and I shared the same blood, albeit somewhat loosely, and sat back waiting for the explosion. It never arrived.

Nearly all of my schoolmates said 'Who??' One did actually say 'Is he no' deid??' (Which offended me but at least showed that he'd heard of McGrory.) I, naturally leapt on the defensive with this traitor shouting, 'No, of course not! He still works for Celtic!' However, truthfully, I didn't know this to be a fact. I mean, he could have been dead, he had to be in his 70s after all but I just hadn't bothered to find out. Some cousiny-grandson, eh? The next time I saw my granda, I asked.

'Sure, he's alive this long time, but I never saw him that much after he got married again.'

Which was wayyyyy confusing! To be that close to a legend and not bother to stay in touch . . . what was that all about? I still wasn't convinced.

'Did you ever see him play?' On this, Neilly was adamant. 'Surely!! Used to go to the home games and then we'd meet up after the matches as well. There was me, my brother Hughie and himself. Rare times; but we lost touch.'

And that was it!

To me, it was like saying that after every game at Celtic Park, Kenny Dalglish and I would get together for a poke of chips on London Road. We'd talk about the match, the penalty that Rangers would surely have been awarded in the last minute, our hopes for world peace or anything else that my cuz, the King, wanted to discuss and then after a few years of this we'd drifted apart like 'The Beatles'!

Unbelievable!!

The Celts were in my blood. . . under my skin. . . pretty much the first thing I thought about when I opened my eyes and the last thing I considered as I lay, head back, on my souvenir '9-in-a-row' pillow case at night. The fact that Celtic-minded Neilly had just let this part of his life ebb away like a Willie Waddell title challenge was hard to take. The next obsession was a simple one. If Jimmy McGrory was flesh-of-my-flesh, blood-of-my-blood etc etc. . . then wasn't it possible, that just maybe, some of his talent had been unconsciously handed down as well???

It was back to 'The Scorcher' again. They also had another story called 'Billy's Boots'. Billy Dane was a schoolbhoy (sorry, couldn't resist) who'd inherited the football boots of a long-gone hero called Dead-Shot Keen. Keen was clearly based on Dixie Dean from the 1930s but because Billy had his boots in the 1970s, he could play like the master himself.

This happy coincidence opened a door to a host of adventures that generally ended with Billy scoring a last-minute winner in any number of school/ county/ international matches. The fact that none of his team-mates, clad as they were in their Adidas or Puma screw-in studs, ever questioned Billy's knackered footwear, never occurred to me as being odd. Hell, the guy was banging them in like our Dixie Deans. . . who would query that?

The upshot was that I started to fashion myself on McGrory in the belief that I could imitate his scoring prowess. However, one day, after yet another fruitless outing in front of goal comparable to the future Tony Cascarino drought, I asked my granda, 'how come I hadn't inherited anything from the McGrory gene pool?'

'Sure you have. . . you, me and McGrory all have the Coll ears!!'

Now, there could be no denying that when it came to the appendages, I was in the company of Mr Spock as was big Neilly who re-christened me after seeing the Vulcan on the only time he ever watched Star Trek. (n.b. Vulcans have green blood. . . no' bad, eh?). But, this was too much to take. Celtic's greatest ever goal-scorer. . . 8 in one game against Dunfermline. . . a manager who had guided the Hoops to the Coronation Cup and engineered the 7-1 'Hampden in the Sun' feast day and all I got from him was a set of sticky-out lugs!!!

Gee, thanks Mr McGrory.

At 12, you think you know it all and so I gave up the ghost that I was, in any way, related to James McGrory. I didn't even think about it on the crisp February morning of my Granda's funeral when I suppose you could have argued that Neilly's famous cousin would have made an appearance. In truth, I was probably too distracted. I'd never dealt with death before on this intimate level and the hurt was mixed with a fascination at the traditions involved when the patriach of a large family is prepared for the final journey. Even the Celts turning over Airdrie 4-0 in the cup replay the night after Neilly had been laid to rest couldn't heal the loss, though Granda Coll would surely have warmed to that 'Tic-tastic' performance.

Jimmy McGrory followed Neilly to that other Paradise just five years later in 1982 and was accorded the kind of sensitive media send-off befitting his status. The newspapers recounted his story, illustrated with reports from the time and a succession of honorary Celts recalled when McGrory had ruled Scottish football. In the midst of it all, one photograph, in particular, caught my eye. It was from the early 1970s and showed Bobby Murdoch being congratulated on scoring Celtic's 6,000th competitive goal. He was joined by Adam McLean (2,000th), Jimmy Delaney (4000th) and one Jimmy McGrory (3,000th). Yet another feat to add to the McGrory canon but, there, in that photograph was a clue. I'd never seen a picture of McGrory beyond the '30s when he was in his prime and naturally, only had an image of my granda in his later years but, by God, the resemblance was uncanny. They could have passed for brothers.

Perhaps Neilly hadn't been 'knockin' the tear from me' as he would have said and that the myth was, in fact, true. At the time, I decided not to follow up on the story, preferring to believe, through the medium of that picture, that secretly, the link was there and would remain just that. . . a nice unproven little episode that life can sometimes throw your way. I continued in this vein, content in the knowledge that what was past, was past, for the next twenty-four years. Turbulent times for the Bhoys, of course, given the highs of the Centenary Double season, the darkest of lows throughout the 'sack-the-board-buddy-can-you-lend-a-dime' era of the '90s, the sweetest of sweet fruit that was Martin O'Neill's millennium crusade and then the treble-winning Gordon Strachan seasons as well. It was only when my wife, Irene, gave me a book for Christmas that I once again, rekindled my bhoyish regard for the story of Jimmy McGrory.

Eminent actor, writer and, to be honest, too many other jobs to count, John Cairney had, somehow, amongst a hectic cv, found time to write about the life and times of James Edward McGrory. This was, clearly, for John, a labour of love and I would recommend the lyrically written 'Heroes Are Forever – The Life & Times of Celtic Legend Jimmy McGrory' to anyone who values his football and cherishes his values. To you, it would be a great read. . . but, to me, it was a moment of validation. For there, in the opening three lines of the very first chapter of a rich life story were Jimmy McGrory's roots. . .

On 25th September 1897, Henry McGrory married Catherine Coll in St Johnston Co. Donegal

The words still engage a shudder in my mind and I have to

admit that, when I casually came across this opening passage, the impact of the sentence quite literally lifted me from my chair. In black and white, John Cairney had opened the story for the reader whilst simultaneously, closing a chapter for me. It had taken thirty years to convince me but Neil Coll had never lied. . . his father's sister had married Jimmy McGrory's father. . . Neilly was a first cousin to the greatest goal-scorer in Celtic's history. . . my granda was genetically linked to the Celtic story as was I. . . and now we had more than just the ears to prove it!

All together now. . . 'They gave us James McGrory and Paul McStaaaayyy. . .'

The inclusiveness
of the Celtic minded

COLIN DEENY

'Auntie Grace was the one who introduced me to Celtic at the age of nine. My dad was serving in West Africa at the time and I felt I was on a big adventure myself when I paid my first visit to Celtic Park on 15 October 1949. I got off to a winning start when Celtic beat Aberdeen, 4-2, with Mike Haughney scoring two goals in the final ten minutes.'   Billy McNeill

And so it is that Auntie Grace is given credit for introducing one of the most important figures in the last fifty years of the club's history to the big adventure of Celtic. I am sure though, that had Auntie Grace not done so, someone else from the Celtic community would have. But what is of note about parts of the Celtic community around the Lanarkshire town of Bellshill, including Auntie Grace and the young Billy McNeill, was the Lithuanian connection. For Billy's mother and Auntie Grace, along with a number of others in the mining rows of Lanarkshire, were the children of Lithuanian immigrants: and they all tended to support Celtic.[1]

So why is it that immigrants from Lithuania, then considered a far and distant country, decided to support Celtic? At first glance on the part of someone unfamiliar with their story it may appear that Lithuanians supported Celtic simply because they were Catholic and Celtic have strong and significant links with the immigrant Catholic community in Scotland. For while Celtic was one of the only football clubs in Scotland – indeed, one of

1. McNeill B. 'Hail Cesar. The Autobiography', London, Headline Book Publishing 2004

the only public institutions – where Catholicism was not only welcome but was an integral part of the club's culture, ethos and identity, it was not a case of Lithuanians arriving off the boat recognising Celtic's Catholic identity and deciding to support them. There is more depth to their affinity with Celtic than that. Rather, their experiences in Scotland meant that they readily identified with the Irish and their offspring, the largest group of immigrants in Scotland, and Celtic was the club of the Irish in Scotland. As a result they readily identified with the inclusive ethos of this Irish and Catholic soccer club. To understand why you have to know some of their story.

Post Reformation Scotland experienced its first substantial wave of immigration from the mid 1800s onwards. At that time the country was dominated by what has been described as 'two great powers'.[2] One was heavy industry, the other Presbyterianism. These helped define the national character and identity. Scotland was in the midst of the industrial revolution and was turning to heavy industries, for example shipbuilding and engineering. These needed coal and as such the period from the mid 1850s until World War I was the age of coal and iron. By 1870 the west of Scotland, including Glasgow, was producing eighty per cent of Scotland's coal. Despite technological advances, the extractive industries still remained heavily dependent on a large workforce. Therefore, not surprisingly, Glasgow's population increased dramatically as deposed immigrants arrived from the Highlands and many more fleeing from the Great Irish Hunger, as well as economic, religious and political persecution in Ireland. Most of the Irish and some of Scottish Highlanders were Catholic. Industry owners took advantage of this vast pool of cheap labour. The arrival of the Catholics – especially the Irish – as others have documented and discussed in the Celtic Minded series, inadvertently challenged the perceived cultural and Presbyterian homogeneity of the native Scots.

Despite the tensions, iron and steel companies continued to recruit abroad. Although the 1880s represented the high point of immigration from Ireland to Scotland, beyond this community, there was a smaller but quite distinct and significant wave of immigration from Tsarist Russia, most of whom were Lithuanians.

2. Kernohan R.D. 'The Many Faces of Scotland' in Contemporary Review Vol.269 pp.234+ 1996

This took place between the 1880s and the start of World War I in 1914. About 8,000 Lithuanians settled in Scotland while a further number, perhaps in the region of 15,000, were resident in Scotland for a short time before moving on elsewhere or returning to Lithuania.[3,4] Most Lithuanians were Catholic with a minority Jewish. The Jewish community joined many Irish by settling in Glasgow's Gorbals area and proceeded to set up craft and merchant businesses similar to those they worked at in Lithuania. The more numerous Catholic Lithuanians took up work in the mines and therefore settled in the mining areas of Ayrshire and, in particular, Lanarkshire.

The Lithuanians' reasons for leaving their homeland can often be seen to mirror that of their fellow immigrant Irish. The Lithuanians were poor, coming primarily from peasant people. They were oppressed. An abortive rebellion against the Russians in 1863 resulted in severe repression and persecution. It was said that the Tsar wanted a 'Lithuania without Lithuanians'. The Tsarist authorities also actively encouraged the colonisation or 'plantation' of Lithuania by Russian immigrants. This 'Russification' went as far as banning Lithuanian publications and books and discouraging the Lithuanian language. Both Lithuanian groups, Catholic and the minority Jewish, experienced religious persecution. The years 1865 to 1905 became known as 'The Forty Years of Darkness'. There was also at that time a further decline in their living standards due to a fall in grain prices and heavier taxation. In other words they were being driven off the land and so they were forced to depart their homes. It is estimated that one in four Lithuanians emigrated between 1868 and 1914 with the main exodus occurring in the 1890s and 1900s.[3]

The Lithuanians' experiences upon migrating to Scotland again mirrored the Irish. Their arrival was perceived as an 'invasion' and provoked almost immediate hostility.[3,5,6,7,8,9] Lunn K. 'Reactions to Lithuanian and Polish Immigrants in the Lanarkshire Coalfield, 1880-1914' in The Journal of the Scottish Labour History Society Vol.13 pp.23-38, 1978 The incoming Lithuanians (loosely described as 'Russian Poles' by many Scots) were the subject of considerable concern and resentment. Of course, there might have been some understandable concerns

> The Lithuanians' reasons for leaving their homeland can often be seen to mirror that of their fellow immigrant Irish

3. Rodgers M. 'The Lithuanians' in History Today Vol.35 pp.15-20 1985 and Duncan R. 'The Mineworkers', Edinburgh, Birlinn 2005

4. Lunn K. 'Reactions to Lithuanian and Polish Immigrants in the Lanarkshire Coalfield, 1880-1914' in The Journal of the Scottish Labour History Society Vol.13 pp.23-38, 1978

about the employment of incomers in the workforce. For example, there was the fact that they spoke little or had poor English, and as such their presence in the mines may have been considered a safety risk. There was also concern that their presence would hinder negotiations and strike actions regarding wages and working conditions. This was because they appeared to have been willing to work for conditions and pay that seemed unacceptable to their local counterparts. However, on many occasions the reaction was knee jerk and the language vitriolic.

Reflecting the tendency of industrialists, capitalists and entrepreneurs to exploit what and where they could as they attempted to increase their profits, as with other raw labour, employers undoubtedly took advantage of the immigrants' poor bargaining status to help reduce their labour costs. Yet surprisingly, a campaign against their presence was led by no less than Keir Hardie, co-founder of the Labour Party, at that time leader of the Ayrshire Miners Union. On several occasions, starting as early as 1887, he campaigned against the presence of the Lithuanians. He stated that 'their presence is a menace to the health and morality of the place and is, besides, being used to reduce the already too low wages earned by the workmen'.[3] Additional comments that demonstrate that the campaign was not entirely about labour relations followed up this remark. For example, Hardie also stated that the only object that employers would have in employing Lithuanians was to:

> . . . teach men how to live on garlic and oil, or introduce the Black Death, so as to get rid of the surplus labourers. Much indignation is being expressed and the upshot will be bloodshed unless a stop is put to the disgraceful proceedings.[8]

When it was pointed out to Hardie at the 1899 House of Commons Select Committee on Emigration and Immigration that more people left Scotland than entered it, he replied:

> It would be much better for Scotland if those 1,500 were compelled to remain there and let the foreigners be kept out. . . Dr Johnson said God made Scotland for Scotchmen, and I would keep it so.[10]

That Hardie by 1899 was a considerable force and indeed a

Member of Parliament demonstrates the level of opposition, bigotry and racism immigrants to Scotland faced. However, he was not alone. The editor of one Lanarkshire newspaper painted the following picture in an article published in July 1900:

> On all questions of labour they are proving to be a menace to the well-being of our own people. . . Then again – speaking generally – they are most filthy in their habits of life, being a source of danger to the health of the community with their primitive ideas of order and cleanliness. . . They are fearfully intemperate in their habits [and] appeal to the knife. . . They are in short a most barbarous people and in Bellshill we seem to have the very scum of their nation.[3]

This statement demonstrates fairly coherently the opinion of the day. The mood has since been described as 'rabble-rousing'[11] and having 'elements of racist assumption or at least ethnocentric shortsightedness'. This is despite the fact that the Lithuanians have since been acknowledged as 'highly-organised and often highly-politicised'[7] and 'good workers'.[4]

The fact that the Lithuanians were predominately Catholic did not help. There was religious friction in the mines and with the Scottish Miners Federation (SMF). The Scottish/Protestant and Irish/Catholic ethnic distinction in the workforce was brought to the attention of the Royal Commission on Labour by the Secretary of the Union. Referring to a strike in 1894, the vice president of the Union stated the Union had been 'crucified between racial and religious prejudices'.[5] This friction was a continuation of the experience of Irish Catholics during the previous generation or so, involving anti-Catholic frictions with Scottish Protestant and Orange elements from Ireland and Scotland. The Free Colliers movement, a forerunner to the Union movement, was a divisive influence, having links to Orangeism and had an anti-Irish and anti-Catholic outlook. As such it alienated many Irish and Catholic mineworkers, who were obviously discouraged from participation.

Despite the difficulties they faced in Scotland, the Irish and the Lithuanians continued to bring their faith with them. John Millar, the son of Lithuanian immigrants has stated that:

> To the Calvinistic Presbyterian country of Scotland they brought

5. Guardian Newspaper. 'Lithuanians in Glasgow', The Guardian Newspaper London, Monday January 23 2006

and diligently pursued the Roman Catholic faith. . . They tended to have a deep faith and rallied to the Roman Catholic Church. They found that the language of the Latin Mass and church rituals, were a universal and familiar part of their life in this foreign land.[8]

With regards to the Lithuanians, an observer from a London-based publication The Slate[8] stated that:

These foreigners are shunned by Scottish workmen as social parasites and not one of them is permitted to put foot inside a Scotchman's door, so that they form a distinct community. Being looked upon as 'dirty dogs' and utterly 'cut' by Scotchmen, the Polish workers have no choice but to herd together in this manner. (The 'Poles' described were in fact Lithuanians.)

Often the Lithuanians formed small colonies and attempted to preserve their culture and identity, sometimes attempting to establish their own parishes.[12] However, due to the outbreak of World War I and political changes, immigration from Lithuania to Scotland halted. In addition to the smaller number of immigrants, this is a key difference that differentiates Lithuanian immigration to Scotland from Irish immigration. The Lithuanian influx was numerically and geographically small as well as limited in terms of time scale. Significantly, Lithuanians in Scotland were cut off from any prospect of cultural renewal or reinforcing or the prospect of further immigration from their homeland due subsequently to the rise of the Iron Curtain in Europe. Unlike the Irish, there were never enough Lithuanians to create and sustain a large football club like Celtic.

In stark contrast, as far as the Irish are concerned, Collins estimates that around eight per cent of all Irish-born emigrants went to Scotland during the period 1841 to 1921 and most Irish immigration to Scotland took place during this time. Irish immigration to Scotland is multi-generational, being small in the early part of the nineteenth century, rising greatly from the period of the Great Irish Hunger, peaking in the 1880s, levelling off and then declining steadily until around 1920, rising again after World War II and then becoming a small trickle into the new millennium. In other words, since the mid nineteenth century there has been a substantial Irish-born presence in Scotland while the offspring of the Irish represented a minor explosion upon the Scottish social profile. Religious, cultural and national affiliations and connections have been reinforced and renewed as Catholics from Ireland and Catholics of Irish decent have intermarried.

In addition, despite many changes and variations, most live in Scotland's west-central belt, many inhabit similar towns and villages, share political and cultural interests and share the same denominational schools within the state system. A huge number also align themselves with the same football club. Although some might argue that aspects of Catholicism and Irishness have in fact been lost or have diminished, as a result of numerous factors Catholics from an Irish ethnic background in Scotland have also managed to sustain many of the things they esteem and value.

For many Lithuanians in Scotland, in the face of the hostility experienced, they just had to 'get on with it'. However, this policy came at a cost. Due to prejudice and discrimination, and like many other Catholics, they had to keep their heads down. Indeed, as a consequence of the prejudice and discrimination many responded by changing their names. This was done sometimes at the behest of their employers, foremen or works clerk to something considered easier to pronounce or write on a pay sheet. Many more chose to change their names so as to avoid discrimination: in other words they hid their roots, culture, ethnicity and identity. Their children were often encouraged to speak English only when outside the home or their own community. Given the prejudice and bigotry against them it was easier to be Lithuanian at home but be 'Brown', 'Smyth' or 'Miller' among the Scottish community. They were frequently forced to assimilate or even 'disappear'. As such it is clear to see that this would invariably result in a loss of Lithuanian culture and identity and crucially, knowledge of their own pasts and community. If Scotland did not acknowledge these people in their own right it would become more difficult for them to be true to themselves.

> they had to keep their heads down. . . many responded by changing their names

If I went forward with the name of Neverauskas plus the name of my [Catholic] school. . . that was it. I didn't get the opportunity. That went for all Catholics, and Lithuanians were even further down the scale. So I became Brown. All my life I've been trying to hide the fact I was Lithuanian.[6]

6. Lunn K. 'Race and Labour in Twentieth-Century Britain', London, Frank Cass Publishers 1986

The Lithuanians joined the Irish in the miners' rows of Lanark-shire and in the slums of Gorbals in Glasgow. Together they occupied a lowly position in society. Whatever event caused dissatisfaction or grievance to the Scots was often blamed on aliens in their midst. In August 1905, for example, the Daily Record and Mail, the leading paper in Glasgow, ran the banner headline 'Alien danger: immigrants infected with loathsome disease'.[9] Lithuanians and Irish along with other, mainly Catholic, immigrants were considered the instigators and reason for many of the ills of contemporary society including immorality, crime, drunkenness, poor working conditions, low wages and unemploy-ment. It has been stated that anti-Catholicism united and agitated many Scots Protestants, reaching a political peak in the 1920s and 1930s, and formed the basis of a distinctly xenophobic or even racist Scottish national identity.[13]

Given that the Lithuanians experienced similar hostility and shared many common bonds as immigrants with the Irish it is no surprise that they 'clicked'. They shared similar struggles of working, getting on with life and raising families in difficult circumstances. In addition, among Irish immigrants and their offspring they were allowed to be 'Lithuanian' and were not ashamed or in fear of discrimination: it was brother with brother and sister with sister in the face of prejudice. Among this community there was no national or cultural 'put down'. They shared a faith, values and politics. The biblical reading from the Book of Ruth, 'Your People will be my people, and your God will be my God', commonly used at Catholic weddings, often applied. In addition in the case of the Celtic football community it can be added that 'Your team will be my team'. And so it was that the Lithuanians became part of the larger Celtic community.

The fact that Celtic is an Irish club and Scottish institution has not diminished the love that Lithuanian descendents have for the team. As a club founded by immigrants, many Scottish-born Lithuanians have understood and appreciated the club's Irish and Catholic heritage and identity. Often these people perceive that they have similar histories of oppression and struggle for independent homelands. Celtic and being part of the Celtic community has given inspiration and a confidence to a

7. Millar J. 'The Lithuanians in Scotland', Argyll, House of Lochar 1998

8. Maitle H. 'Blackshirts across the border' in Socialist Review Issue. p.172, 1994

9. Report from the Select House of Commons Select Committee on Emigration and Immigration (foreigners). Proceedings, minutes of evidence and appendix, Vol. X, xxvi, 113p. (Sessional no. 311) (para. 1491) 1889

people who were oppressed in their homeland as well as in their new country of settlement. In the case of the Lithuanians, it has helped shape their descendants' identity in Scotland.

And so it is not a surprise that Auntie Grace supported Celtic. Nor is it surprising that when my Dad, an Irishman from County Derry, went to watch Celtic for the first time after arriving in Glasgow, he was accompanied by a son of Lithuanian immigrants. Equally it is no surprise that, in the days when many of the players were usually drawn from the club's own supporters, that Alex Millar from Mossend (1935-1940), John Jack from Bellshill (1950-1959), John Kurila from the Gorbals (1958-1962) joined Billy McNeill, also from Bellshill, as the descendants and representatives of these Lithuanian immigrants who have pulled on 'the hoops'.

Celtic is more than a club. It is a community. It is a way of seeing the world, whether political, social or moral. Although a comparatively smaller aspect, part of that community that constitutes the Celtic support is of Lithuanian descent. While many more in the Celtic support rightly celebrate their Irish heritage, background, culture, politics and homeland, and connect with their forebears' struggles and aspirations as immigrants, wherever they are from, Celtic FC and its supporting community also includes anyone else who wishes to buy into all or some of these identities, values and sentiments. Indeed, that is why everyone is invited to become 'Celtic Minded', and to join the celebration.

Although Catholic and Irish at core, and while Catholic and Irishness in Scotland are the unique defining characteristics of the club and its support, inclusiveness has also been a defining feature of the existence and history of Celtic and the Irish in Scotland: crucially this engenders an often wider affinity for the club. Brother Walfrid and his fellow Irish Catholics who gave life to the Celtic story would not have had it any other way.

10. Brown T. 'No wonder half of us think immigration is a problem', Scotland On Sunday Edinburgh 04 November 2007

11. O'Donnell E. 'To keep our Fathers' faith: Lithuanian immigrant religious aspiration and the policy of west of Scotland Catholic clergy 1889-1914' in The Innes Review Vol. 49 pp. 168-183, 1998

12. Brown C.G. 'Religion and Society in Scotland Since 1707', Edinburgh,'Edinburgh University Press, 1997

13. see Brown, C.G. Religion and Society in Scotland Since 1707, Edinburgh University Press 1997

Notes from a Continuing Journey

LEWIS WAUGH

Let's be clear straight away. This piece of writing is more of a travelogue, a story about a journey. It is not a voyage across time and space but more of an account of a passage through ideas and attitudes. Of course there will be a sense of time and distance, places and events along the way but instead of landmarks or panoramas to be seen, there will be viewpoints to be understood.

Let us at least start in a time and place, a point of departure. The point in time is the beginning of the second half of the twentieth century, the 50s and the early 60s. The place is a small village in south-west Scotland. Its name doesn't really matter because in terms of the location of attitudes and values I don't feel that it should be particularly set apart from villages in many other parts of Scotland. The community that I was born and raised amongst had a very strong sense of its own local history. The 'Killing Times' was a period in the south and west of Scotland which some would describe as that of ethnic cleansing, officially sanctioned and carried out by the then upholders of the state and the law. The stories of these times were relayed to us through a strong oral tradition. You may find that whilst the rest of folkloric Scotland sing heartily of 'Bonnie Dundee', in certain areas of the south-west he goes by the name of 'Bluidy Claverhouse'. We also had our local heroes: Burns who needs no explanation and John Paul Jones – pirate, adventurer and the first admiral of the newly formed navy of the independent United

States of America. There were strong threads of Republicanism that lay cheek by jowl with the staunch Presbyterianism that furnished and inspired the cause of the Covenanters. In the weft and weave of these stories and perceptions, a consciousness was informed of who I was and where I had come from. Much deeper and less clearly articulated were other prevalent attitudes. These finer threads are more difficult to define – they were seldom if ever expressed in clear concrete fashion, in the forthright terms of social values. They tended to exist beyond mere words or conscious statements, they lurked somewhere 'between the lines' and were within the realm of 'unconscious identities'. What were those attitudes?

There are many names that could be applied; sectarianism, bigotry, light-hearted banter, anti-Catholicism, 'natural' suspicion of 'difference' or just straightforward anti-Irish racism. From primary through to my secondary schooling I wouldn't have recognised many of those words and phrases but I fine well carried out the practice. Looking back on it all, it would seem wholly inappropriate or even unnecessarily punishing to suggest that my friends or my family were in any way bigots or racists. I find it difficult to equate the politics of hatred with those good folk. But I do recognise that I was brought up amongst prejudiced attitudes the way a fish might grow and move about in water. I cannot imagine that fish, even if they had the mental equipment to do so, would consider deeply or have opinions about water. It's the element that holds them up, shapes both their bodies and their movements and quietly sustains them in their percept-ions. This sustaining environment only becomes notable when it no longer exists, its condition changes radically or it is severely threatened. It is the very unthinking nature of it all that makes such an ill thing of these perceptions. 'Kaffliks!' I knew that word. It went alongside a whole litany of other hateful, hurtful words and phrases.

'Kaffliks! Ye dinnae marry intae thaim – nocht but trauchle and grief. Dirty Irish buggers!! Eyties! Froggies! Papists!'

Whilst I was never aware of having actually seen any 'Kaffliks' – where were they hidin onywey? – I did know an endless stream of nasty wee anti-Irish and nun-priest 'jokes'. I knew the words to 'The Sash', 'Derry's Walls' and the 'Billy Boys'. I knew phrases that, when I see them now, seem to indicate a more sophisticated pedigree, a more 'educated' source than mere street banter. 'Church of England = papist apologists', 'purple whore of Rome', 'carnal idolatry. . .' I could go on, but I really don't think I want to. I ask myself if some of this came from my church? I simply cannot remember. Mind you, some odd things came from the church or should I say churches?

The next step forward on my journey I owe very much to the church. Our village had three churches. In writing this I'm not describing a three-way Jewish, Catholic, Protestant divide. Oh no! I'm talking about Church of Scotland peach pastel, Presbyterian orange and Calvinist mandarin – a real diversity of religious faith. Eh-no?

My journey into the beyond began with the prolonged absence of whomsoever was responsible for leading our Church of Scotland Youth Fellowship. Being farmed out to the radical Presbyterians was better than complete godlessness on a Sunday evening. So there I was, sitting in the front parlour of a different manse, stuck in front of a home movie recently smuggled out of South Africa. I believe I was watching footage of the Sharpeville massacre. This was the beginning of my political awareness, an awareness that was encouraged, guided and fed by deeply felt Christian ethics and principles. There were several international issues that our churches embraced. Looking back on it, I think that it was a bold act showing teenagers footage of white men in neat khaki uniforms, wildly truncheoning black men, women and children. This scene would be repeated many times in the coming years. As I passed from senior secondary to college, the battlegrounds changed but the central issues remained: the suppression of people by people: of deep racial and ethnic hatred. The anti-apartheid movement would continue for decades whilst other freedom movements arose.During the early 1960s the Civil Rights movement in the USA gained international sympathy and support. Again I experienced the sense of disgust that people of one skin colour – my skin colour – could claim to be civilised Christian folk, and yet mete out such ferocious punishment on their fellow human beings? Vietnam burst into conflagration. A wave of left-wing, anti-US demonstrations and rioting spread across Europe. I was studying and living in Edinburgh and involved in those demonstrations, in what at times I felt was just a normal extension of student life. Deep down though, were the ingrained Christian and socialist beliefs that continued to fuel and inform that involvement.

And then came the Civil Rights movement of Northern Ireland: a people who had been disenfranchised socially, politically and economically for it seemed, no other reason than that of ethnic, cultural and religious difference. And again the appalling TV scenes of non-violent, civil rights marchers being viciously attacked by men in the neat dark uniforms of the state police. Men who at other times you might have expected to have been upholders of the law, the guardians and protectors of the public peace. In Scotland and perhaps particularly in the west, we have always lived in the political rain shadow of events in Ireland. This was so much closer to home now. There was no romance of the foreign cause. This was about us.

An Orange Parade had been organised to take place, marching down Princes Street one Sunday afternoon. It found me amongst the ranks of the counter-demonstration. Do they call this bit 'the road to Damascus'? It was almost ludicrous. Suddenly I became aware of different accents here and there around me. 'Oh wait a minute! These guys are Kaffliks! Irish Kaffliks!' And all the while there is a band marching up the street towards us playing one of my tunes! A very odd moment that, a wee bit disconcerting. At first it was like stepping outside myself and watching the interplay of different reactions. You see, over time I had acquired an almost visceral sense of repugnance towards something quite abstract. Its hard to define what that fearful thing was – Catholicism? Irishness? The others? It? The they-it, whoever, whatever **they** were **it** was. But **they-it** were not concrete, not real in any way. **They-it** were much more powerful. **They-it** were a perception, an idea or a story I had been told about in jokes, banter and whispers – the words between the lines.

Amongst the many rich tales, rhymes and songs of my childhood which helped define who I was or who I wanted to be, perhaps the whispers had told me who I wasn't, who I should be very glad I wasn't. I'd watch myself watching myself. I'd catch myself thinking along old ley-lines, seeing the inappropriate thoughts in my own mind, hearing the words and sensing the punch-lines. Then my old self and my new self would get together. They sometimes had a good laugh at I/me/us. I remember one very odd moment on the road of this journey.

I found myself in a situation where I realised that I had forgotten the good advice from my elders regarding the man-woman thing. I had been winchin a lass without taking due precaution. I hadn't found out if she was a 'Kafflik'. So there we were, myself and my bride-to-be, sitting on the bus, chundering its wearisome way southwards from Edinburgh towards my eagerly awaiting family, and I didn't even know which side of the great divide she was on. A long objective look at her only made matters worse. Not only was she wearing a miniskirt, a really, really, short miniskirt such that you wondered why she was bothering to wear a skirt at all, but it was a glorious, rich purple! Jings!!! I had grown up and I'd left my milieu, met different people in different situations. The village boy from the south-west was still there: the strong streaks of Presbyterian doggedness and a deeply cherished sense of humanitarianism. I'd kept a fair amount and I remembered many things, sometimes the not-good-at-all-things, the 'purple whore of Rome' stuff. In one sense the initial discomfort was that of feeling tainted. I could periodically find myself going down paths, feeling and thinking things that had no possible right to be part of a civilised, open-minded person. At other times it was as if I'd just taken off a pair of tinted spectacles through which I'd been peering at the world.

I know it's a cliché, but it's probably a cliché because it does accurately describe a common event. I was seeing and hearing things from a different angle now. As my journey took me towards raising a family with the wonderful wearer of that glorious purple miniskirt, I was both keenly aware and deeply concerned about what my own kids would hear and learn. For eight years I was the 'obligatory exiled Scot', working down in Surrey. By this time I had three children. If football is a focus of sectarian and racist attitudes, football can also offer an immediate and palpable way of sharing, celebrating and expressing a rich diversity of cultures, values and attitudes. I took my kids to see players rather than teams; Pat Nevin, Gordon Strachan, Kenny Dalglish, Joe Jordan, Bruce Rioch. I told them of the famous games that I had seen; when Queen of the South beat Kilmarnock in a Scottish Cup replay – my first pitch invasion, the Battle of Britain – Celtic against Leeds United, the cup finals, the Lisbon Lions and Wembley '67 and '77. I spoke of footballing legends; Pat Crerand, Charlie Tully, Jimmy Johnstone, Jim Baxter and Denis Law. I showed them the near 'holy relics'; the moth eaten scarves, the autographed programmes and the letter from Jock Stein. Their childhood was predominantly lived in southern England and I was determined to keep their Scots identity alive and real. Through the medium of stories, songs and cherished family traditions, I wanted them to share and understand the rich and distinct culture and identity that we came from. At times I had to quite determinedly counter the values and 'education' they were receiving from the environment around them. It was important to keep my family in touch with who we were and where we came from. We were different and this difference was a matter of pride – a sense of worth to be celebrated.

In this I believe that I was no different from the hundreds of thousands of other Scots who have ever lived and worked abroad. Therefore, how strange for me to find in the new millennium such animosity amongst the Scottish detractors of Aiden McGeady's sense of Irishness. We returned to Scotland in the late 1980s – to another village, but this time in the Central Belt. One morning we went down to the main street and saw newly-painted on a gable-end: 'One Queen! One crown! No Pope in this town! Remember 1690!' How odd and how very sad! I'd moved away from my own village and I'd been away from Scotland for nearly a decade. 1690! I felt as if I'd been pulled backwards in time.

Throughout the struggle of my own life, to understand and accommodate the challenges of change I'd either forgotten or hadn't understood the pull of prejudice, the comfort in knowing who you are and who you aren't. At the same time my kids were in receipt of abuse. They may have carried within them a very clear sense of their Scottish identity but after eight years in Surrey their accents marked them out for playground taunts and antagonism. I told them to ignore the words on the wall and the insults at school. I told them that there were other stories, richer stories worth listening to. A friend offered us tickets to Parkhead and so I put the green and white on them and the next Saturday we went to watch Celtic play at Parkhead. Call it an act of self reproach for past sins, call it an arbitrary act of contrariness – Celtic were at that time entering the prolonged period of defeats at the hands of a very dominant Rangers. It's hard to identify why you go along to watch a team in the first place – well I was offered tickets. It's much easier to explain why you continue to do so. The kids learned the lyrics and they sang the songs, they cheered and waved and no-one seemed too bothered about their accents. You looked about you and you could see that in one way or another these folk had been in receipt of antagonism and abuse themselves. But above all we felt safe there amongst the Celtic support who seemed to ask nothing of where we had come from nor why. We could feel part of something that was joyous and accepting.

The European nights were very special, 'away' fans were welcomed and the willingness and ability of my kids to communicate in French, German or Italian was valued by the Celtic support around us. **Més que un club!** – more than a club – is what the cules of the Nou Camp will tell you about their beloved F.C. Barcelona.[1] On the grand occasions this statement is spread in glorious technicolor across their terracing but it always seemed a little too obvious to me. From first hand experience I know that amongst many others; Brechin City, Queen of the South and Heart of Midlothian are all 'més que un club'. Any human organisation has a tendency to be imbued and infused with more than its functional role.

My first job was in a milk bottling factory. It seems that I was so efficient in operating the bottle-filling, capping and crating machines that the manager offered me the ultimate job of working in the yoghurt division. But the way he put it was, 'Are you interested in the company's new brand of yoghurt'? There

1. Cules = Catalan 'the bums'. The first FC Barcelona supporters used to sit up on a high wall to watch the matches affording passers-by the view of an endless row of buttocks

followed a roundabout and very unsatisfactory dialogue wherein I tried to ascertain whether or not I was doing my job well enough? Was the manager: a) wanting to sack me; b) wanting to promote me? He was looking for passion and commitment to dairy products and I just wanted a decent wage at the end of the week. You just can't escape the sub-context. I'll bet that the management of M&S think that their organisation is about more than just retail. So I know that as with any other human activity, going along to watch a game of football is more than about just the game of football. Meaning is everywhere. We create and retell stories about who we think we are, who we want to be and sometimes we even tell stories about who we don't want to be. I have a friend who is a Juventus supporter. He was trying to explain about the roots of the local rivalry between Juventus and Torino:

'Look amico! Juventus is just like Celtic. We are the team of the immigrants. . . from the south. . . the 'peasants' the mezzagiorno. . . the outcasts! As capi?'

'Si! Aie capito!'

The idea of being an outcast, of forming an identity around that very thing, even gaining strength from it, certainly meant something to us during our first season at Celtic Park. In other 'Celtic Minded' articles the writers have appropriately and rightly put their religious faith and their cultural and ethnic roots at the core of their sense of self and club. In those narratives lie the rationale and spirit of Celtic and the core that explains its being.

In some ways I envy this degree of connectedness, of knowing who and where you are. Personally, sometimes this can make me feel an interloper: of not being part of the traditions and communal history that lie at the very heart of Celtic Football Club and its historic supporting community. But such feelings soon give way, because they are probably inevitable as my background and origins are different anyway from the majority of the support.

However, it's at this point I can begin to reflect on the other aspects of Celtic's identity: that within those founding traditions is the open-hearted acceptance that aligns itself with the club ethos of Charity. In this light, the camaraderie, the sense of family and of joy we experienced in those first years at Parkhead has been confirmed again and again. If you are at all perceptive it's easy to see that written deep into the history and identity of this club is a sense of 'the mezzagiorno' (the outcasts). There are pages being written into this history all the time that tell of how people can rise above adversity. The 'against the odds' attitude still exists. I experience, identify and enjoy the certain tendency towards anarchic disreputableness, an irreverence, a cavalier attitude towards the well regulated and 'sensible' things in life. In its most joyous form it comes together in individualistic flair and disdain for 'received wisdom'.

Many writers in football books use individual stories about their experiences to illustrate what their club means for them. Anecdotal experience is a good way – possibly the only way – of people explaining to other people, the very varied motives and meanings which fuel support for their team. I have many such tales but the greatest experience has to be the Seville Iliad. I am left with very clear memories of that event. My oldest daughter and I arrived at Glasgow Airport just after midnight, 21st May 2003 to find the place looking like a re-enactment of Dunkirk without the bullets and bombs: lines and lines of hooped supporters, standing there in sandals, slowly going hypothermic. Hundreds, thousands, patiently and cheerfully waiting their turn to be airlifted out from the West of Scotland Spring drizzle into the dazzling heat of Seville. Keepie-uppie with a ball of rolled up paper and communal singing in the departure lounge. The crazy, surreal humour of our fellow travellers, even when our aircraft had to dramatically and inexplicably take off again in the middle of the landing – we should have been terrified and instead we were crying with laughter. Seville itself, streets not so much invaded by Celtic supporters as being subjected to a huge, vibrant, celebratory transhumance of a people. Some guy in a glittering, green suit strolling towards the Estadio Olimpico in temperatures that made all-out nudity a more viable option. When the final whistle blew, the roar of triumph from the Porto supporters was simply and utterly submerged by wave upon wave of 'Over and Over' rolling down from the terraces. And then late at night both inside and outside the bars, the calm but impassioned post-match discussions, Porto supporters wandering around looking dazed and totally out-numbered – why aren't they attacking us? Walking through the parks towards our bus, seeing families bedding down in the warm Andalucian night on the steps lining the Guadalquivir; the elderly, grandparents, mothers and fathers, bairns in arms, weans in buggies, calm smiles of acknowledgment and resignation. All of these memories are in some way about adversity and more. They are much more to do with a communal act of celebration in the face of it: in the past and in the present.

Having moved beyond partial sight, having gained a clearer vision, I'm not inclined to put on another pair of tinted spectacles. I'm Scottish. I might have an Irish forebear somewhere or other, but I neither harbour the wish nor the need to seek one out. Neither am I about to convert to Catholicism. I really don't think that either of these acts would make me any more or less acceptable or passionate a Celtic supporter. I know many Celtic supporters have Catholicism and Irishness in their backgrounds or have them today as fundamental to who and what they are.

Nevertheless, those same Celtic supporters I stand alongside are defined by their capacity to transcend ethnic animosity and religious bias. They simply celebrate who and what they are. They want to progress from what they have been through. Whilst some may plead or protest that Scotland desperately needs to move on I know that being human, we carry our pasts through the present towards the future. The journey never seems to end.

I still need help on my journey. There are moments, wee lapses. If you're walking down the Springfield Road and you see a tall guy wearing a green and white scarf, a glazed but cheerful look on his face, ploutering along whistling the 'Billy Boys', please don't hit him. Inside he is really singing the 'Ha-ha' lyrics. The glazed look is because he is concentrating on writing a story about a country he could be proud to live in. The cheerful look is because he suspects that there are other people trying to write out different versions of the same collective story, perhaps even a new story. We're living in interesting times.

Michael Davitt:
a man for all seasons

STEPHEN FERRIE

[1] The Official History of Celtic Football Club; a four-disc DVD released in 2008. The DVD is accompanied by a short booklet containing a preface by Brian Quinn, Celtic Chairman 2000-2007. The preface is headed 'More than just a football club'.

[2] President John F. Kennedy of the United States. The quotation in this instance has been shortened from the fuller version, which reads 'History is a relentless master. It has no present, only the past rushing into the future. To try to hold fast is to be swept aside'.

[3] The Official History of Celtic Football Club. On Disc 1, the narrator, Brian Wilson, refers to the many characters who have shaped the club's history as 'legends and heroes'.

'More than just a Club'. That's how former Celtic Chairman, Brian Quinn, begins his introduction to the club's official DVD history that was released in 2008.[1] He acknowledges of course that supporters of many football clubs throughout the world will lay claim to such a lofty statement and indeed, many have distinctive traits. The difference with Celtic, however, is that these words clearly stand the test of scrutiny in social, cultural, religious and political terms. The key to understanding why Celtic is demonstrably more than just a football club lies in an appreciation of its rich history and the enduring sense of common purpose that emanates from it. Speaking of history, the late American President, John F. Kennedy, said: 'History is a relentless master. It has no present, only the past rushing into the future.'[2] So it is with Celtic, where and who we are and what we stand for is largely shaped by what has gone before us.

The history of Celtic, like that of any great institution, has been moulded not just by the many great events that are recorded, but by the people who have left their mark for future generations. These people include club officials, managers, players and ordinary fans. 'Legends and heroes' is how the official club history describes them.[3] In a world of materialistic and commodified excess where the real heroes in life are rarely heard or seen, the 'hero' accolade might be stretching it a little. Nonetheless, among the most prominent legends are people like

Willie Maley, whose service as player and manager spanned fifty consecutive years from the club's earliest days. Others include the club's founding father, Brother Walfrid, along with architects of the Celtic dream such as John Glass, Dr. John Conway and William McKillop. And then there are subsequent generations of managers and players who have graced the stage with such distinction; a litany of revered names – Dan Doyle, Jimmy Quinn, James McGrory, Patsy Gallacher, Johnny Thompson, Charlie Tully, Jock Stein, Billy McNeill, Jimmy Johnstone, Kenny Dalglish, Tommy Burns, Paul McStay, Henrik Larsson and Martin O'Neill . . . to name but a few!

But as with many great histories, as well as the legends, there are also those who have made their mark in a more subtle and less pronounced manner. Those that say something significant about the club and its support but who don't receive the publicity or attention that comes the way of others – for whatever reason. People who have come and gone without fanfare, but who nonetheless have either made a momentous contribution to, or that symbolise something distinctive about, our club. One such character in Celtic's history is Michael Davitt. The chances are that those for whom the name Michael Davitt rings a bell will recall that he laid a sod of shamrock in March 1892 following the club's move from its original stadium to the site of the new Celtic Park; a 'flitting' immortalised in the expression that 'it was like leaving the graveyard to enter Paradise.'[4] However, whilst Michael Davitt has become a celebrated and influential character in Irish history, his contribution to the Celtic story and its significance today remains marginalised.

Michael Davitt was born in the village of Straide in County Mayo on 25th March 1846, just as the Great Hunger was flexing its mortal grip on Ireland. He was one of a family of five children born to Martin and Catherine Davitt who, like millions of others at the time in Ireland, were tenant farmers. As famine took root, so too did the curse of eviction, and the Davitts were eventually forced from their home due to their inability to pay the rent. This experience was seared into Michael Davitt's consciousness. Writing about it years later, he vividly recounts the facts and emotions of it all:

[4] Campbell & Woods, 1987, p. 45

I was then but four and a half years old, yet I have a distinct remembrance (doubtless strengthened by the frequent narration of the event by my parents in after years) of that morning's scene: the remnant of our household furniture flung about the road; the roof of the house falling in and the thatch taking fire; my mother and father looking on with four young children, the youngest only two months old, adding their cries to the other pangs which must have agitated their souls at the sight of their burning homestead.[5]

The Davitt family left Ireland for England in 1850, settling in the Lancashire mill town of Haslingden. Because of the booming Lancashire textile industry of the time, with its demand for cheap labour, the Irish had poured into the town and the Davitts became part of the growing Irish district of Rock Hall. It was from this starting point that Michael Davitt began to make his mark on the world: like so many of his countrymen, an immigrant in new and unfamiliar surroundings.

How then does this seemingly typical (for many Irish people at the time) starting point lead to a connection with Celtic Football Club? More importantly, how does it explain Davitt's relevance to the modern-day followers of the club? Close examination reveals a deep meaning and an even greater significance for this coming together of Celtic and Davitt. The answers to the questions posed above can be found by taking a closer look at the threads that ran through Michael Davitt's life and relating them to Celtic: not just to the institution that is Celtic Football Club, but to the people who formed the club, those who have supported it down the years, and those who carry forward its traditions into future generations.

The first, and perhaps most obvious, connection we see between Davitt and Celtic is famine and emigration. Like Davitt, the people who formed the club and supported it in its formative years knew only too well the experience of famine and the dislocating consequences for those fortunate enough to survive it. Like the Davitt family they too knew what is was to be 'strangers in a strange land'. Like the Davitts they also had to contend with the excessive challenges typically faced by immigrants; putting food on the table, finding work, securing a

[5] Davitt, by Bernard O'Hara, p. 25

roof over their heads and establishing a place for themselves in their new environment. In Glasgow the same immigrants faced the added challenges of suspicion and hostility on the grounds of their religion and ethnicity. Much has been written about the origins of Celtic and the pivotal role the club played in alleviating the poverty and hunger that afflicted the Irish immigrants who flocked to the Glasgow area in search of a better life. These were circumstances that Michael Davitt had first hand experience of and could directly relate to. No doubt they were factors that contributed to his decision to become a patron of the club in the first place and to endorse the principles it stood for: principles of charity, reaching out and inclusion. Undoubtedly also, as an Irish football club and as a symbol of respect, esteem and celebration for the Irish in Scotland, Davitt would have warmed to the invite to become patron.

If we delve deeper into Michael Davitt's life and examine some of the driving forces that inspired him, we begin to see a number of themes that place his life on a similar trajectory to that of the typical Celtic supporter of his era and to subsequent generations of followers. One of these themes relates to the issue of Irish self-determination. History has recorded that Michael Davitt was a key late nineteenth century figure in the struggle for Irish independence. Sharing the same sense of patriotism and desire for Irish liberation as many of his exiled countrymen in 1865 Davitt joined the Irish Republican Brotherhood (IRB), otherwise known as the Fenians. The Fenians were a secret society, dedicated to overthrow British rule in Ireland by armed revolution. Davitt rose quickly through the ranks and became a chief of the local Fenian Circle. It was in this period that Davitt came to local prominence when he helped defend St Mary's Church in Haslingden against an attack by anti-Catholic and anti-Irish bigots, stirred up by the rantings of William Murphy, a notorious sectarian rabble-rouser of the time.

As a member of the Fenians he spent much of his time as an organising secretary and arms' agent, a role that brought him into regular contact with like-minded exiles from across England and Scotland. He was later arrested in London and charged with treason-felony after a surveillance exercise into his activities by the British authorities. On 18th July 1870 he was sentenced to fifteen years' penal servitude after he was found guilty of arms trafficking to Ireland for a Fenian insurrection. After spells in a number of prisons, most notably Dartmoor, he was released in 1877. Davitt's experience in prison had a profound impact on him, and led to him campaigning later in life for prison reform and for an improvement in conditions for all prisoners, including the adoption of a system focusing on rehabilitation rather than punishment. Pertinently, the historian Carla King, in her foreword to Davitt's Collected Writings 1868-1906, remarked that during seven years of a brutal prison regime, Davitt turned, with a greatness of soul and a power to forgive like Nelson Mandela a century later, from a physical force adherent to a constitutional politician. Notably, Davitt also inspired Mahatma Gandhi in his campaign against the British Empire. In this light Davitt's words at the end of his life are inspirational.

> To all my friends I leave kind thoughts
> To my enemies the fullest possible forgiveness.
> And to Ireland the undying prayer
> For the absolute freedom and independence
> Which it was my life's ambition to try and obtain for her

Reflecting such esteemed company as Mandela and Gandhi, today at Straide County Mayo over Davitt's grave next to the museum dedicated to him is a Celtic Cross with the inscription: 'Blessed is he that hungers and thirsts after justice, for he shall receive it.'

The political landscape in Britain and Ireland changed considerably in the latter part of the nineteenth century, and Davitt's desire for Irish independence took him down a new path: that of constitutional politics. When he was released on ticket-of-leave in 1877, he determined to forge a new path to Irish freedom, which had the moral authority of non-violent resistance. The result was the Irish National Land League, launched at Irishtown, Co Mayo on the 25th April 1879, where Charles Stuart Parnell addressed a crowd of about 12,000 people. The Land League was immensely successful in arousing not only the great mass of Irish people but galvanising the Irish diaspora abroad into support for the efforts of the Irish Party at Westminster in their campaign for fair rents and fixity of tenure. Davitt played a significant role in shaping the land reform agenda and in expanding the outlook of the organisation. Initially the campaign for change was centred on County Mayo, but through his foresight this was extended to the whole of Ireland, making it a national issue. His heroic endeavours in this area led to him being referred to, rightly, as 'the father of the Land League'.[6] Related to Davitt's campaign on Ireland's land question the Evicted Tenant's Fund was of course one of the main recipients of Celtic and its supporters' charity giving during the club's early years.

A fitting measure of his success as a campaigner and politician can be found in the remarks of an Irish historian and contemporary of Davitt that he was, at the time, 'second only to Parnell in the leadership of the Irish nation'.[7] Despite an initial reticence to standing as a Member of Parliament, he was eventually elected to the House of Commons as MP for North-East Cork in 1893 just as Gladstone's second Home Rule Bill was being introduced to the House of Commons. Davitt welcomed the Bill in his maiden speech, hailing it as 'a pact of peace between Ireland and the Empire'.[8]

The British government reaction to the success of the Land League was to suppress it in Ireland and close down the Land League clubs in Britain. Davitt, Parnell and other leading nationalists were jailed. They were not released until Parnell agreed to disband the Land League and set up the Irish National League instead, which was more under his direct control. Davitt thought that taking away the autonomy of the Land League was a mistake and he began to diverge from Parnell and develop his own strategy that the way to Irish freedom could be fought by the exiles in Britain making common cause with some in the Labour movement there. Many Irish clubs were set up in Britain during this period and some survivors remain as the Irish Democratic League clubs of Lancashire and Yorkshire. Though the Irish Party had an electoral pact with the Liberals, Davitt was in contact with Keir Hardie and the Irish played no small role in the advance of Labour in Britain and the early commitment of Labour to Home Rule. Although Davitt believed that British colonialism in Ireland lay at the root of Ireland's social, economic

[6] Ibid. The term 'the Father of the Land League' is used throughout the O'Hara's book, but perhaps the most emphatic endorsement of Davitt's role in land reform can be found on p. 114, where O'Hara recounts Parnell's reference to Davitt as the founder of the Land League and 'the life and soul of the movement'.

[7] Ibid, p.54. The quote is attributed to Dr. T. W. Moody speaking of the reception Davitt received from Irish Americans during visits in the 1880s.

[8] Davitt, by B O'Hara, p. 77

and political problems his interests as a politician were not restricted solely to the cause of independence. His close contacts with the Labour party in Britain reflected his wide range of concerns and he became a formidable campaigner on numerous issues.

For Celtic supporters down the generations the issue of Irish independence and liberation has remained an ever present in their consciousness. Indeed, a number of the club's founding fathers, like many of its early players and supporters, were active campaigners for Home Rule. John Glass, president of the club from its inception until its change in status to a limited liability company and a lifelong director, was founder of the O'Connell branch of the Irish National Forresters, as well as Treasurer of the Home Government branch of the United Irish League.[9] William McKillop, another early director, served as MP for North Sligo, holding the constituency for eight years before winning another seat in South Armagh in 1908.[10]

Religiously, Davitt of course shared the Christian/Catholic faith of Celtic's founders and supporters. Although a devout Catholic, this did not prevent him however from taking a stance against Church figures on several issues during his political life, bringing condemnation from influential quarters. One priest Davitt agitated against was Canon Ulick Burke who had threatened to evict his tenants. A campaign of non-payment pressured him to cancel the evictions and reduce his rents by 25%. In this incident an assessment might be made that it was in fact Davitt and not the relevant priest that was imitating Christ.

Davitt was also a great respecter of other faiths. This is underlined by a high profile stance against the Church, this time in support of the Jewish community in Limerick, which had come under attack from a Redemptorist priest who had called for a boycott of Jewish businesses in response to what he perceived as exorbitant interest rates being charged on goods. Davitt took up the cause of the Jewish community and criticised the Priest/Church for their role in the boycott, which was to last for two years, shamefully resulting in the exodus of many Jews from the city.[11] If we look at such examples in the context of the time, where the Church as an institution wielded an almost omnipotent

[9] Campbell & Woods, 1987, p. 18

[10] Ibid p. 19

[11] Davitt, by B O'Hara, p. 118

power over many aspects of Irish life, it is clear that Davitt was a man of great courage and high moral principle. For many in public life, particularly politicians, taking a stand against the Church would not have been a wise career move. Where and when appropriate and right, actions such as these by Davitt required great moral courage and conviction, qualities he had in abundance.

A close-quarters examination of Michael Davitt's life reveals an interest in an extensive range of topics. Many public figures devote their lives to a particular issue, but Davitt campaigned throughout his life on a diverse range of matters and lent his support, sometimes fleetingly and sometimes with fervent and sustained commitment, to many causes. The cause of Irish independence was a major driving force in his life of course but deeply connected to this was the question of land reform. Not surprisingly, the experience he and family endured at the time of the famine, resulting in eviction and subsequent emigration, left a powerful and lasting impression on him. Davitt believed that Ireland's problems were rooted in its colonial relationship with Britain and nowhere was the inequality of this relationship demonstrated more emphatically than in relation to the land. For O'Hara, Davitt's legacy was thus:

> The abolition of the landlord ascendancy in Ireland, Davitt's
> primary objective, weakened the union with the United
> Kingdom, advanced the interests of Irish nationalism, and in the
> process sowed the seeds for a modern democracy.[12]

Consistent with his agitation for land reform, Davitt also devoted a great deal of energy in pursuit of workers' rights in the industrial sector, not only in Ireland, but internationally, with particular emphasis on Britain. In much the same way that his early experience of eviction shaped his beliefs with regard to land, so too did his early working life influence his opinions in relation to the rights of the industrial classes. Having moved to England with his family, he began his working life in a mill near the adopted family home in Haslingden. At the age of eleven his right arm was badly injured in an industrial accident, resulting in amputation just below the shoulder. Subsequently, he campaigned tirelessly for workers' rights and for improvements in the

[12] O'Hara

horrendous conditions endured by the people whose labours fuelled the growth of the industrial era. Here too, we can draw comparisons between Davitt's personal experiences and the reality of many Celtic supporters past and present. The club has traditionally drawn much of its support from the working classes, many of whom will have been all too familiar with exploitation and with the potentially fatal dangers of the industrial working environment. Like Davitt, many of them who arrived as immigrants will also have experienced the shock of adjusting from an agrarian to an industrial society, where field and plough were exchanged for factory and machine tool, and where tight-knit communities gave way to cities teeming with strangers.

Despite his high level of commitment to the Irish national cause and to industrial and land reform, Michael Davitt was still able to devote time and energy to other concerns. He was an early champion of women's rights, supported universal suffrage, believed passionately in education, took a keen interest in international affairs and spoke in many countries. He also investigated anti-Semitic pogroms in Czarist Russia. Davitt was a frequent visitor to Scotland where he was closely associated with the crofters' struggles in the Highlands and Islands. He was also an author of significant note, publishing a number of books on subjects as diverse as his experiences as a prisoner and, as one might expect from his life's great passion, land reform. In 1899 he left his seat in parliament for good in protest against the Boer War, visiting South Africa to lend support to the Boer cause and exposing the cruelties of British concentration camps there. His experiences inspired his book, The Boer Fight for Freedom, published in 1904. Again his interest in the struggle in South Africa was similar to that of many Celtic supporters, players and directors who at the turn of the twentieth century lent their voices and support against British imperialism there. As well as Celtic, Davitt was also one of the first great patrons of Ireland's Gaelic Athletic Association (GAA).

Davitt married Mary Jane Yore in 1886, having met her while on a lecture tour of America a few years earlier. They had five children, the oldest of whom, Kathleen, died in childhood. Michael Davitt died on 30th May 1906. His death, from septicaemia at the age of sixty, was premature. His accomplishments were many and his influence on a range of issues of national importance was extensive. In accordance with his wishes, eschewing the trappings of a State funeral, he was buried in his home village of Straide following a simple ceremony and laid to rest less than half a kilometre from the place where he was born sixty years earlier. It is a mark of his influence and evidence of the high regard in which he was held by people in Ireland that thousands lined the route of his final journey from Dublin to Mayo.

Michael Davitt's association with Celtic might, on the face of it, appear somewhat fleeting and perhaps a little fortuitous, owing much to circumstance and little to considered thought. Closer examination, however, shines a different light on the matter. What we do know is that he was invited by Joseph Shaughnessy, a Celtic director and major player in the founding of the club, to lay a sod of turf at the new Celtic Park in March 1892.[13] The sod was from County Donegal, a place synonymous both with many of the Irish in Scotland and with Celtic Football Club. In an apt and somewhat poetic gesture, this scene was re-enacted more than a century later when a sod of turf, again, from County Donegal, was laid in the centre circle during the latest reconstruction of the stadium in 1995. After making an initial request to the then Chairman, Fergus McCann, a group of around fifty fans from the Rosses Celtic Supporters Club travelled from Ireland for a simple ceremony involving Fergus McCann and goalkeeping legend, Pat Bonner, to lay the first sod at the new stadium and to reconnect with a tradition established by Davitt a hundred or so years earlier.[14]

Whilst we can probably assume that Michael Davitt may not have any great passion for the game of association football, we can be sure that his interest in Celtic was far-sighted and entirely consistent with the values by which he lived his life. And the feeling was entirely mutual. The founders, early directors and supporters of the club regarded him as an individual who embodied everything they and their club stood for. This is evident in the range of values that the early Celtic community and subsequent generations of followers shared with Davitt; values such as social inclusion, charity, equality, national liberation and, of course, the plight of the immigrant Irish.

[13] The Official History of Celtic Football Club, Disc 1

[14] This description of the ceremony is sourced from the website of the Rosses Celtic Supporters Club, www.rossescfc.com

Much has changed since those early days, but those underlying values have remained constant down the years, which leads us to the conclusion that there is much to Michael Davitt's association with the club. He was an honoured and esteemed guest and patron of Celtic and its growing support in the club's first years. The choice of Davitt for Celtic was and is highly significant. His connection with Celtic is likewise. Not only is it noteworthy, but it remains as relevant to our sense of purpose today as it did that day in March 1892 when that famous sod was laid.

The powerful Federation of the Irish League in Scotland voted to join the Labour Party in 1923 and was completely absorbed by it a few years later. In the town of Haslingden in northern England, where Davitt spent much of his early life as part of the Irish diaspora in Britain, people have commemorated Davitt's link with them through the erection of a public monument. The inscription reads as follows:

> This memorial has been erected to perpetuate the memory of Michael Davitt with the town of Haslingden. It marks the site of the home of Michael Davitt, Irish patriot, who resided in Haslingden from 1853 to 1867. / He became a great world figure in the cause of freedom and raised his voice and pen on behalf of the oppressed, irrespective of race or creed, that serfdom be transformed to citizenship and that man be given the opportunity to display his God-given talents for the betterment of mankind. / Born 1846, died 1906.

> Erected by the Irish Democratic League Club,
> Haslingden (Davitt Branch)

'We're better than that'

JACKIE FITZPATRICK

Much of what we have read in Celtic-Minded and Celtic Minded 2 has been well researched and has been a mixture of the 'serious, challenging, witty, informative and reflective'. The two volumes have successfully related important aspects of the story of the club, its players and supporters. We have met people of many classes and creeds and people of various nationalities – all drawn together by their 'Celtic Mindedness', their experiences of supporting Celtic, playing for the club or coming into contact with it in some way. This contact has touched them so deeply that they have taken the time and effort to write about it. Much in the two volumes has been painstakingly researched, drawing on historical documents, oral testimony, secondary sources and statistics, but quite a lot has been personal and anecdotal. My contribution here is of the latter kind. One or two of the areas I touch on may be uncomfortable or difficult for some but I know that Celtic supporters demand honest, critical discussion: because we have proud traditions to uphold we wouldn't have it any other way.

The year 2003 was another unforgettable one for Celtic. We reached our first European final since 1970 and the journey to Seville and the game itself is now the stuff of legend with the twists and turns of the match still the subject of debate. We came back without the cup but the display and conduct of our support won the hearts and minds of the people of Seville – and beyond. We were praised by the city authorities, and soon afterwards officially recognised by UEFA and FIFA who heaped more praise on us with their 'best supporters' and Fair Play awards.

However, the final in Seville wasn't the end of the season for us. We were still very much in contention for the league and many agreed that we deserved something in terms of silverware for our efforts that season. Celtic and Rangers went into their final games of the season level on points and hardly anything in terms of goal difference separating them. We were away to Kilmarnock and they were at home to Dunfermline. It would be results of course but also probably to goals scored on the day. I was lucky enough to get a ticket for Rugby Park and knew we had every chance of winning the league. We missed a penalty but did everything else right. We managed to score four goals without conceding any, in spite of some curious goings on, e.g. there seemed to be only one ball in the ground and when it went out of play the ball boys didn't seem to be in a whole lot of hurry to get it. And then the celebrations at the end, not only by the Kilmarnock support, but also by most of their players and officials: but of course they were celebrating the fact that the result in Glasgow didn't go our way. Dunfermline were beaten 6 – 1 and Rangers had won the league by the narrowest of margins. My feelings towards the celebrating Kilmarnock supporters that day were far from kind.

As we left the stadium the mood was pretty sombre. We walked along for a bit and I heard some raised voices. A few yards ahead I saw the reason for the shouts. A young man and woman, both wearing Kilmarnock tops had found themselves in the middle of the not-too-happy group of Celtic supporters. Normally this wouldn't have raised a whisker but on this day emotion was high, and bitter disappointment and crowds don't always make for the best behaviour. Now I hasten to add that the man and woman in question had not been molested in any way. Nevertheless, they seemed to be very frightened and had sought shelter in a doorway at the bottom of a garden path, presumably until the Celtic fans had cleared. Three or four youths stopped at the top of the path and began to hurl insults at the two Killie supporters and it was clear that this increased their sense of distress. It wasn't a pretty sight but thankfully within seconds the young lads were approached by a number of more mature Celtic fans and were told without ceremony to 'get de f... outa here' The youths obliged but one of them started a stupid argument with one of the men who had moved them on, more or less asking him what the problem was and why were they being told to move. I can't remember the youth's exact words but the answer the older guy gave him has stayed with me ever since. With a certain amount of passion he answered, 'Because we're better than that!' The argument was over. As we walked towards the buses I raised my head and felt very proud to be a Celt, the man's words staying with me: 'We're better than that.'

Now in terms of what we have all seen and heard going to football matches over the years some may think that the above story may not be worthy of comment or offer any original great insight into human behaviour. Were it not for what the man had said the incident itself would not be all that interesting. For me, what he said **was** very interesting and I think it accurately sums up what many of us think of ourselves; we're not only different from other supporters in terms of football culture – who we are and where we are from, what we sing etc. – but we also believe that there is a basic human decency at our core, a recognition that every person on this planet has got the right to be here and is worthy of respect, maybe even when that other person does not seem capable of giving us respect.

I think it's worthwhile having a look at this notion, that 'we're better than that' and consider from where this sense of self-respect comes. Maybe the first thing to bear in mind is that this statement does not say we're better than 'them' – not better than anyone for that matter. What it does say is that we have our own values and standards and it is those that we must strive to maintain and progress: even when some of our own let themselves, the support and the club down – and in the process demean that what makes us what we are, past and present.

The recognition of our exemplary behaviour in Seville gave us a great boost but we didn't need accolades to tell us what the right thing to do was, we had that well worked out ourselves. There are thousands of stories that could be told and re-told

we believe that there is a basic human decency at our core, a recognition that every person on this planet has got the right to be here and is worthy of respect, maybe even when that other person does not seem capable of giving us respect regarding instances of the kindness, humility and charity of collective groups of Celtic supporters. However, I think our sense of decency and willingness to respect others, their religions, cultures, origins etc. comes from Celtic's humble beginnings as a faith and ethnic minority community. Walfrid walked among the poor and I'm sure he must have been influenced by what Jesus says in Matthew's gospel: 'Whatsoever you do for the least of your brethren, you do it for me'. Walfrid was obviously interested in not only feeding the poor of Glasgow's East end, but he wanted to give them self-respect. Being from Ireland he may well also have wanted to add a bit of fun and craic into the mix, and also raise funds for his projects: thus The Celtic Football and Athletic Club was formed in 1887/88.

Now I would be a fool and a liar if I didn't recognise that we Celtic supporters are not all saints and scholars without blemish – few of us will be queuing up to throw the first stone (at least not in the Biblical sense!). We have had some regrettable moments in our past and, while they have to be put in context, we should be ever watchful to uphold the great traditions of our club that embraces people of all backgrounds and creeds and refrains from abusing our rivals' players on the basis of ethnicity or religion. We have suffered too much not to be aware of how harmful such thoughts and actions – written, spoken and carried out – can be towards others.

By way of an exceptional example, the treatment of the black Rangers player, Mark Walters in January 1988 by a vociferous large minority of Celtic fans was shameful and our community's sense of decency was dented big time. That incident stained our support. However, it is also worth noting that those that hurled racist abuse at Walters were in fact challenged by many more supporters at the game and debate raged among fans in the days and weeks that followed. Again, without ceremony, the message was impressed upon the minds of that foolish ignorant vociferous minority amongst us that 'We're better than that'. Such was the anger amongst the majority of our support that this incident has never been repeated. Indeed, it became a watershed for many more supporters who are anti-racist by nature and in terms of their morality and who have clearly decided to shun anyone who thinks or behaves to the contrary. Many Celtic fans have activated their anti-racist tendencies and racists now know they are very clearly unwelcome amongst the support. In this light, numerous Celtic websites and fanzines actively promote anti-racist materials, attitudes and identities.

Now, we didn't need any sanctimonious or hypocritical journalist or chairman or pundit to tell us that the behaviour that day was unacceptable: we worked that out for ourselves. After Mark Walters, the greatest sense of hurt and disgust was felt by a majority of Celtic supporters themselves. It would be simply unimaginable that anything like that could happen now. I was talking about this incident recently to a young supporter in his early twenties who shook his head in disbelief: it was so alien to his experience of being a lifelong Celtic fan that he found it hard to imagine that this had actually happened.

> After Mark Walters, the greatest sense of hurt and disgust was felt by a majority of Celtic supporters themselves.

We have indeed come a long way since 1887/88 but, in spite of opposition from powerful elements in society, we have managed to hold on to our core identities. At the same time we have embraced many of the diverse groups of immigrants who now make up Scottish and Irish society, and, just as important, been embraced by them – we stand as equals supporting our club.

While you can never legislate for what an individual might say or do, we have grown to expect a lot from our support in terms of their knowing the difference between right and wrong. Apart from the barmy, drunken, unthinking and prejudicial minority, Celtic fans always take the side of those who are being oppressed – not those who are doing the oppressing.

Going to a football match is not and shouldn't be the same thing as going to a chapel, a mosque, a church, a temple, a synagogue or a tree-hugging session. It is a time for letting your hair down and cheering on your team. I think we've got to accept some kind of licence in terms of language. And very often strong language and comment on someone's appearance or behaviour is made all the more poignant by an expletive or two. Bad refereeing decisions, fouls, diving, a wee bit of argy bargy, provocative chants or displays by opposition fans are all guaranteed to bring out our creative use of language. Rightly or wrongly, we all accept that and only the seriously naive would expect anything that is different. Some however do indulge in some chants and behaviour that they might want to have a serious look at and ask if they fit in with the positive view we have of ourselves and our sense of decency and fair play that is born out of our historical experience and an awareness of the ideals of our founders.

This is my personal view here and I don't want to join the ranks of those who with great hypocrisy and a holier-than-thou attitude tell us what we should sing or not sing and what flags and banners we should fly or not fly. However, if we see or hear something that contradicts our basic ethos then we shouldn't be worried about discussing and challenging it openly. For example, at some games against our famous city rivals a few supporters around the place have shouted out add-ons to the chorus of The Fields of Athenry that refers to a dead Glasgow Rangers player. I don't hear it at every game against Rangers but it still crops up occasionally – usually from some drunks at Ibrox. I have often wondered about that one. Maybe I'm missing something but I believe sentiments like that about a player who has died should be thrown out – because they're wrong, and we should be more respectful anyway. Thank God that that particular sentiment is not universally expressed by our supporters and it is never expressed by enough to register on TV or radio, but the few people who do use it demean themselves and bring disrepute to our support. 'We're better than that.' Imagine how we would feel if we heard references like that about Johnny Doyle, Jinky or Tommy Burns?

There are some other little ditties about opposition players or their wives that I think we might also consider giving the red card to. As I said before, going to a game of football can bring with it high drama and great excitement and we will need to let off steam and let our players know that we are behind them, but going on about somebody's wife or sister doesn't do anything for the cause. There is of course genuine 'football banter' that sails close to the wind on occasion, and let's be honest some players do bring out the worst in us and if a player behaves like a beast on the park then he shouldn't complain if he gets called 'the Beast' or gets the odd 'boo'. However, I don't think we should involve the wives or families of people who are not our favourites. We have to rise above that kind of behaviour, marginalize it and show that 'we are better than that'.

When it comes to religious and racist abuse in Scotland no group of football supporters have been on the receiving end more than Celtic fans, and our players are not immune from it either: our sins pale in comparison to the mountains of insults endured by us. Our detractors are not only found amongst rival supporters but in Scotland they abound in the popular media and in the establishment throughout the country. In recent years players like Aiden McGeady, Neill Lennon, Sunsuka Nakamura, Arthur Boruc have earned our undying affection by enduring insults and abuse with great dignity and self-respect. Fascist salutes, overt and covert racist slurs, bigoted and prejudicial singing and chants, threats of violence and actual violence aimed at players and supporters, and all of this often 'explained' and excused by some politicians and journalists with even the most murderous attacks being played down in the media. We have seen and have been required to endure it all.

Being human, and in a Christian sense, being sinners, make us prone to wrongs, lapses and faults: we are not perfect. Nonetheless, the dignity and respect – for ourselves as Celtic supporters and for others – that have been integral to our club and its support since our foundation, remain intact. The pillars that this club is built upon, Irishness, Catholicism/Christianity and Charity, are what make us distinctive, as well as inclusive. Our distinctiveness is precious and is the legacy of our founders and those that supported this club from its inception. If the phrase 'keep the faith' is to mean anything worthwhile, then we must work to remain true to the morals, values and identities that set us apart.

> players like Aiden McGeady, Neill Lennon, Sunsuka Nakamura, Arthur Boruc have earned our undying affection by enduring insults and abuse with great dignity and self-respect

PREJUDICE

The Sad Cross
Scotland Has To Bear

GERARD GOUGH

As I began to write my own contribution to the 'Celtic Minded' series of books, the Polish goalkeeper, affectionately dubbed 'The Holy Goalie' by Celtic fans, Artur Boruc had just returned from the 2008 European Championships in Austria and Switzerland, where, it is safe to say, he was the standout performer for his country and indeed one of the best goalkeepers in the tournament. For those Celtic supporters among us who have watched him perform at a high level over the past three years this comes as no surprise. He is without doubt the best goalkeeper I have seen in nearly three decades of watching Celtic. Yet it's not just his technical skill that endears him to the fans, it's his competitive nature, his character and his connection with the supporters, coupled with a seemingly genuine love for the club that makes him such a popular figure amongst the Celtic support. However, this popularity doesn't appear to extend beyond the Celtic support, as many people in Scotland view Boruc in a very different and pejorative light. Although (like some other footballers) he appeared to 'lose his way' a little during the 2008/09 season, this less favourable light might be accounted for in no small part because of his Catholic faith, which is more than a little disconcerting.

This was brought to light after a report, albeit small, surfaced in Glagow's Evening Times newspaper in early August 2006, suggesting that the goalkeeper could face court action over claims he incited violence during a Celtic v Rangers match at Ibrox in February of that year, because he blessed himself.[1] Nearly two weeks later, another report appeared in the same paper inferring that he had indeed been given a warning after blessing himself at Ibrox.[2]

None of the other mainstream national newspapers chose to pick the story up, investigate or expand upon it. However, Harry Conroy, former editor of the Scottish Catholic Observer, was astute enough to do just that and so the story made the front page of the Catholic weekly national newspaper the following week[3] and attracted widespread criticism from within the Catholic Church in Scotland, prominent Catholics such as leading composer James MacMillan and Eddie Toner, former General Secretary of the Celtic Supporters' Association.

The Scottish Catholic Observer article also clarified that Artur Boruc had been issued with 'an alternative to prosecution', which usually signifies that the person has been issued with a fine, or in Boruc's case, a caution. Nobody from the Crown Office contested the fact that the Polish goalkeeper had received the caution for blessing himself, leading a number of people, including many Catholics in Scotland to believe that the Evening Times' assessment of the Crown Office's action was in fact, accurate. Indeed, comments made by John McMillan of the Rangers Supporters' Association in an article in the Sunday Times a few days later, seemed to suggest that the complaints made by Rangers supporters against Artur Boruc centred on the fact that he had made the act of reverence.[4]

'I didn't see the incident myself, but I was aware of a commotion behind the goal and many fans on the supporters' bus saw Boruc cross himself and were angered by it,' he stated. He went on to say: 'We have a particular situation in Scotland, particularly on the west coast, where people are sensitive to such actions.' Boruc, it appeared, was being penalised for a simple act of faith with very few outwith the Catholic community in Scotland and the Celtic support leaping to his defence.

The Scottish Catholic Observer in the same edition, strongly defended the goalkeeper though, and Conroy also launched a

1 'Celt in 'blessing' probe' Evening Times, August 4th 2006

2 'Boruc warned over blessing' Evening Times, August 17th 2006

3 'Scotland's anti-Catholic shame' Scottish Catholic Observer, August 25th 2006

4 'Boruc finds Old Firm rivalry remains stained by history,' Sunday Times, August 27th 2006 (www.timesonline.co.uk/tol/sport/football/article620742.ece)

petition in the newspaper entitled, 'Make your voice heard', which sought an assurance from the Scottish Executive recognising that 'the act of blessing yourself to be treated as a possible criminal act besmirches the good name of Scotland'. The campaign called upon the Executive to 'recognise that the problem arises not from the person carrying out an act of Christian prayer but in the prejudices of those who complain', and also, that the Executive 'take steps to tackle the real problem and to ensure that the act of blessing yourself does not merit, in any circumstances, a police investigation or criminal proceedings'.

Shortly after the Scottish Catholic Observer had given the story the coverage it deserved, it began to travel and receive worldwide exposure from places as far-flung as Australia, Malaysia, Singapore and Canada. Most greeted the apparent cautioning of Boruc, quite rightly, with complete bewilderment. Criticism was also coming in thick and fast notably from Bishop Joseph Devine, SNP Leader (soon to become First Minister) Alex Salmond and also Labour MP Ruth Kelly who also sought reassurances from the Crown Office over the matter. The Crown Office's lack of response was proving to be an embarrassment and eventually they were forced, it seemed, into releasing a statement of clarification on August 28, 2006.[5] It stated that:

> . . . wholly unfounded claims had been made with regard to the action and that the goalkeeper was seen by members of the public and police officer to bless himself. Witnesses describe him smiling or laughing at a section of the Rangers section of the crowd and making 'come on' gestures. This action appeared to incense a section of the crowd to react in such a way that police officers and security personnel had to become involved to calm the situation. The police reported that it took ten minutes to restore normality in the crowd.

Statements were then taken from a number of witnesses and a report was submitted to the Procurator Fiscal in Glasgow, who, after considering 'all the available evidence, including a video recording of the crowd (the incident itself was not caught on camera)', concluded that 'Boruc's behaviour, as described would constitute the offence of breach of the peace **because of its impact on the crowd'** (my bold). The report was also keen

[5] The Crown Office- 'Football and the Law' (www.crownoffice.gov.uk/News/Releases/2006/08/28140026)

to point out that an alternative to prosecution does not constitute 'prosecution, conviction or a criminal record', and also that this 'limited and intentionally private action', was taken for Boruc's 'alleged gesticulation and incensing of the crowd, rather than the act of blessing himself'. Pointedly, the Crown Office added that it wished to 'make it absolutely clear that the prosecution service in Scotland fully respects religious belief and practices and would not countenance formal action against individuals for acts of religious observance, but we would equally make clear that the police and prosecutors cannot ignore conduct which appears to be inciting disorder'.

The delay in the release of the statement from the Crown Office, the previous comments from Rangers Supporters' Association spokesperson John McMillan about the incident and the apparent lack of video evidence of Boruc's action on that day (in spite of many mobile phones now having video cameras as part of their apparatus) possibly led many people to cast aspersions on the reason for the action taken against Boruc. Many no doubt felt that the complaint was made with regard to the goalkeeper making the sign of the cross and the decision to follow it up was an attack on the Catholic faith. This appeared to be confirmed when some 1500 coupons were collected by the Scottish Catholic Observer and handed over to the Scottish Parliament to Labour MSP Michael McMahon, then convener of the Public Petitions Committee.[6] Many were unhappy that the act of reverence could still lead to a prosecution after the Crown Office had stated that it could not guarantee that the act could not be considered a criminal offence in any circumstance as it was 'not possible to speculate on events in the future if such a gesture has material influence'.[7] While both McMahon and the former Scottish Catholic Observer editor Harry Conroy agreed that the act could be used in a non-reverential manner, there was no accord reached over the specifics of how the act could be deemed provocative, with Conroy insisting that, 'legislation should err on the side of the innocent'.[8]

This was not the end of the debacle however, as The Scotsman newspaper decided that after Boruc had performed the same reverential ritual in a match between the two Glasgow sides at

6 'SCO makes your voice heard' Scottish Catholic Observer, November 24th 2006

7 'Blessing yourself could still lead to a prosecution' Scottish Catholic Observer, September 1st 2006

8 Blessing Oneself (PE1005), Public Petitions Committee Official Report 29th November 2006 (www.scottishparliament.uk/business/committees/petitions/or-06/pu06-1902.htm#Col2923)

Ibrox on December 17th 2006, it was an act of provocation.[9] The comment article that accompanied the main news report linked the gesture to the often mentioned, but seldom explained, issue of sectarianism, while at the same time described Boruc's behaviour as 'provocative' and also stated that, 'Mr Boruc is in danger of letting down his club, his sport and his faith'. The Scotsman did not really explore why this might be the case while the assertion was dispelled when Cardinal Keith O'Brien, via the Scottish Catholic Observer, criticised the irresponsibility of the article and comment and launched a formal complaint against the newspaper.[10] Strathclyde Police were also quoted in the article as saying that 'No offence was committed', while Celtic FC also said in the original article in The Scotsman, that they had no problem with Boruc making the gesture.

Those who did have a problem with it though, outwith sections of the Scottish media, were a sizeable number of Rangers supporters, who have been immortalised in a YouTube clip of the incident reacting furiously,[11] one of whom is heard calling the keeper a 'f****** bigot' and boasting that he has him 'on video this time', before adding another expletive. Both The Scotsman article and comments and the YouTube clip did little to help support the original argument from the Crown Office that action was taken against Boruc for other gestures, nor did it allay the fears of many people that the criticism of Boruc was due to the act of reverence, linked to his faith, that he performed before the match.

This belief is not something new, nor is the way in which displays of the Catholic faith perceived or otherwise, have been frowned upon by numerous sections of Scottish society. In a match between Partick Thistle and Rangers on February 3rd 1996, Thistle player Rod McDonald was booked for blessing himself as he left the field of play after the linesman had reported him to referee Jim McGilvray. The player was subsequently sent off after having received two yellow cards. The player appealed the first yellow card[12] and McGilvray resigned,[13] although the latter action was said to be down to feeling forced to book Paul Gascoigne for celebrating a goal.

Shortly after the death of Pope John Paul II, on-loan Celtic

9 'Celtic keeper makes Rangers fans cross' The Scotsman, December 18, 2006 (news.scotsman.com/ latestnews/Celtic-keeper-makes-Rangers-fans.2835999.jp)

10 'Formal complaint issued against The Scotsman' Scottish Catholic Observer, December 2006

11 'Boruc at Ibrox' (http://www.youtube.com/watch?v=yBIC5WABEYs)

12 'Partick made to wait over appeals' The Independent, March 6th 2006

13 'Scots deny crisis talk as referee quits' The Independent, February 20th 1996

striker Craig Bellamy made a faith-filled display in a Scottish Cup semi-final match against Heart of Midlothian on Sunday April 10th 2005. A minute's silence to honour the late Pontiff had to be cut short at just 24 seconds[14] by referee Stuart Dougal after a huge number of fans of the Edinburgh side disrupted the tribute with prolonged racist and bigoted shouts, jeering, swearing and abuse. Conscious of this disrespectful act, when Bellamy scored Celtic's second goal of the afternoon in the 2-1 win, he poignantly pointed towards his black armband, signifying 'his own' respect for Pope John Paul II and disdain for those who hadn't shown any basic and compassionate respect for this much-loved religious leader.

This picture was captured by the photographers and appeared in national newspapers. A friend of mine, who is an avid collector of Celtic memorabilia, including photos of the players, contacted one such photographer to try and purchase a copy of the picture as, for him, it 'summed up a hundred words of emotion'. The photographer apparently reacted with surprise and noted that he had not intended to get caught up in a religious debate by distributing the picture for fear that it may be taken out of context. Instead, he offered to e-mail my friend a selection of pictures of Bellamy that he had taken on the day free of charge. This offer was politely declined, but the photographs arrived in his inbox in any case, with a final comment from the photographer that he wished the matter just to 'die down'. The picture of Bellamy pointing to his armband has apparently since vanished from the public domain.

Two weeks later, in a match between Celtic and Rangers at Ibrox on April 24th 2005, Bellamy scored a sublime goal, which he celebrated by sinking to his knees with his hands cupped to his face. He did not leave the field of play, nor did he make any gestures towards the Rangers supporters, yet he was cautioned by referee Stuart Dougal. This yellow card continues to mystify many Celtic fans to this day and most have, not unreasonably, concluded that he had been booked for appearing as if he was 'praying' in front of the Rangers supporters (indeed I am aware of a number of Catholics who pray 'for' those bigots who can't stand Catholics or Catholicism), which in any case should neither

14 Bellamy silences the jeers' The Guardian, April 11th 2005 (www.guardian.co.uk/football/2005/apr/11/match.hearts?commentpage=1)

be seen as provocative nor worthy of a caution. Both the disruption of the minute's silence for Pope John Paul II and his booking in the match against Rangers, would no doubt have left the striker exasperated and baffled.

Furthermore, in a question and answer session with Mikel Arteta, the former Rangers' midfielder, on his new club Everton's website, in April 2006[15] the player revealed an unsavoury fact about his former employers, with regard to the act of blessing oneself. In responding to a question asking if he was a born-again Christian, Arteta replied, 'I am Catholic. But I have always been Catholic. The people at Rangers didn't really like it, so I had to be respectful'. In other words, like several other of Glasgow Rangers modern signings, he was required to hide that he was Catholic.

These incidents, aligned with the action against Boruc suggest that anti-Catholicism remains a factor for cultural, religious and political assessment amongst many people within the Scottish sports media, the Scottish football authorities, the Rangers' support and quite possibly even within the club itself, as the quote by Arteta could be interpreted as such. Surely if such anti-Catholicism was seen to exist within these organisations, each instance should have been swiftly addressed and each organisation should have been made aware that anti-Catholicism should not be tolerated, accepted and swept under the carpet. Unfortunately, to date, action has not been taken and anti-Catholicism has continued to thrive within Scotland with its victims continuing to suffer and be unfairly depicted and denigrated for a number of their beliefs and identities. Alas, this was again evident in another major incident involving the Celtic goalkeeper.

If we look beyond the small narrow-minded prism of Scottish society we can see that sportsmen and women, in whose lives faith plays a pivotal role, are numerous, and the world of professional football is one such field where many choose to reveal or even exclaim that faith. Brazil's mercurial midfielder Kaka is an evangelical Christian, who, on more than one occasion at the end of matches (including the 2007 Champions League Final against Liverpool) has taken off his jersey to reveal a T-

15 'Mikel's Toffeetalk Transcript' April 19, 2006 (www.evertonfc.com/news/archive/mikel-s-toffeetalk-transcript.html)

139

shirt with the slogan 'I belong to Jesus'. His own faith was fortified in October 2000 after he slipped on a swimming pool slide and broke a vertebra. 'The doctors said that I was lucky to be able to walk normally,' he said. 'They were talking about luck and my family was talking about God. We knew that it was His hand that had saved me.' He has also previously commented: 'I learnt that it is faith that decides whether something will happen or not.'

Kaka's displays of faith even attracted a favourable response from English Monsignor, Keith Barltrop, director of the Catholic Agency to Support Evangelisation. 'A lot of people think religion is quite fundamentalist, so if there is a major sporting figure whose lifestyle backs up his words, it is a positive thing,' he said.[16]

Former Chelsea star, Mateja Kezman, from Serbia is a member of the Orthodox Church and often wears a T-shirt under his jersey bearing a Byzantine image of Jesus Christ. He also sports a tattoo (one of many) with the message 'Only God can judge me', in Serbian, taken from a text by Father Tadej, one of the foremost recent thinkers in the Serb Orthodox Church. He has always worn his faith on his sleeve and has spoken of his desire to become a monk when he hangs up his boots.[17]

Scotland hasn't been immune to having faith-filled players either. Former Dundee striker Juan Sara often celebrated scoring a goal by lifting up his jersey to reveal a T-shirt emblazoned with the message 'Jesus Loves You', while former Rangers defender Marvin Andrews wore a similar garment praising God's role in his team's championship success of 2004/05. 'The things that are impossible with men are possible with God', it read. The Trinidad & Tobago internationalist even refused an operation on a severe knee injury, trusting in God to heal him.

The press coverage attributed to these players and their displays of faith were usually innocuous or even positive, often carrying a curious questioning tone, but were never negative in any way, nor should they have been. Every example of these players' displays of faith suggests that they are appreciative of God's role in their rise to fame, the granting of their talents and

16 'Kaka's outpouring of faith brings joy to leaders within Christian community,' The Times, May 25th 2007 (www.timesonline.co.uk/tol/sport/football/european_football/article1838356.ece)

17 'Mateja Kezman ready to stun Chelsea' The Telegraph, March 29th 2008 (www.telegraph.co.uk/sport/football/2295792/Mateja-Kezman-ready-to-stun-Chelsea.html)

their use of those talents on the field of play, which as a Catholic and a footballer is something I can wholeheartedly appreciate. These players' displays also show that faith is simply a part of everyday life and one's actions, attitudes and identities.

In April 2008 however, at the end of the season's ultimate Celtic v Rangers match, Celtic goalkeeper Artur Boruc, upon removing his jersey to give to a supporter, revealed a T-shirt with the visage of the late Pope John Paul II on it and, in writing above it, the message 'God Bless the Pope': a Scottish media frenzy ensued.

This incident was met with a host of criticism from sizeable sections of the Scottish sports and mainstream media, whose speculative analysis of the goalkeeper's decision to sport such a T-shirt was not only hostile, but was bewildering, saddening and in some cases wholly ridiculous. Thus it's important to look at what was written and said and to reflect upon the criticisms and comments direct at Boruc.

A number of journalists chose to use emotive and offensive language in regard to the incident. Mainstream tabloid newspapers used a number of pejorative terms. David McCarthy and Hugh Keevins of the Daily Record referred to the incident as a 'taunt' and described Boruc as 'the madcap Pole'.[18] Columnist Stewart Cosgrove, also of the Daily Record called the act a 'cheap trick' and twice called the goalkeeper a 'buffoon'.[19] The scathing criticism began to look like an all-out character assassination when The Sun ran with a typically tasteless headline, 'Pope on a dope',[20] with regard to the incident, while Ray Hepburn of the Sunday Mirror made the assertion that 'there is no place for the Pope in football',[21] a markedly more specific and revealing comment than the often favoured cliché of many Scottish sportswriters about there being 'no place for religion in football'.

As a Celtic supporter, I'm glad of the role religion plays in the instance of Celtic, and Catholicism has played generally in football, especially in the history of my team, for without it, it would not exist. Nor indeed would French side AJ Auxerre or numerous other clubs for whom religion played an important part in their foundations and life. Football and its supporters do

18 'Artur Boruc cleared by SFA and SPL over Old Firm Pope T-shirt' The Daily Record, April 30, 2008 (www.dailyrecord.co.uk/sport/football-news/scottish-football/spl-football/celtic-fc/2008/04/30/artur-boruc-cleared-by-sfa-and-spl-over-old-firm-pope-t-shirt-86908-20399772)

19 'Only suckers could fall for cheap trick from buffoon Boruc' The Daily Record, May 1, 2008 (www.dailyrecord.co.uk/comment/columnists/sport-columnists/stuart-cosgrove/2008/05/01/only-suckers-could-fall-for-cheap-trick-from-buffoon-boruc-86908-20400869)

20 'Pope on a dope' The Sun, April 28, 2008

21 'Don't bless this dope' The Sunday Mirror, May 4, 2008

not exist in a social, political or indeed religious vacuum, and football teams the world over managed to pay tribute to the late Pope John Paul II after his death without undue fuss or comment. The language used in criticising Boruc exhibiting a religious T-shirt was also in stark contrast to the reports describing the afore-mentioned players' (Kaka, Kezman et al) displays of faith, which were, by and large, favourable, or simply didn't attract undue comment.

At the more extreme end of the scale, Darryl Broadfoot, chief sportswriter for The Herald suggested, albeit indirectly, that the alleged sectarian abuse and attack on Celtic player Aiden McGeady outside a Glasgow nightclub after the Old Firm match and also the death of Celtic supporter Patrick McBride – who died of a heart attack after being set upon by a hostile gang – could be attributed to Boruc's actions after the match, with the comment, 'suddenly, stoking the fires does not seem such a good idea'.[22] To say that this is a ludicrous assessment of those particular situations is an understatement. However, distinct from anything else, it partly reflects the denial that inhabits much of Scottish society about its problems with Catholics, Catholicism and Irishness in Scotland.

There was also a factual inaccuracy contained within that same report about whether Boruc would face punishment from football's governing body FIFA. Broadfoot, like several other sportswriters, believed this to be the case and pointed to FIFA Rules, Law 4, Decision 1. This reads as follows: 'Players must not reveal undershirts that contain slogans or advertising. The basic compulsory equipment must not contain any political, religious or personal statements.' It goes without saying, a T-shirt with the late Pope John Paul II on it is not part of the compulsory equipment, nor was it revealed during the match. Add to this the fact that FIFA actually had a picture of the goalkeeper wearing the T-shirt on their website and the suggestion that he may be punished sounds like preposterous and malicious scaremongering.

In Scottish media circles the general consensus was that Boruc's action was a unique and calculated move, both in wearing the T-shirt and also taking his top off to reveal it. The implication

22 'Boruc committed no crime, but was still wrong' The Herald, April 30th 2008

also seemed to be that the keeper's faith was of little importance to him and that he was in fact using Pope John Paul II's image in a distasteful manner.

The wearing of a T-shirt with Pope John Paul II on it by Boruc was not unique. He had done so previously for his former club Legia Warsaw. Of course, this was in a country that does not have a history of anti-Catholicism. Moreover, it is true to say that Boruc does not always remove his jersey at the end of the match, but the fact that he did and handed it into the Celtic support, could at the time have been interpreted as a gesture to the fans and an indication that he may have played his last Celtic v Rangers match. Fortunately, that was not the case.

It is also a mistake to speculate on the goalkeeper's faith. He hasn't spoken overtly about his faith, however given that a picture on his website shows him in his flat with a large portrait of Pope John Paul II hanging behind him on his wall and taking into account not only the strength of the Catholic Church in Poland, but the reverence in which the memory of Pope John Paul II is held there, many things would point to the fact that Catholicism and the spiritual shadow cast by the figure of Pope John Paul II do indeed play an important role in his life, despite any faults (sins?) he might have.

There is another point of consensus though, which was mentioned in many of the previous articles criticising the goalkeeper that I do however agree with. I do feel that Boruc wore the T-shirt to provoke a response, but I believe what he intended to do was merely to hold a mirror up to Scottish society and show that the historic profound and defining anti-Catholic streak that has existed in this country, and in the microcosmic society of the football arena, hasn't gone away.

Indeed, I would also contend that anti-Catholicism and its close relation anti-Irish racism are the most important component parts of the so-called sectarianism issue in Scotland. Until that fact is accepted and tackled, then all the initiatives, statements and slogans mean nothing.

Rather than hounding Boruc, we should be applauding him for defiantly refusing to give into bigotry and hatred and for refusing to hide his faith away, as many suggest he should. As a supporter of an inclusive club like Celtic, had a Muslim or Jewish player, for example, chosen to celebrate their faith publicly on or off the field of play, I would have wholeheartedly respected their actions. So too would the media I suspect. However, for many within the Scottish sports media fraternity and for sections of Scottish society, inclusiveness and respect for diversity, does seem to hit a snag when Catholicism is involved.

Neither the reverential act of Boruc blessing himself nor the wearing of the T-shirt with Pope John Paul II's image should have warranted comments of a vitriolic, negative nature. Surely such vehement criticism should be reserved for tackling particularly distasteful racist chanting, like that exhibited by a large section of the Rangers support which through 2008 to 2009 at least, continued to taunt Celtic supporters with their song: 'The famine's over why don't you go home'? Sadly, I can't think of any journalist, print or broadcast who has strongly analysed or highlighted this and tackled it for the racism and prejudice it propounds. Indeed, as some Celtic Minded authors demonstrate so well, maybe some or many of them share the ignorance and bigotry that seems often to prevail.

'One Scotland Many Cultures?' 'The Best Small Country in the World?' I am grateful to Boruc for showing us that neither of these statements are, as yet, factually accurate and a great deal of work remains to be done.

Ignorance and Scotland's Shame

GERRY COYLE

Every so often an episode occurs which reminds us that public manifestations of Irishness are still capable of arousing hostility in this 'best wee country in the world' of ours. The Carfin debacle of February 2001 was one such episode.

That the unveiling of a memorial to the victims of the Great Irish Hunger (significantly the first of its kind in Scotland in over 150 years) by an Irish Prime Minister should be cancelled ostensibly due to the fact that it was to take place in the hours following a Celtic-Rangers football match (we were reliably assured that pre-match would not have presented a problem), might seem a bizarre scenario to rational outside observers. However, to those of us familiar with the Scottish psyche's peculiar confusion regarding football, religion and matters Irish,[1] MP Frank Roy's attempt to justify his advice to the Taoiseach to stay away from his constituency on the grounds that 'if Celtic won, the ceremony (and presumably Mr. Ahern's presence) might be considered as an act of triumphalism, while if Celtic lost it could be seen as an act of defiance', caused little bemusement. Nor was it of any surprise that Mr. Roy had significantly failed to dwell on his damning indictment of Scottish society that his statement contained. Clearly who may adopt such an interpretation and the reason for them doing so was not an issue deserving scrutiny.

Of course Roy may well have genuinely believed that the

[1] Conversely there exists in this country a desire, when it suits, to disengage football from such 'extraneous' influences. The corollary of this view being that Celtic FC should be nothing other than a football club, divested of its culture and traditions i.e. its Irish/Catholic heritage. This desire is not confined to those of an anti-Celtic disposition; it also unfortunately seems to prevail among some small sections of the club's support and employees. Equally of course there are many within the Celtic family who would actively seek to celebrate this tripartite association.

145

Taoiseach's appearance would have created such bloodshed and mayhem as to endanger the well-being of his constituents, the good citizens of North Lanarkshire. One suspects however that, as a seasoned politician, he simply acted as he did because he was confident that his stance would be unquestioningly welcomed in the socio-political milieu in which he was operating. After all, what he was advocating was 'common sense', the much tried and accepted approach of the Scottish establishment when dealing with what are regarded as 'provocative' manifestations of Irishness: inevitably Irishness with a historical/ political dimension – often tagged with the epithet 'controversial'.[2] This approach dictates that rather than challenge the bigots and racists who react negatively, and in many instances aggressively, towards the perceived source of provocation, it is easier and more acceptable to prevent the offending manifestations of perceived Irish/Catholic 'triumphalism' or 'defiance' materialising in the first place. In essence what we are dealing with here in these situations is almost always anti-Irish racism and anti-Catholicism.

It is this approach which led Strathclyde Police, in the aftermath of the Celtic-Glasgow Rangers match at the centre of the Carfin controversy, to close 'Celtic pubs' – hostelries where Celtic fans had gathered to celebrate their team's victory – in Glasgow city centre following a particularly nasty spate of sectarian attacks upon those establishments (a similar approach was adopted by Strathclyde Police following Celtic's Championship triumph in 1998). Interestingly few, if any, of those responsible were apprehended while the Scottish media, in time-honoured fashion, reported these incidents as 'clashes **between** Old Firm fans',[3] conveniently failing to emphasise their more often than not one-sided nature: i.e. ignoring what was in reality, at least for the perpetrators, calculated attacks on a manifestation of perceived Irish/Catholic 'triumphalism'.

So if Mr. Roy was simply following the establishment line in dealing with 'controversial' manifestations of Irishness, why did he and to a lesser extent some of his political colleagues find themselves in the public stocks, pilloried by all and sundry?[4] One would like to think that the ensuing outcry in media and political circles was a laudable desire to support multi-culturalism

[2] A dearth of media publicity and involvement by the Scottish political establishment regarding various other Irish cultural manifestations suggests toleration rather than genuine espousal.

[3] For example, Evening Times 12/2/01, '23 arrests after Old Firm trouble'.

[4] First Minister Henry McLeish exonerated his proposed non attendance at the event by claiming the Taoiseach's visit was at the behest of a group of local business men (which it wasn't), therefore a private event rather than state occasion. Scottish Secretary Helen Liddell initially declined an invitation to attend, as did former Home Secretary John Reid and MP Frank Roy. All four were summarily criticised by the media for 'avoiding' the ceremony and contributing to the cancellation of the Taoiseach's visit. All four subsequently attended the re-arranged visit.

and specifically on this occasion the acceptance and celebration of Irishness in Scotland. The reality, however, was that the opprobrium which descended on the heads of the 'Carfin politicians' had very little to do with any perceived slight to the Irish diaspora and much to do with the antagonism then current towards the Scottish Executive. In truth, the targets were already in place and a queue forming at the firing range long before a suitable arena presented itself in the unlikely form of Carfin.

As the media astutely (due much to its management by other forces) reinvented the Carfin debacle, it is notable how, as the controversy raged on, the Irish Famine, the commemorative ceremony itself, its highly meaningful purpose and the symbolic significance of the Taoiseach's presence became less and less the focus of attention for many commentators. By couching it in generalised political-speak – 'a diplomatic blunder', 'a slight to the Prime Minister of a neighbouring and friendly country' – the issue was divested of its peculiarly Irish historical/political baggage: indeed it was almost sanitised to suit. Viewed in this context the guilty parties were censured for damaging Scotland's standing as a nation on the wider diplomatic stage. Given such unpatriotic behaviour there could be no recourse to appeal.

This perspective, while doubtlessly introduced for the purpose of political point scoring, also had the added advantage of conveniently relegating the 'sectarian' issue, and any anti-Irish sentiment that had become evident, to the sidelines, an advantage not lost on its adherents, anxious to recast Scotland in the image of a modern nation state, rather than a kind of tartan 'Mississippi'[5], rife with prejudice/racism from street level right through to the upper echelons of its political establishment.[6] Any such admission of course had to be avoided at all costs. McChuill's pub on Glasgow's High Street (a favourite haunt of Celtic supporters) lying empty by early evening, its glass front smashed, a memorial standing forlornly and uncelebrated in the middle of a Lanarkshire grotto, however, were images which suggested that George Galloway's infamous analogy of 'Mississippi' was partly closer to the truth than many would wish to admit.

The dust from the whole ignominious episode may now be

> In essence what we are dealing with here in these situations is almost always anti-Irish racism and anti-Catholicism.

[5] George Galloway, 8/2/01. The phrases suggest a parallel with the rabid racism of America's southern states.

[6] Although it may be harsh – indeed wrong by way of intention – to accuse Roy and his colleagues of anti-Irish racism, nevertheless it could be argued that their stance did give that sentiment certain legitimacy.

well and truly settled and Bertie was ostensibly persuaded by the Scottish establishment's pleas of 'haste ye back' that no offence was ever meant. However, Carfin should not be readily forgotten, not least for what it confirmed about the undercurrent of anti-Irish/Catholic prejudice that exists within Scottish society, a prejudice so insidious that it can influence even those from within the community itself. This is crucial to understanding a non-party point scoring assessment, and distinct from the personalities of those involved, of what occurred at Carfin in 2001.

It is important to bear in mind a sub-text of understanding: three of the four main politicians involved were, or had been, Catholic, while two were known as supporters of Celtic. While those things in themselves did not oblige them to support the Carfin ceremony, their conspicuous attempts to disassociate themselves from the event does beg a question: did a fear of being publicly seen as having such credentials and be actively celebrating Irishness, particularly when it brought with it a historical and political baggage (as the Carfin ceremony obviously did), influence their stance?

If such an assessment is indeed correct and circumspection was the guiding factor, it is yet a further reminder that, even within the upper stratum of our political establishment, where the credo has been nurtured and promoted with such gusto, there is an unspoken acknowledgement that, when it comes to 'one Scotland, many cultures', Irishness need not apply.[7] In addition, this raises questions about how open or secret with regards Irishness even 'successful' individuals can be in Scotland. It might be seen as easy to criticise those who feel obliged to adopt such an approach, but perhaps we should instead be reserving our condemnation for a society where anti-Irish/Catholic prejudice is so tangible that such circumspection is deemed to be necessary.[8]

Eight years on, the potential for Irishness of a historical/political dimension to ignite the flames of controversy, particularly in the context of Scottish football, is still evident.

Enter one Jeanette Findlay.

[7] Although Carfin preceded the launch of the 'one Scotland . . .' campaign (2005), this perspective appears to remain unaltered.

[8] Significantly such circumspection seems to be the almost exclusive preserve of those within the Catholic or Celtic communities. Football pundits changing their surname for fear that it would be recognisably Irish/Catholic or former Celtic players turned football pundit, who slavishly adhere to the perceived 'party line', are not hard to find. In contrast those from a Scottish Protestant/Rangers background, who are in the public eye, do not appear to be afflicted by this tendency, as Gordon Smith's controversial utterances aptly illustrate.

Anyone reading the press coverage of the Celtic Trust's Secretary's now infamous interview with Radio 5 presenters Nicky Campbell and Sheilagh Fogarty on 21 November 2007 would be forgiven for thinking that she was advocating the setting up of IRA cells within the Celtic support base and making balaclavas and armalites mandatory accessories for anyone intending to purchase a Celtic season ticket.

Tabloid and broadsheet were as one in their clamorous condemnation of the Glasgow University lecturer's apparent support for 'a terrorist organisation'. 'Celtic Disown Rebel Fans Chief in IRA Row' proclaimed the Daily Record in a piece which managed to present a barrage of criticism of Findlay's views from no less than twelve contributors: a truly heterogeneous mix that included 'Sean from Derry', a spokesperson from Glasgow University, Nil by Mouth, First Minister Alex Salmond and a host of figures from the world of football ranging from Celtic legend Billy McNeill to SFA Chief Executive Gordon Smith (no irony apparently intended), who fortuitously happened to be attending the launch of the Kick Bigotry Out campaign which was taking place on the same day at Hampden.[9] Notably, despite neither the comments by the First Minister nor any of the footballing fraternity making direct reference to Findlay or the views she had expressed, their bland and generalised references to sectarianism – made, one assumes, in reference to the event in which they were participating – apparently constituted sufficient ammunition to counter her 'outrageously offensive' opinions.

The Daily Mail was also quick to get in on the act. 'Fury as Celtic Trust Chair sparks row over pro-IRA Chants' ran the headline.[10] The fury was provided in the piece by the DUP MP for 'East Londonderry' Gregory Campbell (as a member of the Orange Institution, Unionist MP and Glasgow Rangers fan, obviously a good source for objective comment) who condemned Findlay for her 'appalling reference to what can only be seen as a glorification of terror'. Anyone however scrutinising The Mail's offering, looking for any evidence of a 'row' (for which the vigorous expression of opposing viewpoints is surely a prerequisite?) would have been left sorely disappointed. Instead

George Galloway's infamous analogy of 'Mississippi' was partly closer to the truth than many would wish to admit.

[9] Daily Record 21/11/07

[10] Daily Mail 21/11/07

we were treated to the obligatory inclusion of a statement on behalf of Celtic F.C. claiming that the Trust spokeswoman's views 'were totally unrepresentative of the Celtic support' – a glib (one hesitates to use the word ignorant) generalisation surely given a) the comprehensive and complex nature of the views expressed and b) the global and heterogeneous character of the club's support.

when it comes to 'one Scotland, many cultures', Irishness need not apply

Next up came a contribution from the Association of Irish Supporters' Clubs (there's nothing that hurts quite like letting you know that even 'your own' don't want to know, is there?) condemning sectarianism while stressing the desire to preserve Celtic's 'Irish roots' (?)[11] However, no direct comment was given on Findlay's discourse itself, perhaps not surprising given the fact the Association embraces clubs which have named themselves after patriots from Irish history such as Wolfe Tone and Robert Emmet (both Protestants) – ironically a point acknowledged in the article: its implications however, in terms of the credence which it gave Findlay's argument, not unsurprisingly, remained unexplored.

Further Irish 'condemnation' was provided in the form of Irish Foreign Minister Dermot Ahern who pronounced, 'Any singing of those type of songs I wouldn't encourage at all'.

Apparently Dermot's credentials for commenting on the issue stemmed from the fact that his favourite League of Ireland club, Dundalk, was about to embark on its own anti-racist campaign and, of course, the obvious parallel between members of the Irish diaspora communicating their heritage and history through song in a Scottish football arena and the challenges facing the new multi-cultural Ireland: 'If you think in the context of 168 nationalities living in the Republic of Ireland today, to talk about one side or the other is a bit passe at this stage when you see we have a completely ethnic, completely multi-cultural society that we have to grapple with'. Inane, lacking in intellectual rigour, irrelevant even, but apparently all grist to the mill nonetheless.

The following day The Telegraph joined in the attack. It may have been slower out of the blocks and its headline omitting the obligatory emotive reference to the IRA favoured by its tabloid counterparts,'[12] but its piece proved to be equally zealous in its

[11] This phrase is frequently employed by way of acknowledging the Club's Irish heritage, but one which is in effect meaningless given that those who employ it often conveniently fail to acknowledge that a significant part of those 'roots' are also in Irish Republican/Nationalist political identities and attitudes. See Eamonn McCann, Magill, May 1988. Also J. Bradley, Celtic Minded 2, 2006

desire to strike at its designated target. Indeed if anything there was greater venom in the bite. Not content with castigating Findlay for her reported 'jaw-dropping defence of sectarian singing at Celtic' the writer of the piece, Alistair Reid, also saw fit to question her intellectual capabilities. Commenting on Findlay's status as an academic, Reid sniped: 'her specialist field cannot be one that relies on a gift for joined-up thinking'.

His support for the interviewer who had so public-spiritedly exposed Findlay's demonic perspective was equally robust: apparently Dr. Findlay had 'spectacularly' missed the opportunity provided to her by Nicky Campbell to 'give an unequivocal rejection of sectarianism'. After all, had he (Campbell) not 'pointed out that he was not referring to inoffensive ditties from the gentler end of Irish folk music,[13] but blatant support for the IRA'?

No, no doubt about it, the Celtic Trust Chair was caught, banged to rights. Even by taking time to explain that the songs which Campbell was referring to were in fact 'from what was essentially a war of independence going back over a hundred years' she was simply, according to Reid, 'digging herself a deep hole' and providing proof positive that 'Celtic Park is still a hotbed of IRA support' – a claim which Reid obliviously contradicted with his further assertion that in her comments 'Dr. Findlay was hopelessly out of touch with the vast majority of Celtic supporters' (we'll put that one down to a lapse in joined-up thinking, shall we?)

The inner sanctum of the Scottish political establishment was also reluctant to throw up the opportunity that the furore presented to bolster its anti-sectarian credentials. Referring to Findlay a Scottish Government spokeswoman stated: 'Her repugnant views have no place in modern, forward-thinking Scotland. The people of Scotland have had enough of bigotry' – an understandable reaction, one might say, after four centuries of widespread anti-Catholic prejudice in Scotland.[14] In fact so repugnant and offensive were Dr. Findlay's comments apparently that one Celtic supporter and member of her organisation, who was listening to the interview, was 'actually shouting at the radio for her to please shut up'. [15]

[12] A more understated headline alluding to the world of football being the preferred option, as one might expect from an up-market broadsheet: 'Celtic done no favours by Findlay's own goal' (The Telegraph 22/11/08)

[13] See footnote 2 regarding acceptance of 'cultural' manifestations of Irishness

[14] Of course this was, regrettably, not the 'bigotry' the source had in mind. Also, this kind of righteous condemnation was notably not forthcoming from such sources in the aftermath of the sectarian attack on the Sacred Heart in Bridgeton in November 2007 – a very real manifestation of bigotry in 'modern, forward thinking Scotland' one might suggest.

[15] Daily Record 21/11/ 07. Such reactions typify an element within the Celtic fan base for whom any expression of the club's Irish historical/ political legacy is clearly anathema. See Etims Online Celtic Fanzine : What is it with these Findlays?

Overall the battery of comments from the various sources which sections of the media had called upon to denigrate Jeannette Findlay's views fell into three broad categories: clichéd, prejudiced and irrelevant – and almost all could be described as ignorant. In all the coverage of the interview it was clear that few of those who contributed, whether in an official or unofficial capacity, stopped to give a considered and informed analysis of the legitimate and interesting issues Findlay had raised. For example regarding the relationship between sport and politics, a relationship which she points out, is accepted – or at least viewed as reality – quite readily in other countries. It is questionable, from their comments, if they had listened to the interview at all. It seemed in many cases they were responding like a Pavlov dog to the ensuing press coverage rather than what Findlay had actually said.

Any one who reads the transcript of the interview will see that contrary to popular misconception – generated by inaccurate and malicious reporting – Jeanette Findlay did not advocate support for any organisation, 'terrorist' or otherwise. In fact throughout the entire interview she only made one reference to the IRA and then only to correct what appears to be the interviewer's deliberately emotive and misleading use of the term:

> Nicky Campbell: 'I'm talking about actually chanting the IRA and stuff.'

> Jeanette Findlay: 'Well, you are talking about songs about the IRA but again, many of these songs are from what was essentially a war of independence going back right into the 1920s.'

Just why Nicky Campbell saw fit to introduce the issue of Celtic fans singing what he terms 'pro terrorist songs' into a discussion which was set up initially to ostensibly focus on John Reid's appointment as Celtic chairman is itself mystifying. (One must of course suppress any thoughts of 'an agenda' – maybe an opportunity?) Even after completing the gigantic step in lateral logic, which is certainly required if we are even to begin to acknowledge the rationale of introducing the issue in such a context, it still remains a distinct non sequitur.

During the course of the discussion Campbell intervened only on three occasions (the majority of the interview is conducted by his colleague Sheilagh Fogarty), each time pushing the question of the Celtic support's long-standing predilection for singing rebel songs. (Since the birth of the club the Celtic support have sung rebel songs. Some only occasionally make specific references to the IRA. Others refer to times prior to that organisation's founding though almost all relate to resisting the British conquest of Ireland.) Even when Findlay attempts to widen the debate to include a perceptive discourse on politics and football, pointing out an obvious parallel between Celtic and Barcelona, Campbell refuses to be deterred from his fixation with the singing issue:

> Jeanette Findlay: 'Throughout history sporting events are often used as a means of expressing political views or political identities. I don't see anyone criticising Barcelona for essentially being the national club of the Catalan people. But somehow or another when it comes to Celtic there is something wrong with that'?

> Nicky Campbell: 'If I can get back to what some people call the pro-terrorist songs. . .'

Ironically Campbell concludes with the words: 'Jeanette Findlay, we hear where you're coming from.'

Clearly, where Jeanette Findlay was coming from was an attempt to articulate her views, from a knowledgeable and legitimate perspective (not that you would think that, given the hysteria which followed), on a series of issues surrounding the expression of political/historical identity through support for a football club.

What she was not doing of course was kowtowing to the consensual and domineering various 'British' viewpoints on these matters. Having the temerity to hold a view – and moreover, claim that there are others who may hold similar views – which runs contrary to mainstream thinking, is never likely to endear you to the establishment (whether political or media). However, when you are attempting to assist people's understanding and legitimise Irishness of a political-historical ilk in a key aspect of Scottish life (some would say **the** key aspect), i.e. football, in the process, then you can rest assured that demonic status will inevitably be conferred.

Commentators of a 'Celtic Minded' persuasion have noted how aspects of Celtic traditions, most notably the club's Irishness and Catholic identity, are not viewed with opposition and aggression or as having the potential to incite hostility, in environments outside a Scottish context.[16] In fact those traditions are often enthusiastically embraced in many cities the length and breadth of Europe and beyond, whenever the Hoops fans come calling. This is something that clearly irritates those in Scotland who regard displays of the club's Irish heritage (political or otherwise) as acts of provocation.

> (there are) those in Scotland who regard displays of the club's Irish heritage (political or otherwise) as acts of provocation

Following Rangers Champions League match in Barcelona in 2007 radio station phone-ins and fans' pages of newspapers were besieged by Rangers supporters apoplectic with rage. The reason? Apparently some of the Catalan club's fans had turned up for the match at the Nou Camp sporting Celtic jerseys and even had the temerity to produce a large Tricolour in front of the travelling support. Provocation of the most heinous kind, claimed the followers of Scotland's establishment club. Those media outlets which covered the incident of course did not choose to condemn the fans of one of Europe's most powerful clubs for their 'provocative' antics, preferring instead to dismiss the Barcelona fans' actions as 'a wind-up' – apparently a common occurrence at such matches in Europe.

Indeed. Strange then that Celtic do not seem to have encountered similar wind-ups on their European travels (at least not outside Britain). Few opposition fans, whether in Milan, Barcelona, Lisbon or anywhere else, seem to have adopted the practice of donning the blue of Rangers and waving Union Jacks in an attempt to provoke the supporters of the Ibrox club's oldest rivals. One would also have to ask, if winding-up Catalan style is so effective, why is it yet to catch on in the Scottish game? Celtic tops and Irish Tricolours being flaunted by Kilmarnock, Motherwell and Hearts fans whenever Rangers provide the opposition. Yes, well. I think we'll probably wait a while for that one.

[16] See P. Reilly, Celtic Minded 2

No doubt the fans of Barcelona and other European clubs who play Rangers[17] are indulging in an element of 'wind-up', but the means by which they choose to do this i.e. the raising the Irish national flag, clearly indicates their knowledge of the Ibrox faithful's hostility towards such manifestations of Irishness in Celtic's culture – something which doubtless must seem odd to those outside Scotland who do not share such prejudices.

Indeed, Irish symbols are embraced in many parts of the world by those who identify with Ireland through historical experience, religious affiliation or simply love of the country and its people. At no point did those media outlets which covered the 'controversial incidents' of the Nou Camp stop to consider the possibility that what had occurred was simply a demonstration by the Catalan fans of the affinity which they felt with their opponents' greatest rival's traditions and history, not just in footballing, but also ethnic, political and religious terms,[18] while at the same time showing their aversion for those who regard themselves as the very antithesis of those traditions.

Given the acceptance of, and even empathy with, Celtic's culture and traditions throughout Europe – including those manifestations of political/historical Irishness which seem to cause such controversy here in Scotland – is it not strange that the club has come in for scrutiny during the last couple of seasons by UEFA as a result of their supporters singing anti-imperialist songs about Irish independence, as we have been led to believe? Just quite why songs about the Easter Rising or the ten hunger strikers that sacrificed their lives in 1981 should cause offence to our European cousins is difficult to comprehend.[19] Of course, despite the pronouncements by Scotland's domestic media insisting that Celtic, like Rangers, have come under a similar microscope by European football's governing body for their fans' sectarian antics, this is blatantly not the case.[20] The simple fact is that the fans of one club in Scotland and one club only have been identified and duly fined for behaving in a sectarian fashion i.e. causing gratuitous offence to members of the Catholic faith through songs and chants. Clearly this remains an unpalatable fact for some here in Scotland, not least because it exposes some of the anti-Catholic bigotry that exists in this country and denies the 'two-sides of the same coin argument'.[21]

[17] The trend continued to follow Rangers on their travels in the UEFA Cup: Irish tricolours and Celtic tops were clearly visible for instance among the home support when Rangers visited Panathonikos.

[18] See 'Barcelona – President hails Celtic fans', www.Kerrydalestreet.com 18/2/08. Also, A. Pattullo, 'Barcelona happy to play host as Celtic contingent make welcome return', The Scotsman, 4/3/08

[19] The heroic stature conferred on the 1981 Hunger Strikers in Europe and beyond – where memorials have been erected and streets named in their memory – contrasts with their demonising here in Britain. For example several towns in France have streets named after the late Bobby Sands MP.

[20] The Ibrox club was eventually fined in May 2007 for its fans' sectarian antics following a UEFA Cup tie against Osasuna.

[21] Notions of balance re Celtic and Rangers in this and other controversial issues, so favoured by the media in Scotland, does not seem to cut much ice elsewhere.

As soon as UEFA announced in March 2008 that it would officially be investigating – for the first time, it should be emphasised – the Celtic support for alleged sectarian singing in and around the Nou Camp during a Champions League match with Barcelona, there was a tangible sense of anticipation. 'Are Celtic's chickens coming home to roost at long last?' queried Gordon Waddell gleefully in his column in the Sunday Mail.[22] Apparently 'for too long Celtic's self-aggrandising "Greatest Fans In The World" tag has obscured the incessant IRA love-in among sizeable chunks of their away support'. According to Waddell, as with Rangers, 'some UEFA involvement' was what was needed to make the club 'pay more than lip service to the problem'.

Alas, for Mr. Waddell and others of a similar mindset, UEFA's 'not guilty' verdict – delivered with some appropriacy on 1st April – proved to be no 'April fool'. Indeed if anyone was left looking foolish it was the individual responsible for publicising the apparently 'damning' footage and those who were only too quick to seize upon it as proof positive of the Celtic support's sectarian credentials. No, it's just not fair when others refuse to indulge your ignorance and prejudices, is it?

[22] Sunday Mail 30/3/08

The Elephant in the Room*

TOM MINOGUE

Born in England in 1945 the son of an English mother and an English-born Irish father, I moved to Scotland as a small child with my older brother Joe when my parents died. Brought up in a devout Catholic home in Rosyth, Fife, by my mother's brother Jack and his wife, we were taught by these good English people to consider ourselves as English first, then British, but certainly not Scottish, where we lived, and not Irish, our dominant gene.

I don't know why my foster father disliked the Irish but he did, and this made it awkward for my brother and I, as we dearly loved our paternal Irish grandparents with whom we stayed every summer holiday. Growing up I considered myself a Scot, as I had known no other place, but there was no shortage of people both inside and outside of my home to tell me differently. The view on the street generally was that I was an English b****** or a Catholic b******, and if I aired my predominant ethnic origin of Irishness, well that was worse than the other two put together, this brought the ultimate insult – I was a Fenian b******.

My schooling began at an RC Primary school, St John's Rosyth, and then an RC secondary school, St Margaret's Dunfermline. I would say that the majority of my schoolmates were like me with regard to their origin, and Irish names well outnumbered Scots ones in the registers. In 1957, during my second year at St Margaret's the headmaster, Mr Collins, took all the boys to East End Park one Wednesday afternoon to see the Celtic play Dunfermline. This was my first sight of Celtic and that colourful spectacle and the cheerfulness of the fans sticks in my mind to this day.

* The Elephant in the room is an English idiom for a problem that everyone knows very well but no one talks about because it is taboo, embarrassing, etc.

157

This may sound odd, but almost immediately at that football match I felt welcome, at home, and at ease among people like myself. My Irish ancestry and RC religion were, for the first time, not negatives to be hidden, but positive credentials, and in Celtic I saw a rare totem of Irish/RC success in an otherwise Protestant-dominated Scottish society. My confusion over nationality was solved – I was a Celt.

Shortly after this, towards the end of my second year at St Margaret's, my foster-parents transferred me to the local Protestant secondary school, King's Road Rosyth. Let there be no doubt that in those days the school was a Protestant school – not 'non-denominational'. The school padre was a Church of Scotland minister and a very nice man. He went out of his way to welcome me to the school while pointing out that I had no need to take part in assembly or any other religious aspects of the curriculum if I did not want to.

As a Catholic switching to a Protestant school there was a certain amount of hostility towards me – as there was at my RC school for leaving – from some pupils, and from one or two of the teachers, but the vast majority of my new schoolmates were friendly and friendships made then are still cherished to this day. As for differences between the two schools, the main one that sticks in my mind was not religious but historical. At the RC schools many of the teachers viewed the role of Britain in Ireland in a negative way, while their counterparts in the Protestant school saw Britain's imperial rule abroad as an act of benevolence for the good of backward peoples in uncivilised countries.

Occasionally I was faced with outright hostility from a small number of my new schoolmates and was called a Fenian c*** or a papish whatever, but I was by then well used to this, could stick up for myself, and did so when required. On reflection, I had realised from experience at an early age that I should keep a low profile with regard to my Irishness. It was soon apparent that the name Minogue was likely to evince comments such as: 'is that an f*****g Irish name'? Or: 'is that a fenian name'?

As a youth my first line of defence against this anti-Irishness was to espouse a theory that I had heard about Minogue being an Irish derivation of a Spanish name from descendants of the

Armada wrecked off Ireland. If this tack failed then it was off with the jacket. Minogue is in fact an ancient Irish name – it crossed the sea with my namesake and grandfather who came to England from County Kilkenny in 1900 – but the Spanish theory was a useful tool in avoiding trouble if possible. I was not alone in my chameleon-like behaviour. One schoolmate of mine actually changed his Irish sounding Christian name and surname to Scottish ones. Patrick Murphy became Donald McDonald. I later learned that this disguise of Irishness as a means of self-preservation/advancement in Britain was not unique and various others followed a similar path in an effort to be 'accepted' by the majority.[1]

The reason my foster parents had decided that I change schools was the fact that pupils from the Protestant King's Road school were much more successful in gaining apprenticeships in the local naval dockyard. Was this because of the higher standard of education in Protestant schools at that time? Or was it because the interviewers and markers of exam papers favoured schools that did not have a Saint's name? Who knows? It may have been one reason, or the other, or a mixture of both, but in 1960, the year I entered Rosyth Dockyard along with about a hundred of my fellow pupils from Kings Road – not one apprentice was taken from my former RC Alma Mater.

Rosyth was unusual in that each of the Christian denominations had a church, but the Masons had two Lodges. Rosyth Dockyard mirrored the Masonic dominance of the village, and I was soon made aware that to get on in the Dockyard it would help if one joined the 'craft'. I could not think of joining any organisation to get on, and in any case the Masons in Rosyth were almost exclusively Protestant, and often members had joint Orange Order membership or sympathies.

Though having wandered from my faith and no longer a practising Catholic, I had a dislike for anti-Catholic and anti-Irish attitudes and groups, and the Masons were such a group. I was confident in my own ability, needed no leg-ups, and was intent on seeing the world. On the day that my five-year apprenticeship was complete I left Rosyth Dockyard and joined the Merchant Navy.

1 Out of respect for my former classmate the names given are not the actual names.

In 1965 at the age of 20 I signed on with Clan Line Shipping Company of Glasgow, a firm that operated a segregation policy among its staff of white officers and 'coloured' crews.[2] A colour bar was legitimate in Scotland in 1965. Considering that the whole of the southern United States like South Africa was racially segregated, many Catholics in the north of Ireland could not vote while power was manufactured as a Unionist/Loyalist fact of life, and religious and racial discrimination was common in Britain, this practice was not unusual – it was the norm.

As a young man I did not give the question of race much thought. Like most people in the 1960s I was conditioned to accept institutionalised discrimination. My own life view was influenced by having lived and worked with many men who had served in naval bases overseas where the locals were considered to be wogs, kafirs or coolies, and were treated accordingly. My uncle Jack had told me of how, when he worked as a shipwright in HM Dockyards in Egypt during the war, a worker was issued with a cosh to beat wogs if they bothered him. Supervisors were given revolvers! In those days the embers of Empire still glowed bright in Rosyth.

Whilst with the Clan Line, my ship, the MV King George, was the first large vessel to visit the small port of Liverpool, Nova Scotia, to load rolls of newsprint for Australia. I was amazed by the friendliness of the people of this small town, many of whom were of Scots descent. Every night was party night, and locals in their cars draw up on the quayside offering to take us to their homes for dinner and drinks. These offers did not extend to our low-paid Bangladeshi crew, but the mostly Scots officers were treated royally.

Our Nova Scotian hosts were descendants of the Scots exiles who, forced to seek asylum from the Highland Clearances and Famines in eighteenth and nineteenth century Scotland, made the long sea voyage to Canada. Exiles in a foreign land they stuck together to combat hostility and passed on a view of the old country to their children, one that was full of nostalgia.[3] These romanticised views were commonly celebrated in song. My Nova Scotian hosts played and sang such sentimental songs,

2 The certifying authority (normally Lloyds of London) hard-stamped on the steel beams in ships accommodation what the capacity was in terms such as: 'Certified for 1 E or 2 A seamen'. or '1 W or 2 C seamen'. Key: E=European; A=Asian; W=White; C=Coloured. Blacks needed half as much breathing/ living space as whites and this discrimination was literally set in steel.

3 The elusive word nostalgia is formed from two Greek roots: nostos (return home) and algia (pain). The Oxford English Dictionary defines nostalgia as a form of melancholia caused by prolonged absence from one's home or country.

songs telling of a longing for Scotland like 'My Ain Folk', which has a chorus of:

> Tho' I'm far across the sea,
> my heart will always be,
> at home in dear auld Scotland,
> wi ma ain folk'

This is a typical theme of exile, namely distress at being 'over here' when their heart wants to be 'over there' in the old country.

We Scots seamen from industrial Central Scotland could have disabused our hosts of their romantic notions of home, but we politely kept our own counsel, for, as a well-know Irish song says: 'precious things are dreams unto an exile'. The Scots Canadians who entertained us in their homes knew more about Scotland than we did – though some had never set foot in the old country – and together with engineers from Greenock, Govan, and Springburn I tucked into the lobster chowder and Budweiser beer freely provided by our hosts while feigning knowledge of villages in Argyll that their ancestors had come from, but of which, we didn't have a clue.

The highlight of our stay in Liverpool N.S. was a visit to the local ice-rink, which, we were amazed to see, was festooned in tartan, lion-rampant and Saltire flags. Here we witnessed a curling match put on by the local Caledonian society, many of whom wore kilts and spoke Gaelic. That our hosts were more Scottish than those they were entertaining was self evident, as was their prominence in the local community where they were the managers and operators of the giant Bowater paper-making plant. These Canadian Scots were the lynchpins of the local community, and respected as such.

I could not help but draw a comparison between how the Scottish flags flew proudly for the descendants of Scots immigrants in Canada, while in Scotland the Scottish Football Association were trying to force Celtic FC take down the tricolour flag, which flew at Celtic Park in honour of the club and its supporters' Irishness. Later, when I saw the start of desegregation, and the end of racial discrimination in the USA, the same Scottish

Football Association were still studiously ignoring the long-standing anti-Catholic discriminatory employment policy of Rangers FC, Scotland's establishment club. This was a classic example of a Scottish Elephant, although at that time Rangers were just one of a herd.

Leaving the Merchant Navy in 1969 I returned to Rosyth and married a long-time girlfriend who came from Townhill, a small village just outside Dunfermline. My future wife was, and remains, a Church of Scotland Protestant. We have been happily married for forty years and I can say that though we have had our ups and downs, one thing that has never caused us a minute's problem is religious difference.

I was aware however that among some members of my wife's community there seemed to be an underlying sense of superiority towards me as an Irish-descended RC. Sometimes this manifested itself in what they saw as harmless Irish jokes or patronising comments such as 'I have a friend who is a Catholic' or 'we know people from Ireland and they are fine', but the tone was mildly offensive, and at that time puzzling to me: but it was the norm.

Later in life, during my retirement, I sought to understand this subtle bigotry, present amongst even the nicest of people in Fife. I had learned nothing of this at school. My lessons on anti-Irish racism were learned the hard way on the streets and playing fields, but I had long known that a taboo exists on talking about this subject in Scotland. Schoolchildren in Fife would not know of the threat of violence to Irish navvies stated publicly on posters in Fife in 1835, telling them: 'get out of Fife by midnight, or we will attack you with pick-axe handles', whereas a child in England might learn of this as part of their school curriculum.[4]

4 Ireland in Schools, Birmingham Pilot Scheme, English & Irish history for primary schools Version 4, 6th September 2007, What Was it Like to be an Irish Immigrant in Britain in the Nineteenth Century?

I wanted to know and understand more about this and I subsequently carried out some research. I concluded that much of anti-Irish and anti-Catholic sentiment is partly the residual effect from government and church policies. Such policies are typified by the preaching of radical preachers like Pastor Jacob Primmer. Primmer (1842–1914) was a bigoted preacher, who, when parish minister in Townhill Church of Scotland, also preached in the surrounding Dunfermline/Cowdenbeath area. Primmer's rants against RCs and the Irish can be found in his writings which include such literary gems as 'Which is the Greater Evil – Rome or Rum? And the Cure for Both'; and 'Pastor Jacob Primmer in Rome'. Primmer berated the 'racially inferior' Irish who he characterised as lazy criminal drunkards who practised idolatry in a religion headed by a Pope who was the anti-Christ personified. Primmer was not reprimanded by his church for these views, which were not far off the mainstream in a Church of Scotland that had until the late 1930s annually called for the repatriation of the racially inferior Irish. (Maybe the present day cry, 'The Famine is over, why don't you go home' is a contemporary manifestation of this dogma?)

In the days before radio and television, preaching was the mass media, and Primmer preached to sell-out crowds. A celebrity in his day, he was feted, and his son became the Provost of Cowdenbeath and had a street named after him. 'Primmer Place' in Cowdenbeath is today's only tangible physical legacy of the Pastor in Fife, but I think that his intangible legacy lives on in the bigotry passed down through the generations of some families in the small communities where his writ ran.

The belated apology by the Church of Scotland in 2002 for its long campaign of anti-Irish racism and anti-Catholic bigotry went some way towards acknowledging the past wrongs to Catholics of Irish descent in Scotland, but as yet there has been no attempt by that church to proactively address the prejudice their century of bigoted dogma spawned. This, in my opinion, is one reason why this problem has not been eradicated. If we don't examine and learn lessons from the events of history we are doomed to repeat them.

Back to my story, once married I briefly returned to Rosyth Dockyard before leaving to work in the construction industry building power stations, oil-rigs, ships on the Clyde and various other projects. While working at an oil-rig yard, where I was a shop steward, I was involved in a strike which led to me being blacklisted and caused me to take stock. By now I had a wife and two children to provide for, so in 1978 I decided to start my own engineering business and formed Kingdom Engineering (Fife) Ltd.

At its peak in 1985 during the construction of the Moss-morran petrochemical complex Kingdom Engineering employed over 200 workers and had plants in Cowdenbeath and Bo'ness. In keeping with my experience at Rosyth I found that freemasonry played a major part in the engineering industry, but I simply worked my way round this problem by getting work from firms that were not interested in what handshake one had, or what team one supported. This did make life more difficult, but I enjoyed pitting my wits against the perceived wisdom that one had to join the craft to get on. I was, on several occasions, invited to join the Masons always on the basis that it would help me to get on in business/life, but I declined these invitations preferring instead to tread the awkward way.

After twenty-four successful years in business achieved whilst tip-toeing around the twin evils of anti-Irish racism and anti-Catholic prejudice in Scotland and as I approached sixty, two events caused me to re-assess my passive attitude towards bigotry. The first was my arrest as a result of a claim by a Mason in support of a trade rival that, with the help of Masonic bias in the police force, led to me being charged with theft of steelwork. This caused me to spend a great deal of time and money in defending myself (successfully) in what was no more than a commercial dispute regarding ownership of steel components that should never have reached a court – far less a criminal one.

During this incident I faced the prospect of standing trial before a sheriff who, if he were a Mason, had by virtue of his oaths, secretly promised to prefer one of his brethren to any other person in the same circumstances. I decided that this was an unfair situation that I would not accept in silence. By publicly challenging the sheriff in open court on the question of his Masonic membership, I cried, 'Elephant'!

Shortly after this, a second event – in which my late brother Joe was the victim – occurred. Joe's ritual of having a Sunday morning pint (or three) and a game of dominoes in his local club in Kelty was ruined by stories of how in his club the previous evening, Donald Findlay qc had entertained diners at a football event. Local people who had attended the private function – which was on the same day as an Orange walk in the village – told Joe of how Findlay had mocked and ridiculed the Irish, Catholics, and their religion, and how this comedy was well received. Proud of his Irish background and heritage, my brother felt deeply upset that the community he had lived in for forty years had enjoyed this ridicule of him and his kind.

Joe confided in me that he had always felt part of his community, but this incident had hurt and alienated him from people he had long thought he was at one with. I understood his hurt. I don't think those who deal in ethnic jokes or sectarian jibes understand the effect of prefixing their slurs by words such as Irish or Catholic. This intensifies the hurt felt by the butt of the joke, as it has the effect of encompassing their family and forebears, living and dead, in the insult.

Ironically the private dinner at which Findlay had spoke was sponsored by Kelty Hearts Junior FC – a club supported by my brother – and a club that I, through my company Kingdom Engineering, had sponsored for years. Many people my brother considered as friends and fellow supporters of the local team had become estranged from him at a stroke by the intervention of a buffoon telling Irish and religious jokes. Findlay had driven a wedge between members of a tolerant and united village community by inviting one group to laugh at the other's expense – behind closed doors. Of course, that they could relate to this kind of humour also revealed something about the nature of racism and bigotry in Scotland.

Out of respect for my brother's bruised feelings I said nothing about this incident, but some months later, after he died, I again heard what I considered to be Findlay's divisive rabble rousing at a football supporters club. This time Findlay's sectarian stirring took place at a Rangers Supporters Club in Larne in the north of Ireland, a town blighted by bigotry where the last thing needed was for prejudiced or bigoted views to be reinforced or enflamed. So I cried Elephant again by writing and publishing an article on the Dunfermline Town Website called 'Bigotry in Fife', which detailed my brother's tale of hurt and alienation at the hands of the divisive Findlay.

After the first incident, the court case – which hastened my premature retirement – I petitioned the Scottish Parliament to introduce legislation requiring judges to register their membership of societies such as the Freemasons. The Parliament toyed with this petition for about two years before quietly kicking into the long grass without any proper debate.

After the second incident, the Larne affair, I decided to complain to the Faculty of Advocates regarding the anti-Irish, racist and anti-RC conduct of Donald Findlay QC. I argued that as a long-standing customer who had spent a five-figure sum on advocacy services from the Faculty I was entitled to have full confidence in any counsel who may be called on to represent me. In my opinion Findlay by his conduct was incapable of giving me – an Irish-descended Catholic – any confidence in his impartiality. In the event my complaint was upheld and in 2005 Findlay was found by his peers – in the form of a Complaints Committee of the Faculty of Advocates – to have brought the Faculty into disrepute.[5]

I made a second complaint about Findlay, which centres on his reported comments in a book entitled 'How Soccer Explains The World'. In this book Findlay says – with regard to Irish sentiment for the old-country – that his test of British citizenship would be: if a troop carrying the Queen's colours doesn't bring a tear to your eye then you should 'fuck off'. ('Why don't you go home' again?) My second complaint on Findlay's reported anti-Irish racism and anti-Catholic comments is at the time of writing under review by the Legal Ombudsman.

On reflection, I considered that my inaction when confronted with racism in the USA, South Africa, and on Clan Line ships – while others spoke out to bring about change for the good – was something that I was not very proud of. I am a bit too old to be a tree-hugging protester, but I hope it is not too late to remedy my past apathy towards civil-rights and in some small way do my bit to attempt to change things in Scotland. I have promised myself that I will never again silently witness the racism or prejudice that blights this country. I would not go on a safari every morning looking for traces of the Elephant's spoor, but if I came across an Elephant, then I would comment on it.

5 Though Donald Findlay, QC was found guilty of bringing the Faculty of Advocates into disrepute by his conduct at Larne he refused to accept the Complaints Committee's findings with regard to my complaint and the Faculty then took out their own complaint and prosecuted him before a Tribunal at which Findlay was cleared.

However, a word of warning! Elephant spotting is not without its risks, as I found out in 2004. Then I had been irked to see an article in The Herald about a Hearts fan arrested at a Celtic v Hearts match for shouting anti-Welsh racist remarks at Craig Bellamy. I wrote a letter to the editor of The Herald and my letter was published. The gist of the letter was that the police were trivialising the racially aggravated legislation by picking on an isolated incident of anti-Welsh prejudice whilst ignoring the big problem of anti-Irish racist abuse that is evident if not prevalent in many football grounds in Scotland.

The response to my letter was limited to one reply in the newspaper of the following day and I thought no more about it until some days later I received an anonymous phone call from a Hearts fan who told me that there were threats against me on the Jambos' Kickback fanzine website. I checked and sure enough, though most of the discussion was reasonable if robust, there were several pieces that were certainly sinister and threatening.

Postings about me included open threats that I would be visited by thugs at my home (the location of which was given) because I was a RC who had commented on anti-Irish bigotry in Scotland. I took the matter up with the site moderator who was in denial about the nature of the threats and this caused me take the matter up with my lawyers and the police who shared my views on the matter. When my lawyers took action the thread was pulled, most of the moderators quit, and I received a newsletter from Jambos' Kickback condemning bigoted behaviour of any sort.

The Jambos' Kickback incident confirmed to me – if confirmation was needed – that there is hostility in Scotland to Elephant-spotters. My reasonable point on a question of race was pounced on by some and, as can often happen in Scotland, turned into a polemic on religion. My letter which The Herald had entitled 'Zero tolerance needed on anti-racist behaviour' was considered by a major Hearts website as being 'Hearts fans guilty of racist and sectarian behaviour', and my perceived religion was immediately imposed upon my points about racism.

In my experience, anyone who suggests that there is anti-

Irish racism in Scotland risks being the subject of vitriolic attack or patronising accusations of paranoia. One would only require to reflect upon much of the commentary from significant figures in the small world of Scottish football radio punditry and tabloid column writing regarding the widespread singing of the infamous 'Famine Song' (or its variations) to realise to what extent ignorant and bigoted attitudes are shared across various walks of Scottish life.

Of course, some ignorant and reprehensible chants undeniably rise on occasion from a small number of ghastly Celtic supporters: for example, songs (or postings) that appear to threaten other players or that rejoice in tales about certain footballer's family members social (sexual) proclivities. These have no place at Celtic and surely supporters that engage in such chants are far removed from the ideals and dreams of figures like Brother Walfrid, John Glass, Michael Davitt, Willie Maley, Tommy Burns, etc.

Nevertheless, while acknowledging these types of supporters in the context of this chapter to focus on those sad fans would be to miss the point. Of a much more serious nature is ignorance and prejudice shown by racial comments from respected public figures such as Jimmy Reid who mocked those who followed Celtic singing about 'Erin's green valleys' that he said they had never seen. Would my Scots Canadian friends be treated to such scorn even if they had never been to Scotland? Would a Jimmy Reid of the Americas demand that Scots Canadians/Americans lose all traces of their Scots cultural identity by total assimilation, and foreswear their tartans and saltires for the Maple Leaf or Stars and Stripes? Similarly would journalists in the Americas ridicule the sound of the bagpipes as 'diddle dee' music from 'plastic Jocks' and tell the pipers that they should stop playing such 'tosh' and if not, 'there is a place called Scotland, go there'.[6] The recent homecoming campaign on the part of the Scottish government and tourism industry depended entirely on the concept of the Scottish diaspora abroad, utilising as it did ideas of heritage, history, origins and geographical and emotional ties.

Would a Canadian James Traynor dare tell my good Scots Canadians to stop their cloyingly sentimental longing for the old

6 All of these terms have been used to describe the Irishness of the Celtic support in Scotland. See Celtic Minded, Celtic Minded 2 and Bradley 2009 for references

country? Would he say that clinging onto, and protecting their Scottish heritage seemed mawkish? Would he warn them that if they persisted with their reminiscences about their ancestors being driven from their Highland homes then they shouldn't expect sympathy if others saw this as anti-Canadian and mocked them in racist song? Would he tell those who objected to such racist mocking:

> Go. Go on, just gather up your prejudices, take your suspicions and pack your loathing of Canada. Go find a better place to live and leave us to get on with the job of making something good of this country.[7]

The answer to these hypothetical questions is an emphatic no, but it is symptomatic of the residual anti-Irishness in Scotland that such negative and hostile remarks can be made about Irishness in Scotland, Scots-born Irish, Scots of Irish descent, the Irish diaspora or Celtic fans, by omnipotent commentators in today's Scottish media – without demur. All such hostile and intolerant comments, with regards the Irishness of the Celtic support in Scotland, and many more, are published regularly in the columns of Scottish newspapers and broadcast on television and radio.

I say it is time that we Celtic-minded folk did our bit and challenged the oft-repeated mantra that there is no longer any anti-Irish racism in Scotland and these things are history. We can meet the challenge by highlighting anti-Irish racism in whatever form and wherever it occurs. It would be nice if the majority community took a lead in this matter, but (with a few notable exceptions) there is little sign of this happening. It should not be left to outsiders such as UEFA to let us 'see ourselves as others see us'. We have to do this for ourselves, and for the benefit of future generations, who should not have to put up with the ignorance, prejudice, bigotry, silence, evasion and shame that we, for too long, have endured.

I believe that if we all work together much can be done to change entrenched attitudes in this country. I know for sure that if we all do nothing the status quo will prevail. The problem will not be solved if it is not spoken about. Spot the Elephant anyone?

7 The Dailly Record carried an article that said something similar to people of Irish descent in Scotland. See Sports Section, p.24, 22/9/08

Seeing is believing: How television changed the reporting of football

PATRICK REILLY

I first began to read George Orwell seriously when at university in the 1960s and one of the works that particularly caught my attention was an essay called 'Looking Back on the Spanish War'. Orwell had gone to fight in Spain as a volunteer on the Republican side and the essay was a reflection upon his experience of the conflict. In particular, Orwell was both shocked and frightened at how the war had been reported, especially in the English press. It was his first encounter with the alarming power of rampant, unbridled propaganda:

> I saw newspaper reports which did not bear any resemblance to the facts. . . I saw great battles reported where there had been no fighting, and complete silence where hundreds of men had been killed. I saw troops who had fought bravely denounced as cowards and traitors, and others who had never seen a shot fired hailed as the heroes of imaginary victories, and I saw newspapers in London retailing these lies and eager intellectuals building emotional superstructures over events that had never happened. I saw, in fact, history being written not in terms of what happened but of what ought to have happened according to various 'party ' lines.

John M Feehan in his book 'Bobby Sands and the Tragedy of Northern Ireland' (1983), Liz Curtis, 'Ireland the Propaganda War' (1984), Brian Murphy's 'The Origins and Organisation of British Propaganda in Ireland 1920' (2006), Jonathan Bloch and Patrick Fitzgerald's 'British Intelligence and Covert Action'

(1983), and Patrick Magee's 'Gangsters or Guerrillas? Represent-ations of Irish Republicans in "Troubles Fiction" ' (2001), all studiously reflect on similar processes in relation to the historical conflict concerning British political and military involvement on the island of Ireland.

For Orwell, it was the spectacle of reality being invented and truth being stood on its head that so unnerved him.

> This kind of thing is frightening to me because it often gives me the feeling that the very concept of objective truth is fading out of the world. After all, the chances are that those lies, or at any rate similar lies, will pass into history.

In which case, the lie becomes truth. When all the original eye-witnesses of an event are dead and only the printed version survives unchallenged, this becomes, by default, the sole, unimpugnable account of what happened. History is written or, if you prefer, constructed by the winners and the winners are those who control the media. Whatever is printed is true – unless there is a competing printed version of the same event.

Spain was Orwell's window upon the terrifying possibility of this truthless, propagandist future. Long before the Spanish War he had remarked upon the unreliability of newspapers and grown used to their lies and suppressions. But in Spain this reached to a nightmare extreme – the creation of an alternative reality prevailing over and replacing the actual objective world. In the beginning was the Word. In Spain the word became incarnate as propaganda. Truth was replaced by lies that could neither be tested nor refuted. The verification principle – testing an assertion of what happened against what actually happened became for Orwell, the most serious casualty of the war and the most ominous threat in the modern world: 'the very concept of objective truth is fading out of the world'.

The degree to which this tormented Orwell is attested by the frequency with which he refers to it. In 1944, when the full horror of the newly liberated death camps was breaking upon the West, Orwell declared – for many it must have seemed an outrageous valuation – that the injury to objective truth was even more abominable, an atrocity even greater, than the gas ovens.

> The really frightening thing about totalitarianism is that it attacks the concept of objective truth; it claims to control the past as well as the future.

The holocaust itself is less chilling than a world that incinerates truth. From the millions of corpses littering the age, Orwell identifies truth as the gravest casualty. It isn't camps or genocide, wars or slavery, frightful though they are, that unnerves Orwell so much as the almost universal mendacity, the ubiquitous doublethink, of the times. He carried these thoughts to their nightmare conclusion in his most famous work, Nineteen Eighty Four, in which what is truth changes from minute to minute, depending upon what the dictator wants it to be: and the dictator can do this because he has total monopolistic control over all the means of communication – nothing can be spoken or printed or screened unless he approves. Thought itself is imprisoned, for how can you think for yourself when every public access to reality is blocked off and truth is a no-go-area?

Of course, there never has been and (please God) never will be so consummately totalitarian a state as Orwell's Oceania: Orwell was simply extrapolating from certain alarming trends in his own time to a nightmare scenario which perhaps he himself never believed could come to pass. But 'Looking Back on the Spanish War' is an altogether different matter. Far from being far-fetched, what he tells us there is now so obvious as to be almost trite. Every modern government, of whatever political hue, censors the information available to the public. The Vietnam War was the first and last occasion when full, unrestricted media access to the action was allowed, with disastrous consequences for the popularity of the war in the USA itself. Margaret Thatcher, by contrast, was careful to let the British people know only as much about the Falklands/Malvinas conduct as suited her purposes until after its successful resolution. From Northern Ireland to Iraq, there have been numerous occasions when successive governments, for reasons of national security etc, have ensured that the press, radio and television were permitted to report only what it suited governments to tell. No one disputes this today, not even those who did and still do the censoring.

But when Orwell wrote his essay in 1942 this wasn't the truism that it is now. Coincidentally, it was about that date that I first began to take a serious interest in football – going to watch games, listening to the radio, reading the papers. There was, of course, still no television, let alone televised football, something that will be of importance to the argument I wish to present. If you didn't attend a game in person, there were only three ways of finding out what had happened: ask someone who was there, read the paper or listen to the 'wireless'. This explains why I was so interested in 'Looking Back on the Spanish War', because, at a much more serious level, Orwell was describing something with which I was already familiar – he 'spoke to my condition', to borrow a phrase from an old tradition of sermon literature. I had attended football matches in Scotland and had then read reports in the press which, apart from getting the score right, bore little resemblance to what I had seen happening. Nor was it simply – and this needs stressing – a difference of opinion over the interpretation of facts: the facts themselves were the victims. It was just as Orwell said: things that had happened went unreported while things that hadn't happened were presented as fact. If your only source of information was the radio or the sports pages, it was impossible to separate fact from fiction – you had as much access to the truth as a Tibetan living under Beijing. If you had seen the game and challenged the official version, you were dismissed as irrational and prejudiced. Paranoia was not at that time an everyday term, but the idea was already available for trashing the views of any dissenter from the prevailing orthodoxy.

Time for a disclaimer. Not for a moment am I proposing a parity, an equivalence, between Orwell's dilemma in Spain and my frustrations in Scotland. No one was ever more egregiously wrong than Bill Shankly when he said (tongue in cheek, one hopes, for his sake) that football is more important than life and death. Orwell was talking about life and death, on a massive scale. Football, however absorbing for its devotees, is trivial in comparison. What I am saying is that the fabrication of reality can occur at any level, high and low alike. I am also saying that my youthful experience of the Scottish media's treatment of football gave me a head start, a privileged insight, into understanding Orwell's predicament in the far more momentous matters that concerned him.

It was taken for granted in those television-less days that journalists and broadcasters were men without preferences or prejudices, completely objective, imperturbable, rational and impartial. Truth was what you heard on the radio or read in the paper. The idea of fans with typewriters or microphones was still in the future. It followed that if you challenged this truth, you were a fantasist and there was no more to be said. Allegations of paranoia are, admittedly, still liberally slung around today. Nevertheless, one major development since the dark days (literally as well as metaphorically) of the 40s and 50s has significantly changed the balance of power and altered the relationship between the erstwhile omnipotent broadcaster journalist and his hitherto captive audience. Today we have television. No longer is it a case of take it or leave it, no longer do the broadcaster and journalist possess the monopolistic power over the reporting of major games that was once theirs in the days before we could see for ourselves what was happening. They can, of course, still write and say what they like, but they do so knowing – and this is what is new – that their words have to stand the scrutiny of reality. The all-important benefit of establishing the truth aside, this can also be very revealing.

From a host of examples, I shall choose one. In the fully televised C.I.S. Cup Final between Glasgow Rangers and Dundee United (won by Rangers after a penalty shoot-out) in March 2008 the referee failed to award a 'stonewall penalty kick' for United when they were 1-0 ahead. For many people, there was no scintilla of doubt about the award – the tackle would have led to a charge of assault had it occurred on the street. During the post-match discussion in the television studio BBC pundit Dougie Donnelly proposed in mitigation that the referee's view had been obstructed and that this explained why he was unable to see what was otherwise impossible to miss. Subsequently, and unfortunately for Mr Donnelly and his explanation, the replayed television pictures showed the referee with only ten yards of unoccupied grass between himself and a perfect view of the incident – thanks to television, the obstructed view theory was out. (It was, incidentally, the same referee, who, the season before, failed to award an equally glaring penalty when Neil Lennon was felled in the box at Ibrox, so why Mr Donnelly didn't proceed to a defence based on recurring temporary blindness while the ball is in the Rangers penalty area is something only he can tell.)

The real point is that sixty years earlier Mr Donnelly could have gone on insisting that the referee was unsighted and no one could have said him nay. If some supporters believe today that things are still bad as far as referee decisions are concerned, they should try imagining just how immeasurably worse they were in the dark days (in every sense of the word) before television. Injustices still occur – England's third winning goal against Germany in 1966, Maradona's infamous 'hand of God', etc. etc. – but they can no longer be ignored, denied or ridiculed, because we can now see the pictures replayed. (I can't resist adding that Mr Donnelly, left to make the best of a bad job, took refuge in one of the most fatuous remarks ever to fall from the lips of a distinguished and well-paid pundit: 'maybe they would have missed it anyway'. True, but it scarcely constitutes a reason for denying a team a penalty kick they deserve.) Nothing beats seeing for yourself: in football, as in most other things, we are all Doubting Thomas. There is a story about a wife who catches her husband in flagrante delicto with another woman. Later, still protesting his innocence, the errant husband asks his still incandescent wife: 'who are you going to believe – me or your lying eyes?' What her answer was I don't know, but I think I do know what every Celtic supporter in the land would reply if confronted with the same question.

Today, as in the pre-television past, a game is history the minute it's over. History is not what happened a thousand, a hundred or ten years ago; it's any past event, even if that past is only hours old, because it's now irrecoverable, gone forever. In the 1940s, if you had watched the match, you knew that the reporter was mistaken, perhaps even worse, but you had no way of proving this, for his word was as good as yours, indeed better, given his more authoritative position and his appropriation of the right to call anyone who disagreed with him deluded and unbalanced. All you had was words, and words by themselves are not evidence. But when words become print, they somehow acquire a new authority, a higher accreditation – 'but it's in the papers' – and will usually, as Orwell discovered, carry the day against their merely spoken equivalents.

Television changes everything: a picture is worth a thousand words. Seeing is believing – it's why we spend billions on CCTV cameras. There is now a permanent body of visual evidence in football to which appeal can be made in support of whatever views are being advanced. If those views are outrageously absurd or hopelessly paranoid, a simple replay of the contentious material should go a long way towards settling the question. Football being football and not some precise mathematical science, there will always be ample scope for honest disagreement – even followers of the same team will often take sharply divergent views of the same incident: who would wish it otherwise? But the old habit of ignoring what happened while inventing what hadn't – that, at least so far as fully televised games are concerned, is no longer an option.

Edited highlights are a very different matter. In a league game at Celtic Park in April 2008 between Celtic and Aberdeen, the referee disallowed what television later showed was a perfectly good goal for the visitors in the dying minutes. The referee got it wrong and Celtic survived to win the game instead of draw. However, in the after match descriptions of what occurred not only was it under-emphasised in media reports the fact that the referee had blown for an infringement against Aberdeen seconds before the goal was scored and that Celtic defenders had slowed down or stopped accordingly and this may or may not have had an impact on whether the goal was scored or not, but not one of the television, newspaper or radio commentators who trumpeted this referee blunder to the heavens thought it worth remarking that the referee had also previously disallowed two goals for Celtic. To find out about the disallowed Aberdeen goal you only needed to be alive, with eyes or ears, in Scotland. To find out about the two disallowed Celtic goals, the non-attendee would have needed a friend to be at the game. We all know that editors exist to leave things out, but a selection policy that focuses on a disallowed goal for one team while totally ignoring two disallowed goals for the other seems less than even-handed. Those prone to suspicion might even be tempted to sniff a whiff of bias about the whole affair.

Nevertheless, despite some reservations, it is unarguable that television has brought to football a welcome transparency that was sorely lacking before its advent. No longer is it an option simply to ignore complaints about injustices or to dismiss the complainants as suitable candidates for psychiatric treatment. The arrival of video recordings has made it necessary to evolve a new strategy for dealing with the ever-recurring allegations of raw deals and this has been found in recourse to statistics, probability theory and the law of averages. It is no longer denied that Celtic are sometimes the victim of bad, even blatantly bad, refereeing decisions. This is now freely conceded, but only when coupled with an insistence that so, too, in equal measure, is every other team in the land. It's what happens in football, we are told: sometimes the breaks go for you, sometimes against, but there is definitely no question of deliberate malice or discriminatory intent, and we are assured that over the course of a season there will be, indeed there must be (see the theory of large numbers) an equal distribution of both good and bad luck. The only losers in the long run are those who are not good enough to win.

Above all, there are no favoured teams. You can say today, without being reviled, that the Prime Minister deliberately told lies to lead the country into an illegal invasion of Iraq, that Prince Philip conspired to assassinate Princess Diana, that some Catholic politicians in Monklands were corrupt, and special enquiries will be instigated to determine the truth or otherwise of these allegations. But the merest hint that a referee on occasion might have been less than fair – as opposed to making a mistake – is greeted with howls of indignation. If there still is a sin against the Holy Ghost, this is it. One recalls how Lord Denning, the then Master of the Rolls, one of the highest judicial offices in the English/British legal establishment, adamantly refused to allow an appeal by the Birmingham Six against their conviction for terrorism on the truly unbelievable ground that it might unearth police brutality, prosecutorial corruption, and the deliberate falsification of evidence. Lord Denning thought it better that innocent men and women should continue to rot in prison than that an English court should be exposed for perverting the course of justice: for how could the legal system survive such a revelation? Better by far to prevent such a revelation being made. A similar mindset is discernible in the horrified repudiation of any suggestion that some team or teams may get preferential treatment within Scottish football. You must not even think this, never mind say it – it is, to use Orwell's term, thoughtcrime.

There are no favoured teams. Neither are there any fortunate teams, since, on the theory of equal breaks for all, every team in the long run is equally fortunate – and equally unfortunate. It all evens itself out. Don't complain when the decisions go against you – your turn will infallibly come and then you will be the beneficiary of the lucky break or the doubtful decision. It seems, on the face of it, a plausible and persuasive argument. The idea of a team being 'unlucky' every week seems at odds with our everyday commonsense view of the world: if your opponent is repeatedly cutting a higher card, it might be wise to inspect the deck. Nevertheless, for obvious historical reasons, Celtic supporters may need a good deal of persuading that there is no bias in Scottish football, that what they regard as injustices are really just slices of bad luck, and that they should embrace the theory of equal breaks for all. Let us assume that you encourage them to do this, and, that, grudgingly, they agree.

At this point a very strange thing happens. The devotees of the theory, who have been exhorting everybody, Celtic supporters in particular, to adopt it, suddenly turn against it. As long as the decisions are going against Celtic, everyone seems happy: the theory is enthusiastically endorsed and there are no calls for referees' heads. But the moment a doubtful decision goes Celtic's way, a storm erupts among those who were previously assuring us that it's always and necessarily a case of equal breaks for all. All their customary equanimity, their indulgence towards erring referees, disappear. The facade of impartial indifference crumbles, the high-sounding rhetoric about long-term fairness for all is heard no more, referees are being arraigned for judgement. No longer are the commentators on those untainted heights above the conflict, indifferent gods serenely contemplating the struggle below. Startlingly, they are now down in the arena, laden with all the dust and heat of the contest, as openly partisan and committed as any denizen of the terracing.

One need only contrast the very different reactions of the same pundits to decisions in favour of Rangers with decisions in favour of Celtic. I have already referred to the refused penalty kick in the C.I.S. final. In the semi-final of that same competition against Hearts, the opening goal was scored by Barry Ferguson after he controlled the ball with his hand – no one denies this because it was plain for all to see on television. These were major decisions that were also major 'mistakes', yet they were treated by the Scottish sports media as trifles, mere afterthoughts: one suspects that they might not even have been mentioned at all, but for the fact that television made them impossible to ignore. The real point is this: there was no subsequent media witch-hunt against the offending referees, rather a cheerful consensus that this is what happens in football, that the breaks 'even themselves out', and that the culprit officials are, after all, 'our best whistlers'. As our minds and focus are pushed in the well-established direction of 'mistakes' and 'these things happen', it all ends with three cheers for the theory.

However, the direction and focus of the media spotlight is frequently ultimately determined by which teams are actually involved in whatever the incident. This is crucial in how the relevant discourses are shaped. Importantly, there is no such latitude, no such genial forbearance, for those referees unwise enough to err (if indeed they do) in Celtic's favour. The referee (Ian Brines) certainly did err in disallowing the Aberdeen equaliser in the game referred to – though he may also have erred twice earlier in the same match in Aberdeen's favour with the two disallowed goals for Celtic that terrestrial television (though Setanta did) chose not to show.

In the same period, at Love Street in a league game against St Mirren, Celtic scored the winning goal direct from a disputed free kick awarded by Eddie Smith almost thirty yards out – clearly a gift since hardly anyone ever fails to score from such a distance? Referee Craig Thomson's performance in the 3-2 victory over Rangers at Celtic Park produced Derek Johnstone's sour comment that Scotland is now afflicted with the worst crop of referees in years – strange, for I can't recall him being at all critical when Rangers won four in a row against Celtic, two of them in this same season that is now the target of his condemnation. (In one of these victories, the referee booked a Guinness-record number of **nine** Celtic players, but he, too, was one of 'our best whistlers'). Steve Conroy's transgression – and this may have you shaking your head in disbelief – was to give Celtic a 'disputed corner-kick' (no more than a disputed corner kick) from which they scored the winner against Motherwell at Fir Park. It was Celtic's 'first' corner-kick of the game. If I say that Motherwell had already had eleven corner-kicks from which they had not scored once, it may indicate the statistical probability of scoring from a corner, disputed or otherwise. A corner-kick, for heaven's sake! Any day now, expect to see a referee excoriated for giving Celtic a doubtful throw-in.

This is surely carping on a microscopically nitpicking scale. Where is the referee who will survive undamaged such an unforgivingly censorious scrutiny – which of them, to quote Shakespeare, 'shall escape whipping'? It is the more baffling when we recall the leniency with which far more serious infractions are treated on other occasions. Blatant handballs in semi-finals, blatant penalty kicks in finals – all brushed aside as peccadillos – referees are only human, after all, and in any case, these are the best referees we have: meanwhile, what are, at worst, possible mistakes over relatively minor matters like disputed corner-kicks seem to warrant a Scottish public enquiry, judging from the ensuing media commotion. It's on a par with hammering some motorists for parking on double yellow lines while cheerfully dismissing others who drive at a hundred miles an hour while under the influence of drink. Serious derelictions on behalf of one team are glossed over, while the most trivial lapses on behalf of the other are pursued with an inquisitorial zeal. Any referee who thinks about it might well conclude that it is safer to blunder for Rangers than to give even a 50-50 decision Celtic's way. Certainly, Messrs Brine, Smith, Thomson and Conroy will have to make amends in future if they are to restore their tarnished reputations with those who write and talk about the Scottish game.

Yet why should their reputations be tarnished at all? Why should that air of sweet reasonableness and gentle indulgence that generally prevails, suddenly vanish when a decision goes Celtic's way? Isn't this what's supposed to happen? Well, no, seems the answer. All is changed. A monstrous, an irreparable wrong has been done, and nothing can compensate the victims for the injury they have suffered. The hapless referee, up to that point an agreeable man, vulnerable, as we all are, to making a mistake, is suddenly transformed into, if not a malefactor, a crass incompetent who should be forever parted from his whistle – Craig Thomson might reasonably fear for his future if Derek Johnstone has any say in the matter. Celtic supporters must be forgiven for feeling bemused at such an unpredictable turnabout.

They have every right to be perplexed. What has become of that sacrosanct law of averages, that inviolable axiom of statistical probability, in which they were invited to seek solace when decisions went so outrageously against them? Why did the media console the aggrieved managers of Aberdeen, St.Mirren and Motherwell over the irremediable injustices they had suffered, instead of telling them, as the theory dictates, to stop complaining, because next week they will be the beneficiaries and their opponents the losers? Where was/is the sympathy for Maley, Stein, Burns, Strachan, et al? Doesn't the Scottish sports media believe its own theory? After all, it's what they tell Celtic. Are Celtic supporters to conclude that every other team in the land is entitled to these breaks, these gifts from the footballing gods, but not their own?

There is certainly nothing in the reaction of the pundits to make them think otherwise. These normally affable, imperturable men, confronted with a mistake (it need only be a possible mistake) in Celtic's favour, suddenly become the most draconian of judges, mandated from on high to search out and chastise refereeing ineptitude. They do not tear their garments and strew dust upon their heads when every other team in the league (and one in particular) benefits from dubious or even undeniably bad decisions. What is it about this one team, Celtic, that sets them apart and causes them to be treated so differently? Why should this be?

Once again there is a clue in Orwell, in particular, his concept of doublethink. Doublethink means the ability to hold simultaneously, in one's mind, totally contradictory ideas without being aware that one is doing so. This is the kindest, most charitable explanation of the bewildering inconsistencies and double standards exhibited every season in Scottish football by those employed to comment upon it. We must assume, in charity, that they sincerely believe in their theory of equal breaks for all. But why, then, are they so upset when a decision goes in Celtic's favour, since this might go some way towards confirming their theory's truth? Why aren't they happy? – because happy they are certainly not. Read their words in the papers, listen to their words on radio and television, and ask yourself: are these the words of happy men rejoicing in the vindication of their theory? If not, why not?

Remember, it is their theory; my guess is that a considerable majority of Celtic supporters are skeptically unconvinced. But those who most vociferously espouse the theory – surely they are committed to it. It is they who insist that every team gets their fair share of the breaks, so why the resentment when Celtic are the recipients? Or is it that, as they see it, Celtic get more than their share, too many 'lucky' breaks, too many doubtful decisions? This would explain why Derek Johnstone and others are so disgruntled with the present state of refereeing in Scotland. Or (and this is a speculation that Lord Denning would veto) might it be that even one break, one doubtful decision, for Celtic, is already one too many and that the whole theory of equal-breaks-for-all is a fraud and a sham? The theory is already in trouble if the Johnstone insinuation that Celtic is the favoured team (too many decisions going for them) is true, for the theory insists that there are, and can be, no favoured teams. If Johnstone is right, then we are back once again with that dreadful conspiracy spectre which the Scottish football establishment has been strenuously trying to exorcise for all of my lifetime and long before. Celtic, of all people, a favoured team! Are you having a laugh? seems the only possible response to so absurd, so preposterous, a supposition. But if Johnstone et. al. are wrong and Celtic are not being favoured, why the fury in the media whenever a decision, however slight, however minuscule, goes their way? If this isn't doublethink, it's something even more sinister.

There is something very puzzling here. Perhaps the real clue is to be found in the nature of the society in which we live. The most cursory acquaintance with Scottish history since the coming of the Famine Irish after 1845 indicates the existence of persistent latent, but occasionally explicit, anti-Irish, anti-Catholic sentiment among us. Cardinal O'Brien recently criticised the media in Scotland for their consistently negative attitude towards Catholic schools. It would be remarkable indeed if our football was somehow miraculously immune from this contagion, and, of course, it isn't. Who can forget the shameful behaviour of the Hearts supporters in a Scottish Cup semi-final against Celtic at Hampden in 2005 when they shockingly violated the minute's silence arranged to commemorate the death of Pope John Paul II? In England, on the preceding day, the minute's silence had been observed at a number of leading football grounds with more or less the utmost, unblemished respect. Hampden, by contrast, was the stage for an exhibition of raucous, moronic obscenity, pictures of which were beamed round the globe (that plaguesome television again) from New York to Beijing. 'From scenes like these old Scotia's grandeur springs'. It is not, I think, what Burns had in mind.

More regrettable still was that some leading figures in our society chose to blame, not the odious perpetrators of the outrage, or the bigoted traditions 'they' sprang from, but the SFA for 'imposing' the minute's silence in the first place, thereby foolishly providing a platform for advertising to the world at large the kind of society we are. But for the SFA's blunder, the nation would have been spared the mortifying international publicity to which it was exposed. In this light, the important thing, it would appear, is to keep the shame 'in house' and not let the wider world find out about it.

It would be temptingly easy to relegate this bigotry to an underclass, a lumpen proletariat, whose pitifully low IQs might be submitted in part extenuation of their deplorable conduct: 'forgive them for they know not what they do'. Easy, but mistaken. Bigotry is not always the bedfellow of a low IQ. The journalist who alleged that Celtic supporters turned against Gordon Strachan because he was not the kind of 'bead-rattling' manager to whom they traditionally give their affection, does not belong to the lumpen proletariat – his article, the gratuitously spiteful religious insult aside, is competently written and appeared in a quality newspaper – but might he be as much a bigot as any of the canaille who routinely disgrace themselves on the terracing? He must be abysmally ignorant if he really believes that Celtic supporters continue to revere Jock Stein as their greatest manager because he was forever reciting the rosary in the dugout during games. Much more probably, the sports journalist just couldn't resist the opportunity to deride a religion he obviously despises. After all, if Catholics or Celtic supporters object, doesn't that simply confirm how paranoid they are?

The article is, admittedly, an especially nasty public example of trawling the depths, and we should be grateful that we don't regularly encounter this sort of muck – at least in the 'respectable' media. But at least part of the shock came from confronting attitudes – explicitly, crudely and brutally expressed – that are normally kept discreetly under wraps, or expressed on websites and fanzines, etc, though we suspect that they are always there more widely. There is an ongoing anti-Catholic, anti-Irish, anti-Celtic strain in our society and there can be no eradicating it till we admit that it's there.

Hence the need to jettison once and for all the old, hoary, decrepit jibe about paranoia. It is – a moment's thought should suffice to alert us to this – a particularly absurd term to apply to many thousands of people and their football club. Paranoia is, by definition, a solitary affliction that affects, thankfully, only a small scattered minority, setting these scanty victims apart from the mass of their fellows: it afflicts individual, isolated sufferers. It is difficult to conceive how such an essentially private delusion can affect a whole community, a whole people, thousands upon thousands of ordinary folk. If it's just a joke, then it's a poor and insensitive one and it should be dropped. If, however, there is a serious intent behind its use by those who use it, they should find another name for such a bizarre malaise. It's despicably easy to stigmatise those who disagree with us as dreamers and fantasists: the pictures, I repeat, are there for all to see. And so it seems to me a pity that the Rev. Stuart MacQuarrie the Church of Scotland chaplain at the University of Glasgow, writing in a collection of essays on Glasgow Rangers, should have seen fit to besmirch Celtic supporters in the mass as a multitude of martyr-junkies, in love with their role as victims, hooked on the idea of being persecuted, and forever cosseting their addiction. Are they really as sick as that?

There is, however, a grain of truth in what Mr. MacQuarrie says and it has to do with the occupational hazard of what I shall call victimdom. (There is no such word, but in the circumstances the coinage seems justifiable.) When maltreated people are repeatedly told over many years that there is no such thing as bias but only bad luck, they have an understandable tendency to react by believing that there is no such thing as bad luck but only bias. The one erroneous extreme inevitably produces the other, but, of the two errors, I think I know which is the more pardonable. The Church of Scotland, to its great credit, recently found the courage to admit its fault in scapegoating Scotland's Irish Catholics during the 1920s and 1930s and apologised to them for the injustices this had caused. It deserves to be commended for this. But it is surely high time for other great Scottish institutions, football included, to follow suit. There is something amiss with our football as well as with our society and it will no longer serve to go on saying that it's all the fault of people whose injuries exist only in their imaginations.

Let Orwell – amended – have the last word: all Scottish teams are equal but one is more equal than all the others. When this has become a superannuated witticism, then, and only then, tell us that the breaks always even themselves out.

P.S.
Sidney Smith once saw two women arguing with each other from open windows in two tenement buildings facing each other across a London street. He turned to a friend and said, 'they will never agree, for they are arguing from 'different premises'. Smith's witticism came to my mind as I reflected on the quarrel between Craig Levein and Gordon Smith apropos the referee, Mike McCurry, in an important league match in May 2008 at Ibrox. They, too, are arguing from irreconcilably different premises.

Mr Levein presents a body of impressive evidence designed to prove his contention that Dundee United were deliberately, wilfully cheated by the referee who had already made up his mind, before a ball was kicked, that, if possible, Rangers were going to win the game. For Mr Levein it is a question that can be addressed only by examining the evidence of what actually happened during the game. If this is done, he has a very strong, perhaps incontestable, case. How can one man over the course of ninety minutes so consistently make a series (not one or two) of major mistakes in favour of one team against another? It defies all the laws of probability: it smacks of design, of intent, rather than of luck or accident.

Mr Smith comes at it from an exactly antipodal position. For him, evidence, no matter how abundant or compelling, is completely irrelevant. He knows, on a priori grounds, simply by thinking about it, that there can no more be a cheating Scottish referee than there can be a square circle: it's a logical impossibility, an intellectual absurdity. Since it cannot happen, Mr Smith is not interested in examining the evidence, even were it piled as high as Mount Everest. He does not care, because it matters not, if a Scottish referee disallowed a dozen goals and refused twenty penalties: no amount of evidence can convict him of corruption because he is simply not convincible. The legal maxim that 'the King can do no wrong' is extended to every Scottish referee: he cannot be accused of cheating because it is impossible for him to cheat. What happens in shady places like Spain or France or Italy is perhaps another matter – who knows what kind of depradations these foreigners get up to? – but it is inconceivable that such a thing could happen in our unfallen Scottish football Eden. Mr Levein simply wastes his own and everyone else's time as he parades the evidence to prove that his team was cheated, because in Scotland a team cannot be cheated. We no more need discuss this than discuss whether a circle can be square. The football establishment in Scotland is in precisely the same position as was Lord Denning with respect to the English judicial system in the case already alluded to in this essay. How can the system survive if the allegation is even admitted for investigation? For what would happen if – horrendous thought – we found out that it was true?

A Tommy Burns Supper

JAMES MACMILLAN

A few years ago I was invited to be a guest speaker at the nineteenth annual Tommy Burns Supper, hosted by Heriot Watt and Edinburgh Universities' Celtic Supporters Club. Based on, but rejecting the traditional Rabbie Burns Supper model, it turned out to be a deliciously raucous clash of cultures. They had billed it, embarrassingly, as their 'highbrow' supper, because Dr Joe Bradley of Stirling University, the unusually erudite footballer Pat Nevin and I, were speaking at it. As far as my invite was concerned they knew there had been a curious interface in my life between Celtic and composing, and they wanted to hear more about it.

There has been an extraordinary love affair between some twentieth century composers and the beautiful game. Dmitri Shostakovich was a fan of Lenigrad Zenith and regularly attended games. This was very much in my mind during the 2008 UEFA Cup Final in Manchester when they played and beat Rangers, with all the expected attendant hooliganistic chaos from the usual suspects. (I sought out Shostakovich's great Leningrad Symphony and played it at full volume to drown out the appalling sounds from the terraces. This was the work he wrote to give sustenance and encouragement to the people of Leningrad as they endured and overcame the bestial onslaught of the 'German' Hun.)

Martinu was a supporter of Sparta Prague and his orchestral work 'Half Time' is dedicated to them. There has even been an opera written about football – 'Playing Away' by Benedict Mason in which the ball has an aria. Elgar was mad for Wolverhampton Wanderers and attended many games at Molineaux in the 1890s. Mark Antony Turnage is Arsenal-daft and has quoted some of the Highbury chants in 'Momentum', the work commissioned by Sir Simon Rattle to open Symphony Hall in Birmingham. Michael Nyman's 'The Final Score' was, he claims 'anthemic enough to lift Queens Park Rangers immediately back into the Premier League'. That was in 1991 and they are still languishing in a lower division.

Some music though does obviously have an effect for other teams. Osmo Tapio Everton Reihala, a Finn, has made a special series of Everton compositions including, I kid you not, 'Barlinnie Nine', dedicated to Duncan Ferguson. The premiere was on April 20th 2005 in Helsinki, performed by the Finnish Radio Symphony Orchestra, and incredibly, that night Ferguson scored the only goal of the game in Everton's win over Manchester United.

Tommy Burns, the principal honoured guest of the afore-mentioned evening, was unaware that he and his colleagues from past and present have been a constant source of inspiration for me, and some of my works over the years have celebrated them. In September 1989 Tommy and the team flew to Belgrade to take on Partisan in the UEFA Cup. Celtic were beaten 1-0 but returned with high hopes that this could be overturned in the home leg. That game in Glasgow turned out to be one of the most extraordinary in Celtic history, when the entire Celtic family experienced every football emotion from confident apprehension, tension, frustration, elation and ultimately despair. The team was characteristically passionate and frenzied in attack, careless in defence. The dazzling, exhilarating display was ultimately futile, for although they won 5-4 on the night, they lost on the away goals rule. It struck me as a vivid illustration of the facility in these parts, in these tribes, for shooting ourselves in the foot in sporting, and for that matter, political endeavours. It reminded me of stories about ancient Celtic and Viking 'berserkers', warriors who would work themselves into an aggressive frenzy on mead and magic mushrooms, plunging headlong into wild, often suicidal attacks. My piano concerto, 'The Berserking', came about in response to this game and I am proud to say, is the only piano concerto in the history of classical music to be inspired by the away goals rule.

An observation of the wider contemporary Scottish dimension has had unexpected musical results. A recent work, 'A Scotch Bestiary', premiered in Los Angeles in 2004 and then at the London Proms in the same year, attempts to portray notable Scottish archetypes in the guise of animals, much in the tradition of earlier portrait pieces such as 'Carnival of the Animals' by Saint-Saens and the Enigma Variations by Elgar. In my researches for this work, I came across the extraordinary red-handed howler monkey that became a model for one of the portraits. And so the third section of the first movement is entitled The Red-Handed No-Surrender Howler Monkey, which could have been modelled on thousands of delightful Scottish individuals.

Just as my emotional and spiritual roots in the Celtic family have proved important to me, so also did I grow up, whether I wanted to or not, worshipping at the altar of the other Burns, the secular demi-god, and Masonic saint, Rabbie. Unusually perhaps for someone from my background, I am thoroughly embedded in the Burns cult, although I've grown increasingly sceptical of it as time goes by. That's why it was so refreshing to experience an alternative Burns Supper a few years ago. No interminable Immortal Memories, no misogynistic Address to the Lassies, no ideological hijacking of a narrow proportion of the poet's work for political propaganda (such as the earth-bound A Man's A Man), no dodgy handshakes, no narrow definition of what it means to be Scottish.

In 1977 in my final year at school in Ayrshire, as chairman of the debating society I was invited to deliver one of these interminable Immortal Memories for the senior Burns Supper. This was a baptism of fire. The school hall was decked in Masonic insignia, borrowed from the local lodges. As is the practice in deepest darkest Ayrshire, Masonic bonding songs such as The Star O Rabbie Burns are used in these liturgies. The Ayrshire Burns Supper is unmistakably a Parody Mass with its liturgies of The Word and The Eucharist. Homilies and invocations are used to evoke 'sacred' memory', 'epiclesis' is called down on a sacrificial victim in the sacramental shape of whisky and haggis, which is pierced by a knife and then consumed, communion-style by the assembled congregation. My Immortal Memory didn't go down too well that evening I seem to remember, and it may have had something to do with the fact I was beginning to suss out what the whole Burns cult was about.

Nevertheless, Robert Burns provoked sublime music from the likes of Haydn and Beethoven, who both set his poetry. Tommy Burns, a poet of a different dimension, may be a stranger inspiration for a composer. However, I can fully understand the comparatively eccentric fascination held by Shostakovich, Martinu and so on for the beautiful game, especially when played as beautifully, and as exhilaratingly, as by the virtuosic, flame-haired maestro: may he rest in peace. He and the other great Celtic personalities have been, and will continue to be the source of artistic flight in music, poetry, literature and song. This does not surprise me. Tommy Burns' soul burned with the legacy of devotion – a mixture of faith, family, community, culture and identity – handed down the years from Brother Walfrid: a gift from a history of dreams and aspirations shared by many of us. He lived the dream and lived it well. He shone as his maker intended and requested. People such as Tommy Burns and his like are the ones that have made this cold, dark and sometimes inhospitable little country a better place for people like me to live and to imagine.

DIASPORA AND IRISH DESCENT

Irish identities, history, public silence and the Celtic singing tradition*

JOSEPH M BRADLEY, BRONWEN WALTER,
MARY J HICKMAN, SARAH MORGAN

Formal narratives of history are central to the construction of national identities.[1] But diasporic peoples, particularly the offspring of immigrants in another country, are cut off from the representation of an important strand of their histories by a series of absences from spaces of cultural reproduction, in education, memorials and popular culture more widely. Although this can often be experienced most severely amongst the second generation it can also be felt for subsequent generations of offspring. At least some aspects of this culture are passed on in the intimate space of child rearing, but at school age in particular the children, grandchildren and great grand children of immigrants are thrust into a public sphere where their background culture is underrepresented or may be missing altogether.

For colonised populations this may entail a more active suppression of dissident identities in order to avoid contestation and speed up the process of incorporation into the national mainstream – and with this the adoption of the national identity of the host nation. Hickman shows that Irish history has been conspicuously excluded from the curriculum in Britain since the nineteenth century, not only of majority state schools, but also from distinctive Catholic schools, where the majority of children

* A version of this paper was published in the journal Ethnicities in 2005. By kind permission of Sage Journals

1 Johnson 1992

of Irish descent are educated.[2] She argues that this has been a key element in the denationalisation of the Irish in Britain and their construction as 'good' Catholic British (English or Scottish) citizens.

However, there is evidence to suggest that knowledge of their cultural background in Ireland cannot entirely be erased. It continues to be handed on to British-born Irish offspring both consciously and unconsciously. This knowledge can also result in significant Irish identity being manifest amongst those of Irish descent in Britain. For example, Bradley has utilised the case of Celtic Football Club's supporters to demonstrate how people born in Scotland can have a passionate affinity for, and disposition towards, Ireland, their country of origin, culture, history, community and family.[3] In this context the Irishness around Celtic may also be seen as an outward expression of the way cultural, national and identity impositions can be resisted and alternative ones maintained, sustained and celebrated. This chapter reflects on some aspects of this resistance and how Irishness, particularly elements of an historical and political Irishness, is central to Celtic supporter culture and identities.

In this light, the first part of this essay explores some of the ways in which Irish histories are passed to the second generation in particular, enabling them to acquire a different perspective on the national story being told in the 'diaspora space' in which they live. Because the national stories of Britain and Ireland continue to clash as a result of centuries of British colonialism in Ireland, this de-centred knowledge has an ongoing political significance for people of Irish descent in Britain. One of the key purposes of the introduction of the Prevention of Terrorism Act in 1974, for example, was to dissuade British residents from expressing views sympathetic towards Irish nationalism in Ireland and questioning the British state's political and military strategies in 'the North'. Since 'the propaganda war' ensured that strict British censorship was being practised in the public sphere, access to alternative constructions was largely confined to private – family, community, cultural and, in the case of Scotland, football – sources.[4]

This chapter initially reflects on the production and repro-

2 Hickman 1996

3 Bradley 2004 & 2006

4 Cathcart 1984, Curtis 1984, Bradley 1995

duction of narratives of Irish history amongst second generation Irish people living with predominantly English neighbours. It will subsequently refer to this specifically amongst generations of Celtic supporters in Scotland. This reflection shows that in particular contexts these constructions may emerge in strongly oppositional ways to those that dominate. Boyle identifies a situation in the urban west of Scotland where he claims that:

> Across the past decade there has been a qualitatively important development in the currency of particularly virulent and potent memories of Ireland's past, among at least some sections of the Irish Catholic community.[5]

He is referring to the 'rebel music scene' in the west of Scotland where mainly young men (but not solely) gather in venues where bands perform songs that remember and celebrate perceived patriots and 'freedom advancing' events in Irish history. This is of course a qualitatively different version of the Irish-British colonial conflict from that which dominates throughout much of Britain, particularly in much of the British media.[6]

This work forms part of a wider research study, the Irish 2 Project, exploring the identities and experiences of people born in Britain to one or two Irish-born parents and in Scotland, also to those with one or more Irish-born grandparents. Five geographical locations in Britain – Glasgow, London, Manchester, Coventry and Banbury – were selected in order to construct a sample including with a wide range of regional and local backgrounds. In this first part we focus attention on the smallest centre, Banbury and explore the public/private duality of Irish identity experienced by people who have spent at least part of their lives in this very 'English' context.

Banbury

Irish migrants have settled in England on a large scale at least since the early nineteenth century. Although certain centres have attracted significant clusters – particularly London, the North-west region of England and in the post-World War II period, the West Midlands – there has also been a wide spread across all

5 Boyle, 2002, p. 174

6 Curtis, 1984, Murphy, 2006, Bloch and Fitzgerald, 1983

195

counties.[7] In large part this has reflected subsequent migration following the continuous redistribution of job opportunities. Those living in large centres can choose to be more securely ensconced within an Irish 'world', with provision of community meeting places, regular cultural activities and schools where the majority of people share a similar heritage and work networks.

In smaller centres, by contrast, Irish people are more isolated, interacting with the majority population in all spheres of life. The experiences of this sample are the most varied in the research study, including people born and raised in much larger Irish communities, who have subsequently migrated, and those who have lived only in a variety of smaller ones, including Banbury itself. Without specifically labelled Irish meeting places many people may be unaware of the presence of other Irish people in the town and often do not meet them.

On the edge of the South East region of England, between Oxford and Coventry, Banbury remained a small local centre until the 1960s when it was designated for 'overspill' housing expansion from London and Birmingham. In 1967 a large food manufacturer General Foods, now Alcan, moved from Birming-ham and brought many employees, including Irish workers. At this time large public housing estates were built in the town. The presence of a number of Irish people led to the construction of a new Catholic church (1968) and school in these parts of the town.

However the numbers of Irish people remained a very small proportion of the total. Respondents laughed when we asked them whether Banbury could be regarded as an 'Irish' town in any way. The only connection they drew was with the Catholic churches where they knew or assumed that the congregations included many people of Irish descent. But there was no specifically Irish provision in the town, though at times in the past there had been Irish dancing classes. The only named Irish activity was the Banbury Irish football team where young men were mainly recruited from the Catholic comprehensive school. St Patrick's Day was not celebrated in any communal way. Very few could identify an 'Irish' pub.

7 Walter 1980

Public accounts of Irish history in Britain

Respondents were asked about their knowledge of, and interest in, Irish history. For most people the study of national histories is primarily connected with compulsory elements of formal education, possibly supplemented in adulthood with voluntary activities including courses, reading and other popular media forms. The mass media is a further significant source of learning. However the most striking aspect of the Banbury participants' encounters with Irish history outside the home was its absence from the school curriculum. Even in Catholic schools history lessons were about British history and they could not remember Ireland being mentioned. Unusually one person used an option in her A-level Sociology course to make a video about Northern Ireland. This absence has been analysed closely by Hickman in her study of the experiences of London and Liverpool children of Irish descent.[8]

In the Banbury sample it was women in particular who described themselves as 'ignorant', a term often tinged with guilt and regret, or as 'a bit interested in Irish history but not very knowledgeable'. Men did not admit this as a lack, but described ways in which they had increased their knowledge. The realisation that this has been a missing part of their cultural knowledge has come to the respondents later in their lives. All the respondents who grew up with an Irish-born parent were to varying degrees interested in filling in some of the gaps. Many now describe themselves as self-taught. Often an impetus is to gain an understanding of the Northern Irish Troubles, which they feel in particular have been missing from the British culture in which they grew up.

Interviewees used a variety of formal and informal methods to gain an understanding of Irish history as adults. Participation in taught courses on Irish topics was rare. Only one interviewee, a woman who trained at a Catholic teacher training college, had enrolled in an Irish history option. Another respondent had been awarded a place at Ruskin College, Oxford through his trade union activity. He chose the topic of James Connolly, the Scottish-born second generation Irish trade unionist and Irish nationalist, for his dissertation topic. One man in his 50s had recently enrolled

8 Hickman 1990, 1993

in an Irish language class in London.

A larger number reported searching for Irish history books in the public library or finding websites. But without guidance they sometimes found it difficult to know where to start. Most respondents made a point of watching documentaries and dramas about Ireland when they were shown on television, as well as going to see films such as 'Michael Collins'. Louise made immediate connections with her own family:

> I went to see the Michael Collins film a few years ago when it came out. I know it wasn't absolutely accurate, and I remember walking out of the cinema and saying to Peter, to everybody else: 'They have just watched a film, I have watched part of my family history'.

Family stories: private accounts of Irish history

For many families, the family home is a place where Irish issues can be most safely discussed.[9] However the knowledge that people had acquired about Irish history within the family was fragmentary in most cases. But even where there was little factual knowledge of wider historical events imparted on the part of parents and grandparents, children often grew up with a strong sense of an alternative story in their family's past.

> Marie: Mum remembers an old lady where she lived [in Ireland], having all her possessions thrown out in the street, because her sons were members of the IRA. (Born London 1951)

> Tara: My parents would often mention political history going back even further than that. My dad would get really incensed if anybody went on about how marvellous Winston Churchill was. I'm not entirely certain of the political details, but he was no friend of the Irish, and go back even further to Oliver Cromwell. He was really dragging them up, and how Oliver Cromwell had massacred all these hundreds of Irish. (Born Dover 1967)

But many people also experienced silence at home and only picked up more indirectly on the sense of an oppositional history.

> Not even my father [spoke about Irish history]. . . I don't think he was interested in Irish history as history, but he was

interested in the feeling of Irish nationalism. . . when I was filling
the form out, I took out the family documents. Amongst them
was one of the first things I remember associating with my
father. The cigarettes he smoked then used to have flags of the
world on a bit of silk. I still have with me Irish Free State, and
that's the one my father kept and I ended up with. It is valued
and it is an emotional thing. (Born Leigh, Lancs 1942)

Some parents made a deliberate decision to put things behind
them, especially those that had painful personal connections.
One man contrasted his own curiosity as a child with the silence
of his parents.

Brian: Because of the troubles, that is what has triggered me to
find out why is there turbulence in that country. To find out, my
[Irish-born] parents had never spoke about it, I had not known
about any Irish history. [My parents] must have been interested
as it must have affected them. My parents are very quiet people,
it was a mystery to me, why is this going on in the British Isles, I
wanted to find out. . . There was nothing before the 1970s no
real news, but it must have always been there. . . I bought
books in the book store. . . I remember my father was born in
1920, when I asked him he said the black and tans came and
burned the hay stack and killed the cow, and that was all he'd
say. (Born London 1952)

Memories of British rule in Ireland have remained strong for
people whose parents were brought up in the north of Ireland:

Grace: So when I was little they were talking about it before the
current thirty-year troubles started, I was brought up to think
that the British in Ireland were a bad thing. Then there were the
B Specials, how anti-Catholic they were, and heard lots of tales
about people being stopped. Lots of stories about how
impossible it was for a Catholic to get a good job in Ireland, you
only had to answer the question of which school did you go to,
and they would know. You then had no chance of promotion in
the civil service or any career prospects at all. So that is what I
remember as a child. (Born Letchworth 1946)

Some children, however, were actively discouraged from
asking questions. One woman explained that family history was
not discussed in her household. It was considered rude for
children to ask adults questions about their background. A

reluctance to talk about the family's past in Ireland was also related to family 'secrets'.

Most second generation children augmented their fragmentary knowledge when meeting their Irish families face-to-face on holidays to Ireland. These were important occasions for a reintegration of families split by emigration and a chance to hear stories at first hand from relatives who had remained. However there was a clear bi-modal division between families who kept close physical contact with Ireland and those who rarely visited. Amongst the latter considerable regret was expressed by respondents that they had been deprived of close family connections.

The accounts given by the Banbury sample illustrate the wide variation in family knowledge about the national past of their Irish-born parents and grandparents. These relate to the placing of the family within the context of political events as well as to customs, attitudes and continuing contacts. Gender differences in both the givers and receivers of accounts were also identified. But the national story being painted, however faintly, for children in households that were to some extent 'Irish' was often different from that being absorbed from the English culture around them.

Irish history and the west of Scotland

Notable amongst many of those involved in the Irish 2 Project was the groups themselves providing an atypical space for second and third generation Irish people to explore their senses of cultural difference. The Banbury interviewees were amongst those that expressed their pleasure in having the opportunity to discuss issues of Irish identity and experience with others from similar backgrounds. None of them knew each other before the meeting but they discovered many common strands in their lives that had not previously found a more public forum.

Geographical isolation also holds for Scotland and people of Irish descent can live where there are few people from a similar Irish ethnic background as most areas are as might be expected, Scottish/British in the same way that Banbury is English. Nonetheless, in the west central belt there exist numerous districts that contain significant numbers of people of Irish descent as a result of nineteenth and early twentieth century Irish immigration. For example, a number of towns such as Coatbridge, Dumbarton and Port Glasgow, villages like Carfin, Croy, Glenboig and Clelland, and areas of Glasgow such as Govanhill, Garngad, Kings Park, Toryglen and Castlemilk, all include notable numbers of second, third and fourth generation Irish: much more than found in other parts of Scotland.

In the case of the older part of Croy on the outskirts of Cumbernauld/Glasgow, this is a village almost entirely comprised of people of Irish descent. A few miles away, with a population of around 45,000, Coatbridge contains more Irish-descended people per head of population than anywhere else in Britain. Indeed, people from an Irish background represent a majority of people in the Lanarkshire town, which is a unique statistic for a place of its size in Britain. Tangible markers and indicators of Irish ethnicity in Coatbridge can be seen in the existence of several specific Irish organisations; a branch of Comhaltas Ceoltóirí Éireann, the Irish traditional music organisation, a Gaelic football club with a vibrant youth section, six Irish Dance Schools and a St Patrick's Week festival that is the largest in Scotland and one of Britain's biggest. In 2006 a survey reported in The Times pointed to Coatbridge having the highest per head percentage of Irish surnames in Britain.[10] Other signs of Irish ethnicity that largely derive from the Catholic make-up of most of the Irish that originally migrated to the area include nine Catholic Church parishes, two Catholic high schools and eight Catholic primary schools. The town also contains numerous Celtic supporters' clubs as well as thousands of individual fans. Coatbridge is but one example of a story and context that can be replicated in smaller numbers in numerous areas of the west-central belt. Such high figures for Irish-descended people living in the west-central belt also partly demonstrates the multicultural and ethnic character of significant parts of modern Scotland.

Such incidences of Irishness also increases the likelihood of 'alternative' identities remaining, developing or being manifest, in contrast to those that dominate in other Scottish locales which reflect more prevailing indigenous Scottish/British identities. In

10 The Times, 10/9/06

addition, the Banbury research informs us of the potential for a greater awareness of 'Irish' history amongst this section of the British population than is usually found. Although throughout Britain people of Irish descent have not been able to access the histories of their country of origin through formal channels of education, and although individuals and families occasionally overcome this, it is the case that in Scotland a unique space exists to access aspects of these histories that are otherwise difficult to find. Doyle says:

> There are many political, social and cultural forces which exert and have exerted an influence on the formation of national and cultural identities, such as religion, family, community, mass media, art and literature. . .[11]

With this in mind, as reported in the research on Banbury and elsewhere throughout the Irish 2 Project, beyond the family's influences and outside of possible consequence of Catholic schooling, added to close community networks arising from similar patterns of Irish migration and settlement, for many Celtic supporters the historical narratives, awareness and counter culture that has been intricate to the club since its foundation is significant. This is critical to the acquisition of knowledge and understanding regarding alternative versions of the Irish-British historical cleavage and struggle from those that dominate in Britain (via inclusion or exclusion).

Of course, various Irish nationalist identities, feelings, attitudes and activities have characterised the Irish in Scotland beyond the Celtic environment and were witnessed prior to the foundation of the club in 1887/88. Today individual and family Irish nationalist identities, feelings, attitudes and activities retain a strong resonance amongst parts of the Irish-descended community in Scotland. As such, rather than a separate development, Celtics' founding, evolution and sustenance are a reflection and aspect of the story of the Irish in Scotland. As a football club founded by men of fervent Irish nationalist disposition, followed by many people of a similar outlook, and where since its foundation corresponding attitudes significantly shaped the club's character and culture, Irish nationalist ethno-cultural and political identities remain markedly relevant to understanding Celtic. It is

11 Doyle 2002

the case though that in recent decades this pertains more to its dominant supporter culture rather the club as an institution.

Although Boyle mentions 'Irish rebel culture' as a phenomenon of the past decade, in reality Irish social and political awareness, as well as Irish nationalist and/or republican identities have been prominent features of the Irish diaspora in Scotland and in other centres with a history of Irish immigration since the nineteenth century. The strength or manifestations of these vary in time and context but research shows that identities that challenge dominant British interpretations and representations have long been present amongst the Irish in Scotland.

Although the days of mass meetings, demonstrations and activities in relation to Irish nationalism are decades gone from the Irish scene in Scotland,[12] resistance against loss of Irishness and the assertion of diverse historical perspectives and understandings from the mainstream can take other forms. The clearest public evidence of this is manifest through singing Irish songs that reflect and resonate with themes around Irish historical events and patriotic personalities that are ultimately concerned with challenging British colonialism in Ireland. The remaining part of this chapter reflects on elements of historical and political Irishness uniquely existing as a significant aspect of Celtic supporter culture.

History, political identities and football

Most football clubs reflect facets – economic, social, religious, cultural, symbolic, ideological and political – of prevalent and ascendant features of the wider society that they inhabit. Although all football clubs and their fans are distinctive in their own terms, to a greater or lesser degree most share the ideas and identities that govern and reflect for example, widespread and established religious, ethnic and state identities as well as in relation to the prevalent ideologies of the national mass media and relevant political landscape. In such a terrain having or acquiring a collective identity that deviates markedly from the relevant central and dominant socio-cultural tendencies is something that creates and constitutes an unconventional and

12 Bradley in The Irish Parading Tradition: Following the Drum. Ed T G Fraser, pp. 111-128, 2000

nonconformist distinctiveness for a football club and its support.

Many countries have examples of such clubs. The most relevant parallels to Celtic drawn from the likes of Barcelona (Catalonia/Spain), St Pauli (Germany) and Athletico Bilbao (Basque country/Spain) demonstrate that intense social and political experiences, rationales, awareness and identity contribute to a 'differentiation' that is fundamental to the spirit of these football clubs and which makes them stand out from the majority. Such clubs are frequently part, a demonstration or a reflection, of alternative political identities (often leftist or/and socialist or/and alternative nationalist in orientation) that are at variance with those that dominate at the wider state level and that are reproduced or manifest as ethos, ideology and identity.

Physical markers of distinctiveness can be manifest as club colours, flags and emblems. More significantly such individuality emerges as a result of origins, geographical area of club location and from where its support arises, an encompassing of minority ethnic, national and religious identities, the person or people who gave a club birth and/or, a result of events during the course of a club's history. Although manifestations of each club's political character can vary, chiefly in relation to the relevant climate and context, this can be a definitive feature of a club and its support. Of course, change can take place with regards any institution socially constructed and conceptualised, but this would generally occur as a response to social, cultural, economic and political conditions, including new ownership. If such change takes place then the relevant club would for many people cease to exist, forthwith surviving even flourishing as something else: albeit possibly with the same name and location but as a new creation markedly distinctive from its former self.

Understanding the uniqueness of Celtic requires us to reflect on the vast majority of its support being part of the multi-generational Irish diaspora in Scotland: a factor that in itself makes Celtic a distinctive institution in the space that is British professional football. This multi-generational Irish diaspora in Scotland is largely cut off in society from positive and informative representations of their past family and community histories 'by a series of absences from spaces of cultural reproduction, in education, memorials and popular culture more widely'. As Hickman has demonstrated elsewhere with regards the Irish-descended in England, for the multi-generational community of Irish descent in Scotland knowledge of their cultural background in Ireland is partly erased through the state education system. Added to this we should also acknowledge exposure to the media and its role as a primary source of information and knowledge, shaped largely by British/Scottish centric specifics and contexts.

However, just as the family unit can be viewed (as with the Banbury research) as a counter cultural influence in relation to the acquisition of a different perspective on amongst other things, the centuries-long Brtitish-Irish colonial and anti-colonial struggle, the Celtic football environment is a 'diaspora space' that has long provided this community with alternative narratives that challenge British versions of Britain's military, political, economic and cultural participation in Ireland. In a communal and public sense, as with many in the wider community of Irish descent, much of the character of the Celtic support reflects interpretations and positions more akin to the assortment of Irish nationalist thinking that exists, rather than the more dominant colonialist and British unionist ones more frequently reproduced in the wider society, particularly through Scottish/British families, communities, education and media.

In addition, as far as Celtic is concerned, political awareness and identities are not solely limited to Irish-related affairs. Since at least the 1970s (though as the chapter on Michael Davitt shows and Celtic's history reflects, these concerns go back to Celtic's earliest days), much of the Celtic support has been partly characterised by 'alternative' notions and identities with regards other ethnic, national and political conflicts. Amongst the causes noticeably sympathised with, promoted or supported within the confines of the Celtic support during this time, have been those of black South Africans (particularly anti-Apartheid and pro-ANC), Basque separatists, Nicaraguan Sandinistas, Catalan nationalists and the Palestinian cause against the perceived colonialism and hegemony of the Israelis. Consciousness concerning, and/or support for these causes is often manifest amongst fans through dressing in specific clothing (t-shirts), waving flags and wearing various scarves and badges, as well as within the narratives of numerous Celtic fanzines, websites and other supporter discourses, including through music and song. At a club level in 1968, Celtic, under the chairmanship of Robert Kelly, refused to travel to play in the then Soviet Bloc because of the invasion of Czechoslovakia by Warsaw Pact (controlled by the Soviet Union) countries. On this occasion Celtic showed its moral support for the Czechs and Kelly stated that such 'things for Celtic [are] more important than money'.[13]

Just as Louise in the Banbury interview group spoke of having an unusual opportunity to embrace 'her history' by watching the film 'Michael Collins', many within the Celtic support experience and consume not only standard, typical or dominant state-media education and information, but in addition, alternative forms of knowledge and understanding that speak to them about elements of their own pasts. A range of interviews and other evidence clearly demonstrates that for a substantial number of the multi-generational Irish community in Scotland, particularly amongst the Celtic support, contemporary films – often non-mainstream – like Michael Collins, but also, Bloody Sunday, In the Name of the Father, Some Mother's Son, The Wind that Shakes the Barley and Hunger are avidly viewed and seen as more reflective of personal, family and community ethnic histories and also more objective and/or accurate accounts of 'what really happened'.[14]

Apart from clothing, literature and discursive interests etc, it might be argued that alternative Irish memories, histories, narratives, likings and relevant identities are most clearly witnessed in the music and songs that have since the foundation of the club characterised the Celtic support. In beginning to understand this culture it should be noted that in Britain, some Manchester United, Aston Villa, Liverpool, Arsenal and Everton supporters for example know and also sing Irish, often 'rebel' Irish, songs. Indeed, this has occasionally been witnessed by Celtic fans when visiting the relevant cities: an experience generally explained by virtue of some Manchester United, Aston Villa, Liverpool, Arsenal or Everton fans having an Irish background, heritage and cultural identity and drawing on this when socialising

13 Kelly 1971, p. 118

14 Liberation struggles, particularly when significantly charactersed by armed uprisings, are morally complex and related ideas and opinions have numerous layers involved in their understanding. Historically and contemporaneously, they are also highly contested affairs. Nonetheless, it is clear via research conducted by the editor on several projects involving both Celtic supporters and others with Irish ethnicity, including the Irish 2 Project, that alternative and often oppositional ideas exist with regards the British-Irish colonial struggle from those that frequently dominate in mainstream society.

with Celtic supporters. However, this is highly fan specific and is a reflection of Celtic supporters meeting other like-minded Irish-descended football fans from areas of high Irish migration, in circumstances generally conducive to such micro communications, experiences and expressions. In this sense these Irish-descended fans of other clubs exist as individuals or in small groups and their Irishness is relatively privatised, not visibly or vocally represented as part of a club's fan culture and is usually, as indicated in the Irish 2 Project interviews for England, a reflection of family and individual learning and experiences.[15]

The situation in Scotland differs in that the Irish origins and foundation, history and contemporary identities of Celtic and its support are unique, not only compared to any football club in England but also within the Irish sporting diaspora worldwide. Celtic and its supporting community's Irishness has no parallel in the world of professional sport. For this reason there is no football culture in Britain where a defining aspect of its individuality, distinctiveness and existence is Irish, and where identity is expressed in the collective and communal act of singing Irish songs, sometimes of an anti-colonial 'rebel' variety. As part of the history of the Irish community in Scotland and as with almost all sorts of similar events of their time, such songs would have been sung at the first meetings that formed and established Celtic, and they continue to characterise the Celtic support today.

Many popular Irish tunes, songs and ballads reflect a wide array of aspects of Ireland's anti-colonial struggle against invasion, conquest and plantation on the part of England from the twelfth century and subsequently Britain – England and Scotland – mainly post-1603/1707. These rebel and revolutionary songs refer to a struggle for Irish liberation and independence. They are listened to and sung by the Celtic support and reflect an alternative reading and interpretation of individuals, groups and events in Irish-British history from those excluded, or referred to, via British school education, the military-political complex and media. In many ways such readings are unsurprising as to a large extent the existence of an Irish community in Britain is a direct result of the centuries-long colonial problem between Ireland and Britain. Many thousands of people of Irish descent

15 In Celtic Minded 2 Joe Horgan notes how his support for Birmingham FC could not be expressed in Irish terms while he envied how Celtic fans could do this as individuals and as a collective. Horgan says that his club were not Irish in relation to 'community, family, background, heritage, identity, songs, culture, colours or social or political preferences'.

in Scotland come together and express these alternative identities in the context of the culture that surrounds Celtic Football Club.

There are many different kinds of 'rebel' songs, their variety infused with contexts and narratives relating to poverty, love, family, death, despair, celebration and aspirations. Many can be categorised in terms of the periods they refer to, the patriots and events reported and the information they contain and convey. As alternative accounts of the historical cleavage and conflict, they can be defiant, joyous, thought-provoking and celebratory: they can also refer to the sacrificing, defending and/or taking of human life.

So for example, the song 'Grace', a love song about Grace Gifford marrying 1916 Proclamation signatory Joseph Mary Plunkett in Kilmainham Gaol the night before he was executed, differs in tone and content from Crossmaglen, a song celebrating the armed Republican volunteers that made that part of Ireland so difficult for British soldiers during the period of the recent Troubles. Different also is the Fields of Athenry, a well-known love song with its context of the Great Hunger as a consequence of that aspect of British colonialism in Ireland and Sean South of Garryowen, a ballad that remembers an armed attack on British/ RUC military barracks in the late 1950s. Rebel songs vary in their laments for people who have sacrificed their lives in the past (Robert Emmet, Wolfe Tone and Terence MacSwiney) or the near present (the ten hunger strikers of 1981), about uprisings in 1798 (Kelly the Boy from Killane), 1867 (Down by the Glenside) or 1916 (Off to Dublin in the Green/Merry Ploughboy), about defence of people, villages and towns under attack from British military personnel (Irish ways & Irish laws) and about attacking those same forces of perceived oppression (Boys of the Old Brigade). Others, like A Nation Once Again, On the One Road and Only Our Rivers Run Free are aspirational in their intentions.

Some of these songs as well as many others have been in the Irish charts over the past forty years. In these songs themes can be viewed as related or similar while the tone and the contemporary relevance and meaning varies with context and time: they also represent contested terrain. Depending on knowledge, understanding, moral standpoint and political perspective, sometimes songs from the distant past will be seen differently from those that refer to contemporary events and thus as worthy or unworthy of celebration. Nonetheless in some manner countless Irish songs, rebel or otherwise, address or refer to the anti-colonial struggle against perceived British imperialism in Ireland. In general they encompass or encapsulate a sense of Irish freedom and liberation from centuries-long British colonialism.

Since the birth of the club and as an important part of the Irish diasporic community in Scotland and beyond, Celtic supporters have collectively sung Irish rebel songs. This has evolved at varying family and community gatherings as well as publicly whenever Celtic play or privately on the many more occasions where and whenever supporters gather. As Warfield and Daly note, historical-ethnic-cultural-political songs have characterised the Celtic support throughout its life.[16]

In the same way that the Irish 2 Project recognises not only 'alternative' Irish identities from those of mainstream British/Scottish/English ones, but also identifies how family and community can be seen as additional, and alternative forms of education and knowledge regarding Irish history and politics, so also the Celtic supporting environment provides a site for learning, cross-generational communications, a sharing of collective memories, histories, alternative understandings and identities in relation to several ethno-cultural and political conflicts and struggles: none more so than Ireland, the country where most of them have their ethnic origins.

Conclusion

Diaspora spaces include by definition peoples with different cultural backgrounds. For those whose difference is marked by visibility, for example skin colour or clothing, or by audibility, including language or accent, these cultural differences are acknowledged (positively or negatively) by the majority. They may indeed be over-determined in the case of assumptions made on the basis of skin colour. Min and Kim describe the painful but

16 Warfield & Daly 2008

gradual establishment of an ethnic identity amongst second generation Asian-American professionals who had managed to hide their ethnic culture and 'non-white' characteristics during their early school years but were not allowed to do so in college.[17] But for 'white' groups raised and educated in Britain whose language patterns have become almost indistinguishable from the 'white' majority, such cultural difference is unrecognised. For many people, 'whiteness' signifies sameness with the 'indigenous' English/Scottish/British mainstream.

Yet within the diaspora space of Britain a significant 'white' minority population has not shared the political and historical understandings of the British-origin majority. These different and sometimes oppositional views have been contained by the exclusion of knowledge in the public sphere and its encapsulation within the private domestic sphere. Such memories cannot be erased altogether. They re-emerge through the connections people make about the relationship between their individual, family and national identities.

Second generation Irish people in Banbury took as their starting point family stories, closer to the oral history tradition of Nora's 'milieux de memoire', which he describes as 'unselfconscious, commanding, all powerful, spontaneously actualising'.[18] However they also felt a need to place these stories within a wider national picture so that 'lieux de memoire' in the form of secondary academic and media historical accounts were being actively sought in their adult lives. Although several expressed interest in pursuing family history through genealogy, it was the broader political context that attracted them most. This group of 'English-born Irish' or 'Irish-English' people strengthened their sense of a shared national heritage by an individual search process.

The sharpened awareness of their national past highlights the 'unfinished business' of de-colonisation of Ireland, both in traumatic memories of the violent accomplishment of partial independence in 1916-22 and in the re-ignition of the Troubles in the north of Ireland after 1968. Mary Lennon, Marie McAdam and Joanne O'Brien reviewed the lifestories of Irish-born women in Britain in Across the Water:

17 Min and Kim 2000

18 Nora 1989, p. 7

A sense of our own history is very strong amongst Irish people in a way which people in Britain often find mystifying. Most women we talked to felt this. The need to locate ourselves historically also appears to be reinforced by living over here and confronting that lack of information which so many British people have about Ireland and also, about their own history.[19]

Those who are born and raised in Britain inevitably encounter elements, if very muted, of 'an imperial mentality' that has 'penetrated everyday life, popular culture and consciousness'. The authors of the Parekh Report argue that this too remains an unresolved issue.

It remains active in projected fantasies and fears about difference, and in racialised stereotypes of otherness. . . There has been no working through of this collective imperial experience.[20]

Perhaps the clearest indication of this is in the different historical memories retained within families. What distinguished all but one of the respondents from their English neighbours in Banbury was an empathetic response to war and suffering in the Northern Ireland 'troubles' and a willingness to educate themselves about the underlying causes of the violent incidents presented in the media. They had access to different sources of historical memory that challenged the censorship and propaganda which produced a hegemonic belief in Britain that the 'problem' was not a well established colonial one, and further, was the inability of two religious tribes to live peacefully together, which necessitated the peacekeeping input from even-handed, justice-loving Britain.

Such censorship and propaganda is clearly vigorously challenged (in terms of the worldwide Irish diaspora) by those from the multi-generational Irish communities in west-central Scotland who incline towards the various forms and genres of Irish rebel music, song and culture, especially manifest in the Celtic supporting environment. The culture around Celtic is a site of struggle for ethnic and political identities that provides the Irish-descended in Scotland with a space to express and celebrate their Irishness, to resist hostility against Irishness in Scotland, and to remember people and events that have partly

19 Lennon, McAdam and O'Brien 1988 p. 13

20 Parekh Report, Runnymede Trust 2000 pp. 24-25

shaped who they are, why they are, and where they are. Celtic allows those of Irish descent in Scotland a sense of empowerment difficult to acquire in other spheres of Scottish life. The findings of the Irish 2 Project along with knowledge and understanding of the identities of the Celtic support challenge notions of assimilation amongst the offspring of Irish migrants in Britain and point to the need for more nuanced understandings of 'white' diasporic identities.

A study of the Irish-descended in England: with reference to the Irishness of Celtic supporters in Scotland*

MARY J HICKMAN, JOSEPH M BRADLEY,
BRONWEN WALTER, SARAH MORGAN

Introduction

Brubaker has argued that when considering racial, ethnic or national groups it is not sufficient to refer to them as socially constructed entities: what is required is a linking of macro-level outcomes with micro-level processes. In other words, we need to be able to specify how and when people identify themselves, perceive others, experience the world, interpret their predicaments and orient their actions in racial, ethnic or national terms.[1] The research presented here is based on data collected as part of the Irish 2 project that examined processes of identity formation amongst the second and third generation Irish population in England and Scotland.[2] The findings can be deemed insightful with regards an exploration and understanding of the otherwise unrecognised and marginalised as well disparaged and vilified Irishness of many Celtic supporters in Scotland.

The Irish 2 project focuses on a group of people often perceived to have assimilated within multi-ethnic Britain but who

* Some of the material for this paper arises from research conducted by the authors for a paper published in Scottish Geographical Journal in 2002, to whom acknowledgement is given.

1 Brubaker, 2001

2 An ESRC-funded research project 'The Second-Generation Irish: A Hidden Population in Multi-Ethnic Britain' (reference number: R00023836); see [www.apu.ac.uk/geography/progress/Irish2]

have recently been recognised in the public domain as a distinct constituency. In the case of the second and third generation Irish, their white skin, local accents and assumed cultural similarities have been taken to reflect the reality of a population easily assimilated to the 'white' English/Scottish/British majority.[3] Consequently most reference to the Irish in Britain is to those who were born in Ireland, the first generation migrant community, assumed to be distinguishable by their accent and place of origin.

However, some of the assumptions of white ethnic homo-geneity in Britain have been under critical review by numerous academics in recent years.[4] In addition, the Commission for Racial Equality published a report on discrimination and the Irish community in Britain,[5] establishing Irish racialisation, social disadvantage and discrimination. Three years later, the Runny-mede Trust published The Report on the Future of Multi-ethnic Britain.[6] This was a landmark commentary on a number of counts, one of which was that its analysis of minority ethnic groups bridged the black/white binary for understanding racial and ethnic exclusion in Britain:[7] it featured data and commentary on the Irish and Jewish populations in particular. The introduction of an Irish category to the ethnic origin question in the 2001 British Census was another landmark, albeit a problematic one, in marking the distinctiveness of the Irish component of the British population and diversity within whiteness. (The form of the question was not as recommended to the Office of National Statistics by those who sought the inclusion of an Irish category for second, third and subsequent generation Irish, see Walter, 1998.)

3 See Modood, 1996; Goulborne, 1998

4 See for example, Brah, 1996; Lewis, 1998

5 Britain Hickman and Walter, 1997

6 Parekh, 2000

7 See also Modood et al., 2002.

8 For example, see Harding and Balarajan, 1996

To some extent recognition of the problematic experiences and positionings of many of the Irish-born has led to a reconsideration of post-first generation Irish communities. For example, data on the health of the Irish in Britain noted the cross-generational impact of health penalties such that the second generation experience levels of poor health and excess rates of mortality compared with the British population that cannot be explained by class or age.[8] Two surveys of second generation teenagers in the 1980s highlighted the importance of Irish identifications for this group. In Philip Ullah's studies over 75%

of his sample of second generation teenagers in Birmingham self-identified as either 'half-English, half-Irish' or as 'mainly Irish'.[9] He concluded that the second generation Irish thought they belonged to a group who were viewed as of low status. Ullah said:

> I found that anti-Irish prejudice was widely experienced, and that questions relating to identity formed a major issue in the lives of many of these people. It was clearly not the case that they had been assimilated to a greater extent than other minorities, or that they had escaped the many problems associated with second-generation youth.[10]

Ullah argued that because they are (predominantly) white, second generation Irish could if deemed necessary, use the strategy of 'psychologically leaving their group' (consciously or unconsciously), thus distancing themselves from situations likely to reveal or emphasise their Irishness and the anticipated resultant unpleasantness, awkwardness, stigma and problems. It is by making use of such analysis that we can begin to uncover some of the long term negative social, cultural, political and religious consequences that arise from the problematisation of Irishness within and around Scottish football, as well as beyond in wider society.

As a consequence of the problematising of Irishness in Scotland, over several generations this has resulted in a frequent denial, evasion and privatisation of their ethnic background and heritage by many of those of Irish descent. Such actions are a consequence of specific social, cultural and political contexts and wider socialisation processes. For instance, racial, ethnic and religious prejudice and opposition to Irishness can produce such actions and conduct. For those of Irish descent who deny, evade or privatise their Irishness (to a greater or lesser extent), such responses resonate with an endeavor to gain social acceptance in Scottish society, to evade detrimental labelling, social, cultural and political prejudice, and to acquire employment and avoid discrimination in the workplace. Such experiences have been added to in recent decades via the effects of prejudicial and discriminating discourses on the part of a Scottish sports media that negatively label Irishness in Scotland on the basis of

9 Ullah's studies, 1985 & 1990

10 Ibid, 1985, p.310

uninformed and prejudicial notions of 'sectarianism'. In this sense, a view dominates whereby Irishness is in effect frequently, mechanically and instinctively associated with a narrow concept of 'sectarianism' in Scotland. What can also be recognised in such discourses is a socialisation process that is designed – consciously or unconsciously – to form a national identity that emphasises Scottishness or Britishness and is bereft of esteemed public recognition of Irishness for the Irish-descended in Scotland.

In a wider sense, the idea of 'leaving the group' (to whatever degree desired) should be recognised as a contextualised response to social and cultural learning, knowledge, circumstances and experience. For example, the perceived need or want to leave, deny or ignore one's family and community history and heritage might not be as pressing or may not exist in other social settings. An argument utilised by many Scots-born Irish in discourses concerning social experiences in Scotland is that they would be/ are more readily accepted as Irish in Australia and the USA, but not in Scotland where such ethnic identification invites hostility. An additional point relevant to socialisation, and returned to later in the text, is that the strength of Irishness in a given area is affected by the immediate social and cultural environment experienced, particularly by the high or low number of people who share Irish origins and heritage in any given geographic locality.

Mary Hickman has argued that whereas education has been a prime way in which the public mask of Catholicism has rendered Irishness invisible in Britain, the family has often provided a counterpoint to the state school and its incorporating strategies of turning out young people who learn little or nothing about their family and community's Irish ethnicity and national origins or history.[11] Indeed, in a British context they more often than not learn an historical narrative that ignores, marginalises or opposes their Irish ethnicity, origins and history.[12] The family and local community play a similar role in Scotland of course, but there are other significant cultural influences within and beyond that are important for the survival, maintenance and celebration of ethnic Irish identity. In Scotland the narrative that is Celtic Football Club is one of the most compelling and obvious examples of a site and space for such resistance.

a view dominates whereby Irishness is in effect frequently, mechanically and instinctively associated with a narrow concept of 'sectarianism' in Scotland

11 Hickman, 1995

12 See Celtic Minded, pp. 59-80

The study discussed here is mainly concerned with the meanings and constructions of ethnicity by individuals of Irish descent in England and Scotland via the ramifications of the presence or absence of Irish ethnicities in political and public policy discourses and practices. This study challenges the assumptions of white homogeneity that predominated in the literature on ethnicities in Britain up until the late 1990s, by excavating the forms of Irish identification submerged by the hegemonic category 'white' in Britain. Second, it helps develop a framework for analysing the responses (or lack of responses) to the Irish option in the ethnic question of the 2001 British Census, by exploring the interpretations or narratives embedded in the responses of second generation Irish participants in the research. This chapter of Celtic Minded 3 mainly utilises work on the Irish in England, as revealed in discussion groups conducted in Banbury, London, Manchester and Coventry.

Identifications and positions of the second generation Irish

At the beginning of each of the discussions, participants were asked how they would identify themselves (they were also shown a copy of the 2001 ethnic question). A participant in one of the Banbury discussion groups was unclear about how he wanted to respond but very clear as to the dilemmas the question encapsulated for him (all names have been changed). Early in the research he signalled issues that were to arise many times in all locations.

> James: It is a question that has arisen, because I have been cornered almost, are you English or Irish? It reminds me that there was a bit in It Ain't 'Alf Hot Mum, the porter is asked by one of the soldiers, 'are you in favour of Indian independence or not?' and he said 'well it depends who I am talking to at the time'. It feels a little bit like that sometimes. It's like an England–Ireland football match, who do you support? I normally support Ireland, is that just an Englishman wanting to support the underdog, it is difficult isn't it?

The form of the census question with its sub-categories of 'British', 'Irish' or 'Other' under the conglomerate category of 'White' echoed the challenge faced by many second, third and subsequent generation Irish people when giving voice to their ethnic, social and cultural distinctiveness in their daily lives. Several themes were regularly alluded to by participants including: the challenge from English and Scottish people when an Irish-descended person differentiated themselves from 'the English/Scottish/British'; comparison with the situation of other minority ethnic groups; reference to the strategy of varying self-presentation according to context or to the people being addressed; reference to sporting allegiances as a way of gauging 'who you really support' (and therefore 'are'); also the sometimes derision with which claims of 'being Irish', by people with English and Scottish accents, can be greeted by some people in Ireland; and the insistence of not being English/Scottish/British primarily because of differences in upbringing.

A variety of identifications were voiced by the participants from Banbury and broadly these are represented by five different positionings: 'being English'; 'not being English/British'; 'being Irish'; 'being half-Irish and half-English/British'; and 'being local'. These are identifications that individuals can hold at any one time, but it is also clear that individuals can move in and out of them over time or juggle simultaneously a number of different positionings. Each positioning is in turn a hybridised identification. We are not arguing that these positionings represent a continuum along which it is possible to chart the degree of assimilation of an individual or group, rather at any one time or in a particular context or at a particular point in the life cycle, one of these points of identification may represent the narrative that an individual may utilise in response to the question 'are you Irish or English (or Scottish)' or as a response to their difference being denied or rendered problematic. The problematising of being Scots-born Irish for many Celtic supporters in Scotland is a case in point.

On 'being English' and on 'not being English/British'

There was a small number, all in Banbury, that represented themselves as 'being English', which also suggests that issues relating to the numerical and cultural 'strength' of local multi-generational Irish communities can be important. In this sense, the propensity to say, or have the 'confidence or knowledge' to answer 'Irish', if one comes from an Irish background and lives in Coatbridge, Glenboig, Hamilton, Dumbarton, Greenock, Port Glasgow or parts of Glasgow such as Govanhill, Kings Park, Toryglen or Castlemilk for example, would be different from Banbury where Irishness is not as prominent a feature as it is in these parts of west-central Scotland. These Banbury 'Irish' were positioned in comparison with people who primarily addressed their identity in terms of the impossibility of 'being English' or 'being British'. Those who said they were 'English' were initially clear in choosing their identity but, ultimately, in conversation these seemingly straightforward declarations were qualified in various ways. For example,

> 'if I am with Irish people I will mention it [I am Irish]'; or
> 'I always stipulate I am English. . . where there is an Irish presence, then I would raise the point, and talk about how I am half Irish'.

Some of those who said they 'felt' English contextualised their selection, by referring to negative experiences as children when they became aware that as members of a second generation: 'You are not as Irish as everybody else who is Irish;' or: 'When we were younger we termed ourselves as plastic Paddies, half there but not quite'. These caveats reveal carefully calibrated decisions about when to declare an Irish background. They also demonstrate concerns about the authenticity of claiming to be Irish when this is not accepted by 'everybody else who is Irish' and clearly locates the non Irish-born Irish community in Britain differently to the Irish-born.

One man, Kieran in Banbury described why he would select English or British as his identification. He revealed that his motive to be identified as English might stem from a desire to distance himself from anti-Irish jibes as a child as well as a distancing from an Ireland, which had 'rejected' his father who had been in the British Army during the Second World War. In contrast, one man in Coventry who identified himself as a 'Coventry kid' and as Irish, of which he commented 'the only true "Coventry kid" is the man with a shamrock in his turban', had the following to say about not being English:

> Patrick: I find I can't throw any allegiance behind England whatsoever, although I do feel I am a member of the wider community, including the Scots, English, Welsh, Irish and Asians . . . I think the most important thing, although we don't often admit it, or look at it hard enough, or ask hard questions about what it means to be English. But, an essential component part of being English is being white. The lad up Friars Hill road stays an Asian, regardless of wherever he is born. If he is born in Coventry and wears a turban he is a 'Paki' or an Asian, he carries a certain Asian identity regardless of his birthplace. Afro-Caribbean people remain West Indians, Jamaicans regardless of their birthplace. English for me seems caught up with being white at the moment, Cliff Richard was born and raised in India, and has no problem at all selling himself as an Englishman does he? Although it might be nice to be English in the future, I say until they want the Asian, I don't want the English.

Later in the same discussion a woman described how a tutor on her nurses' training course identified her Irishness by her name and 'he was absolutely disgusted'. In response to her, Patrick gave an account of how, when he got an apprenticeship in the local car factory, he was identified as an Irish Catholic. He was immediately subject to remarks such as 'how many nail bombs have you made'. His response was 'I didn't know which way to turn, what to say, I was 16 just, and I thought to myself is this how people really think of us'. So his apparent mature exercise of choice about being English or not takes on a different resonance as does his earlier description of how when he was 17–18 years old 'I tried to be English, I thought I am from England I must be English, it must be my nationality. I tried it a lot for a while, and it didn't fit properly, it felt like acting, 'rule Britannia', and I couldn't get any inner feeling about it at all'.

Patrick is effectively mobilising both a local identity and the Irish identity available to him amongst a number arrayed against 'being English' in order to exclude himself from an Englishness which is characterised by a set of practices around whiteness with which he does not want to be associated. He recognises that Englishness as an ethnic identity is mobilised to exclude Asians so he is mobilising Irishness to distance himself, because he is white, from this racialised 'discourse of Englishness'. He is simultaneously grounding both himself and the Asian 'lad up Friars Hill' into a local context. His act of solidarity can be fully understood in the context of his own experience of racialised verbal attacks for being an Irish Catholic when he was a young worker and in the light of his unsuccessful attempts 'to be English'. Juxtaposing the accounts of both Kieran and Patrick of their early experiences of anti-Irishness reveals how their different responses can be understood in terms of family background, local context, and political frameworks.

On 'being Irish'

Participants in the discussion groups characterised 'being Irish' in two main ways, both of which related to their early developing awareness of 'difference'. As children, either they observed responses of people they took to be English to their parents, which marked the family's difference, or they became aware of differences in cultural practices, by visiting or staying in friends' homes or by observing others in the neighbourhood. These cultural practices became what they associated as distinctively 'Irish' and what they often celebrated. For some people both these processes occurred, sometimes intertwined. A discussion in one of the Manchester groups illustrates this. One man spoke of his own feelings about being Irish and the impact of something his brother observed.

> Liam: I was very aware of it [being Irish], but I always felt intensely positive about it, and very defensive about it and my mum and dad. My brother had a story of when he was a little boy on the bus, the bus conductor said 'move along there, Paddy' in an unpleasant manner. My dad just looked at him, but it was a pivotal event in my brother's mind, he wanted to scamper up and kill this bus conductor, so I was really aware of being different.

The witnessing of incidents in which Irish-born parents and

grandparents experienced negative responses once identified as Irish (accent usually being the trigger) could have a searing impact. Audibility is the prime marker of Irishness in England, confirming the assimilationist assumption about Irish offspring.[13] However, as this extract demonstrates, children (and grand-children and beyond) can 'experience' the anti-Irish hostilities that may be generated in their parents and grandparents' everyday encounters.

In a later part of the discussion of the same group, observations were made about cultural practices. Here the participants discussed the social contexts in which they became aware of 'difference'. These individuals have grown up in areas where they met or went to school with people they identified as 'English'. Difference for them as children was marked by accent, artefacts, habits, atmosphere, opinions, food, hospitality and sociability. Awareness of how different they and their families were came about through their own observations, emotional responses and as a result of the comments of others.

> Liam: I was only about 6. My best friend at school, I went to his house, he lived in Stretford, he wasn't a poncy middle-class at all, but he was English. I was struck by how different the environment felt in his house to mine. I remember flags and emblems and things, it felt really weird to me. . . I was in the same lad's house when I was 13 when the first hunger strike was called off in 1980. I was starting to become aware of things then, and I remember the dad saying, why did they call it off, they should have let them all die. I remember the feeling of complete and utter revulsion. I was so annoyed.

> Eilish: One thing I noticed where my mum lives, we were the only ones that went out on a Sunday morning by car to mass. Everyone else was washing their cars, we were the only ones that went to mass. . . You are going to get a picture, a crucifix, a sacred heart, some ornament. Cooking, there is always cooking going on of some sort.

Liam's intense response to his friend's parents, their environment, and political views was not remarked upon by other group members. His remarks are politicised and form a rupture in this conversation which returned for several minutes to the

13 See Walter, 2000

'safety' of the Irish characteristic which is both celebrated and almost a cliché: in this case, the abundant hospitality that would emerge in the Irish household compared to an English one. Even a number of years into the peace process in Northern Ireland, the habits of steering clear of political discussion in public spaces can still have effects for people with Irish identities in Britain.[14]

Later in the discussion, the social spaces of pubs or music venues were cited as the places where a gregarious Irish culture was enacted in which people from an Irish background could 'find each other'. This need to search out places where Irishness and a communal sense of belonging could be expressed is discussed in terms of the advantages of being Irish. In a similar sense, despite frequent hostility and antagonism in the wider social and cultural setting, within the confines of the Celtic environment in Scotland Irishness can offer a degree of reassurance, confidence and sense of community and celebration: a place where like-minded people can 'find each other'.

'On being half-Irish and half-English/British'

A majority of participants in the English-based discussion groups struggled in one way or another with proportionality when responding to how they would identify themselves. In one of the Coventry groups, a woman tries to express her positioning, acknowledging as she does the extent to which she is within 'the grip' of official discourses and is frustrated by them:

> Tricia: I feel that I have only very recently been able to identify my Irish heritage in a positive way. Because, anything I have ever written down, they have never asked me what my cultural heritage was. I have been white UK, British, white European, nobody has ever asked me until recently, the recent [2001 British] Census. In social work, they are now incorporating Irish as a separate ethnic identity, which is completely new. So I feel really by and large formerly it has gone hidden, and people just guess and ask, people say I look Irish, but would just assume I was English most of the time. Most of my life I have felt between the two cultures, and consequently I can really identify with the English part of my life. As I am maturing, I have really come back and feel much stronger towards my roots, than I did in my 20s, and early 30s. I have started to realise how strong

14 Hickman, 2002

the Irish is in me, but I do feel between the two cultures and always have done I suppose.

A number of other people commented on how their identities changed as they got older and more confident, in most cases they were able to claim Irish identities in a way that had been difficult for them previously. This is a phenomenon that has been noted before and challenges assimilation assumptions.[15] This is particularly so in relation to relevant aspects of some hostile academic assertions that challenge Irishness amongst the second, third and fourth generation Irish in Scotland, or which ignores their existence altogether, a position that in itself can be considered bigoted and prejudiced.[16]

In the Manchester discussion group, people struggled for terms in which they can express what is to many the self-evident 'truth' of being, in Liam's words, 'a separate identity from Irish from Ireland, and British'. People struggling with proportionality generally spoke from a position of the relevance of 'British' as a civic identity, although they also used English as a term for this. The reference to not having 'any organisations' is an acknowledgement of the public invisibility of second and subsequent generation Irish people in Britain. As a counter to this, in a Scottish context, and distinct from any other Irish cultural organisations or related bodies, the importance of Celtic Football Club as a cultural resource for many Irish-descended can be understood and recognised: a resource where and when Irishness can become significantly less privatised, relevant and a community space and focus for celebration.

Partly related to Liam's point, what was also indicated in the English-based group interviews, was the extent to which the research invoked by the Irish 2 project was positively perceived as a public raising of issues previously only discussed within the family or in other 'Irish' arenas.

James: It is recognition, though, that is the main thing. I have found this tonight to be really interesting. The only other opportunity I get is if I am talking to cousins, who like me were born here [in England]. Then when you sit down and start talking to them about it, they understand, they know what you are talking about.

15 Lennon et al., 1988

16 At a conference held at the University of Stirling in January 1997, consideration was given to a number of pertinent social and political questions that focused on the historical and contemporary position of Catholics in Scotland. Apart from a small number of indigenous Scots, and others with origins in countries such as Poland, Lithuania and Italy, Catholics in Scotland largely originate from Ireland and relevant issues were expected to be a part of conference proceedings. Nevertheless, during the discussion, two academic professorial speakers expressed the view that the Irish in Scotland could be referred to historically but not contemporaneously. Only after a number of exchanges did one concede that discussants could talk about 'the ex-Irish' in Scotland. The Chair of the conference, as well as his supporting professorial colleague, offered a view that talk of the Irish in contemporary Scotland was illusory and that the greatest single immigrant grouping in society had 'ceased being Irish'. Along with several others, these academics have frequently published

Bradley has also found this in Scotland where numerous Celtic supporters interviewed have frequently stated; 'I've never been asked these things before', 'This is the first time I've been able to say what I feel' and, 'it's good to know other people feel the same way – I've always felt so isolated'. In one of the Banbury discussion groups, one interviewee clearly showed an incipient desire to have Irishness publicly recognised. This yearning additionally underlines many of the narratives of despair reported by Celtic supporters concerning their Irishness not being legitimately accepted and recognised, or where it is labelled and besmirched by negativity. Indeed, these Celtic supporter narratives reflect a strong perception of Irishness being frequently attacked, particularly by other football fans and by many from within the Scottish sports media.

On 'being local'

In the English groups interviewed identifying with a local area emerged both as a way of avoiding identification with Englishness or Britishness (although the latter was seen as relevant as a legal identity and as representing citizenship), as a way of describing being half-and-half in the absence of a category to describe that, and as a resolution of the problems of invisibility and the need for recognition. A participant in Manchester put it like this:

> Liam: I wrote Irish Mancunian [on the Census form]. The reason for that is I identify very strongly with Ireland, I also identify very strongly with Manchester. I don't identify at all with the notion of Britishness or Englishness.

In Coventry an exchange took place that encapsulated a common dilemma. With no public recognition of the specificity of an Irish background, children experience pressures not to stand out or have to explain what all these 'big green ribbons' or badges were that they were expected to wear on St Patrick's Day by their family.

> Tracey: . . .Coventry Irish usually I class myself as. But that has actually changed as I have grown older. I didn't go to a Catholic school, with my mum being disabled she couldn't take me. So I

Celtic supporter narratives reflect a strong perception of Irishness being frequently attacked, particularly by other football fans and by many from within the Scottish sports media

material that denies, ignores and marginalises 'the Irish' in Scotland. This denial of Irishness in Scotland is a frequent occurrence in the popular Scottish media and beyond reflecting a broad ideological position that is partly shaped via the legacy of Britain as one of the world's former great colonial powers, Scottish anti-Catholicism and a growing anti-Christianity in a rapidly secularising Scotland.

225

very much hated my name O'Gara when I was young, I really got picked on because of it. Especially at the time when all the bombing was going on, I remember my dad coming home from work saying quite a few things about it. I really hated my name then, but as I got older and became confident and sure about myself, then I really identified with being Irish. I suppose that happened when I was about 15/16: it has changed.

Confidence as an adult can lead to greater powers of self-assertion in terms of ethnic identity, both feelings about who they are and how they are prepared to express these identities change over time.[17] Events, circumstances, awareness and coming into adulthood are among the experiences that can often determine Irishness. Outlined here are the different identifications which British-born Irish people can either claim, utilise, or struggle to mould or represent what they feel, especially when asked or challenged to define their ethnic identity. There exist multiple positions from which the British-born Irish speak and how they are positioning themselves. All of these identifications represent positionings in terms of the national hegemonic domains of Scotland/England/Britain and Ireland. Many British-born Irish are at an intersection of two hegemonic domains of rootedness, nation, and authenticity with themselves, constituted by their family's past migrancy and their own duality located in particular places. Scotland/England/Britain is represented by birth, education, employment, locality and citizenship while Irishness fills the space occupied by many other features of identity, for example, distinctive Irish names, music, holidays, personal readings, social activities, musical tastes, affiliations and identifications, and of course in Scotland and beyond, being part of the culture around Celtic Football Club.

Pressures 'not to be Irish'

The contesting of Irish identities by others surfaced in all the discussion groups. As far as this research in England was concerned, and other investigations in Scotland confirm, most prevalent was a sense that nothing is done, or is largely unavailable, to support or encourage Irishness and that if an individual articulates an Irish identification, they meet resistance, sometimes

17 See Walter et al., 2002 for further analysis of this finding

to the point of argument and estrangement. This also raises questions about possible discrimination akin to that experienced by their Irish-born past relatives. In Banbury, Kieran gave an example of the pressure to conform to 'being English' in the work place. He identifies as English and British but explains the fall-out of someone being identified as British-born Irish at work:

> Kieran: . . . at work it came up in the last 6 months . . . They probe for one's weak point, they are PE teachers. Delia Cronin is in the office, and she bites all of the time, and I tell her please Delia don't bite. They found out that Delia is second generation Irish and they go on and on about 'you are English'. I got involved in that in explaining to them, actually I'm in the same situation. Oh OK, what do you say you are, 'I'm British', so in some ways it made it worse. It has raised an awareness about cultural backgrounds amongst the people there, and now they're talking about Irish, and Scottish and the rest of it.

Delia's 'bite' is something to be controlled. Kieran, sensitive, as someone of an Irish background who identifies as English might be, tries to control her impact himself; in fact sees this aspect of her as symbolising his distance from Irishness. She is what he is not. However, he gets caught up in the fall-out from the discovery that she is second generation Irish. Her colleagues' constant repetition to Delia that she is English is a way of attempting to exert control and regain the secure landscape of homogenous white Englishness. In Coventry, one man described the context in which he thought the second generation were struggling over their identities in the following way:

> Tom: there is no positive reinforcement of that [Irishness] in this culture. I imagine it is the same for black people when they are growing up in England, they wish they were white, stuff like that. . . they have not really been encouraged by this society. . . I get a very 'what do you mean, you are Irish?' Like as if I am stupid or have got a problem. So you don't want to make an issue of it, I find I don't want to make an issue out of it. I think what is the point of getting into arguments and hassle, things like that, so I don't think it is an easy thing to do.

This man identifies what others recount as their experience, that there is no support in the institutional structure in Britain for Irish identities, and under pressure about their identities some choose to maintain a low profile. In Scotland the experience of facing comments about Irishness can't simply be put into a category of feeling that one is 'stupid or you have a problem', although this can be part of the experience. It is also likely that for a person of Irish descent in Scotland, who esteems and prioritises their Irishness, that they will encounter suspicions and accusations that reverberate with popular and dominant notions of what in recent decades has been constructed as 'sectarianism' in Scotland – particularly by the Scottish media. In this sense being Scottish-born Irish has been ideologically constructed as oppositional, problematic and is widely experienced by those of Irish descent as being unacceptable in much of wider Scottish society. For many of these Irish in Scotland, this experience is exacerbated and intensified if support for Celtic is also part of their Irishness.

being Scottish-born Irish has been ideologically constructed as oppositional, problematic and is widely experienced by those of Irish descent as being unacceptable in much of wider Scottish society

Discussion

This analysis uses the self positionings and voices from amongst second generation Irish people in England and the interrelated ways in which they are positioned by others to demonstrate similar issues that exist for many Scots-born Irish. Work carried out by Bradley reflects this as well as numerous other similar issues for this community in Scotland. Whiteness can also be seen here as limited in power as a guarantor of the discourse of Englishness (and Britishness and Scottishness) when disrupted by white people 'born and bred' in England who claim strong allegiances to Ireland: the boundaries of Englishness are not always determined by colour but are also predicated on notions of cultural belonging which do not allow any hybridised identifications.

Throughout the Irish 2 project there was substantial and consistent evidence that the second generation Irish are positioned as having to, amongst others things, defend charges of inauthenticity from those pressuring them to be English, Scottish or British and from denying their Irish identifications. From the English part of our work, it seems that England cannot countenance any dilution of whiteness or weakening of the hegemonic subject and thus also insists on their 'qualified' (?) Englishness. This might be seen as similar to Scotland, but additionally the Scottish context also introduces stronger notions of religion and a seemingly greater awareness of politics and history in relation to the troubles that have evolved in the North of Ireland as a result of the conquest, plantations and incorporation of Ireland into the British Empire. The hegemonies we are discussing are those which surface when people identify themselves, perceive others, experience the world, interpret their predicaments and orient their actions in racial, ethnic or national terms.

Some of the material here reveals the instability of any 'hard and fast' drawing of a colour line to explain patterns of acceptance and belonging in multi-ethnic Britain. The daily ruptures of it by white people born and brought up in England who assert a claim to differentiation, to possibly being British (more rarely English) by birth and nationality, but to having Irish identities and heritage, or to 'being Irish', are resisted strongly by English friends or work mates/colleagues. Their allegiances to Ireland are not acceptable and disturb the universe of white Englishness. These ruptures reveal the limitations of whiteness and the boundaries of Englishness and de-authorise the hegemony of Englishness from within the circle of whiteness. 'Visible' minority ethnic groups must stake a claim for full acceptance as British in a context where their 'difference' is designated/recognised 'on sight'; they are involved in a constant process of asserting their belongingness in a context which does not assume it. This exercise, reflecting the constant denial of the difference of people with white skins and 'English' accents who assert Irish identifications, reveals the weakness and vulnerability of Englishness and reproduces the positioning of intimate betrayer accorded the Irish within historical memory of British-Irish relations. Importantly, this research adds to understandings of the position of Scots-born Irish, particularly those from within the Celtic support that esteem and refuse to relinquish, hide or dilute their Irishness.

FAITH, HOPE, CHARITY & FOOTBALL

Was Shakespeare a Celtic Supporter?

Roisin Coll and Robert A. Davis

> Exit, pursued by a bear
> Shakespeare, The Winter's Tale, 3.3, 57.

In recent decades a fierce debate has taken place in Shakespeare studies over the nature and extent of William Shakespeare's supposed Catholic connections. Opinion has divided sharply in the assessment of Shakespeare's Catholic upbringing, the secret Catholic allegiances of his father and other family members, his likely association with a network of recusant Catholic households in the north of England and his coded expression of sympathy for persecuted English Catholics in his plays and poems.[1] No settled view of Shakespeare's Catholicism has emerged from this controversy (and it seems probable that Shakespeare's personal relationship to religious faith was uncertain and conflicted), but the critical focus on such an iconic literary figure has brought home to the British cultural establishment something that Catholics (both indigenous and immigrant in origin) in Britain have recognised for several generations: that the dominant narratives of identity, belonging and achievement in British culture have been for the last few centuries fundamentally Protestant ones, with Catholic affiliation and Catholic heritage routinely marginalised as the religious and ethnic 'other', deviating dangerously from a normative Protestant axis around which modern Britishness has maintained much of its manufactured cross-border coherence.[2]

[1] For a broad overview see R. Dutton, et al, (Eds), Lancastrian Shakespeare: Theatre and Religion. Manchester: MUP (2004); J. Pearce, The Quest for Shakespeare. London: Ignatius Press (2008)

[2] R. Wilson, Secret Shakespeare: Studies in Theatre, Religion and Resistance. Manchester: MUP (2004); P. Lake and M. Questier, The Antichrist's Lewd Hat: Protestants, Papists and Players in Post-Reformation England. New Haven, Conn: Yale University Press (2002)

Moreover, the frequently heated Shakespeare dispute of the last fifteen years has also demonstrated the extent to which the investment of British cultural identity in a Protestant conception of nation and people has survived the decline of the confessional state, enduring in an account of cultural attachment Alison Shell has tellingly called 'secularised anti-popery'.[3] If adherence to Catholic tradition – and to the broader popular beliefs and practices associated with day-to-day communal Catholic life – represents the superstitious Other from which the Protestant polity freed itself, then the onward post-religious advance towards enlightenment, progress and liberation, so firmly associated with being modern, is also irreducibly an anti-Catholic narrative, further underlining the status of Catholics and their culture (whether elite or vernacular) as alien and subversive.

In Britain the recovery of Shakespeare's Catholicism – the appreciation of his immersion in an older ceremonial worldview the sudden loss of which his writings at the very least question – compels a reappraisal of the character of that historic Catholicism more generally understood: the depth of allegiance it once commanded; the nature of its hold over the imaginations of its adherents; its permeation of the rhythms of daily behaviour; and also its unexpected post-Reformation survival amidst great persecution, in actions such as storytelling, oral transmission, underground literatures and those diverse activities of 'unregulated' memory and popular piety fashioned to preserve a legacy menaced by the constant threat of erasure.

Understanding of these hidden processes has been powerfully enriched as a consequence of the questions summarised at the outset of this essay. In consequence, assessing whether William Shakespeare was a Catholic or not has turned out to be less about examining Shakespeare himself and more about rediscovering the depths of a forgotten Catholicism, one quite deliberately consigned to the fringes of cultural recognition, to a shadowy domain of learning and devotion largely despised by mainstream English-speaking culture.[4]

The work of reclaiming Shakespeare's Catholicism, however that task might finally be concluded, has lent legitimacy to the exploration of a whole region of experience shared by minority

[3] A. Shell, Catholicism, Controversy and the English Literary Imagination, 1558-1660. Cambridge: CUP (1999), 9

[4] A. Shell, Oral Culture and Catholicism in Early Modern England. Cambridge: CUP (2007)

Catholic communities across Britain (including Irish, other migrant and indigenous) over many generations of isolation and hostility. The act of raising the question, focused as it is upon a touchstone of cultural excellence, has given permission for voices to be heard and loyalties to be explored that previously were shrouded in ignorance and suspicion. The complete revaluation of traditional Catholic identities in Britain beginning to emerge from this intervention teaches important lessons about the ways in which historic prejudices create frames of intellectual analysis and enquiry which persist long after the prejudices have themselves become outworn, and even officially disowned, in the centres of cultural production. The Catholic Shakespeare debate has revealed that even in those quarters where religious intolerance has for some considerable period been officially renounced, habits of thought and interpretation rooted in older, almost instinctive, anti-Catholic sentiments have gone on shaping some of the key terms of reference in which all sorts of literary, cultural and even ethnic discriminations continue to be made. [5]

At its mildest, this attitude of mind takes a condescendingly hierarchical view of Catholic culture as something eccentric and anachronistic, remote from the mainstream progression of British thought and ideas. In more strident forms, it assumes a genuinely aggressive anti-Catholic posture, hostile to the supposedly 'anti-modern' ideas and values to which Catholics habitually ally themselves and determined upon disembedding many of the social and cultural practices associated with historic Catholic communities from the religious beliefs and values out of which they originate.[6] It is acceptable, for example, for Catholics in Britain today (who come from native Scottish/English traditions but also from predominately immigrant ones) to be campaigning socialists wedded to the pursuit of justice and peace. It is not acceptable, however, for them to be campaigning socialists who are opposed to abortion, because secularised anti-popery perceives such a combination as illustrative of the icy grip of an outmoded illiberal theology on the Catholic mind. In the same vein, Catholics are free to support any football team they might wish, but should they seek to encompass that support in terms of a more comprehensive set of memories, principles, allegiances or experiences at variance with the approved formulae in which

[5] C. G. Pestana, Protestant Empire: Religion and the Making of the British Atlantic World. Philadelphia, PA: University of Pennsylvania Press (2009), 66-100

[6] R. J. C. Young, The Idea of English Ethnicity. London: Wiley Blackwell (2007)

contemporary footballing affiliations are authorised (mostly linked to approved class and regional identities), then once again they have simply manifested that regressive cast of mind for which their fellow-citizens have for centuries feared them.

Asserting the right to locate specific social, cultural and recreational practices in a broader context of heritage and belief has been a prominent theme in the expression of sporting loyalty in many national and regional settings. When seeking to understand, for example, the rivalry between Barcelona and Real Madrid, it has proved pivotal to appreciate the profound influence of their respective Catalonian and Castilian roots in shaping the destinies of the two great football institutions. Both teams are inextricably linked to the expression of ethnic, regional and linguistic identities, often in the most highly charged political terms. To suggest that these factors are somehow incidental to, or regrettably parasitical upon, the experience of the two teams – and of the intense competition between them – would be arbitrarily to decouple the expression of footballing loyalties from the narratives that accord such loyalties meaning and validity in the first place. [7]

Yet in the Scottish context, to argue that the experience of supporting Celtic Football Club resonates with a **Catholic** identity, and with the historic memories of a people and a faith implanted in that identity, prompts frequent derision, provoking levels of denunciation inseparable from the suspect, marginal perception of the broader Catholic heritage and its awkward relation to the patterns of contemporary mainstream Scottish and British cultural life. The repeated journalistic exhortations to Celtic and its support to detach themselves from an irrelevant and outdated past often masquerade as a simple, ethically high-minded call to reject sectarian bigotry (ethnic Irishness and partisan Irish nationalist politics are prominent in the mix as well, of course) in the name of civil democratic pluralism. In reality, however, these injunctions to the club and its fanbase repeatedly rehearse the age-old scorn of Catholic difference, its historically subversive associations and its departure from some of the dominant norms of contemporary secular society, which implicitly conceives itself as the post-confessional successor to the Protestant state that supposedly threw off the shackles of popery and priestcraft in

> The repeated journalistic exhortations to Celtic and its support to detach themselves from an irrelevant and outdated past often masquerade as a simple, ethically high-minded call to reject sectarian bigotry in the name of civil democratic pluralism

[7] R. Llopis Goig, 'Identity, nation-state and football in Spain: the evolution of nationalist feelings', Soccer & Society, 9.1, 2008, 56–63

the sixteenth and seventeenth centuries. To be rid of those older affinities and sentiments is, in effect, to put aside in its entirety the idea of any publicly-affirmed Catholic culture, acknowledging its ultimate incompatibility with the requirements of living harmoniously in a supposedly pluralist and non-religious society.

> In reality, however, these injunctions to the club and its fanbase repeatedly rehearse the age-old scorn of Catholic difference (and)its historically subversive associations

Against the backdrop of this prevailing climate of scepticism, recovering the legitimate continuities between faith and football in the experience of supporting Celtic is more than an act of misplaced cultural defiance. It is, instead, the positive articulation of the reciprocal relation between commitment to a football club and the embrace of a set of powerful values with a meaning and resonance radiating well beyond the confines of sport. Appreciation of these values neither diminishes football as a purely sporting pursuit nor denigrates alternative expressions of the possible linkages between football and identity. You do not have to be Catholic to support Celtic. You can fervently support football teams with roots and traditions extending well beyond the boundaries of sport in all sorts of other religious and non-religious directions. It does nevertheless unequivocally argue for acceptance that a vital element of the essence of supporting Celtic – emotional, communal and spiritual – originates in the historic experience of a Catholic culture which continues to impress itself on the story of the football club and the character of its fanbase. Certainly, values may be transgressed as well as upheld. Dispositions towards religious faith especially may shift, sometimes to the point of abandonment. Nevertheless, the imprint of that Catholic experience remains, supplying much of the symbolism of the club and its fortunes.

Symbolism that is familiar to, and embraced by, the Celtic fanbase, contributes to the anchorage of an identity that is shared not simply in Scotland, but around the world. For example, the emblem of a cross chosen for celebrating the club's centenary year, and still found on the neck of every current Celtic player and fan donning the official strip, is indicative of the club's recognition and avowal of a continued Christian heritage. So too the image of the Pope on a certain Celtic players' t-shirt, or a minute's silence for the death of Pope John Paul II, can be seen as meaning something to most of the Celtic support in a way that it does not to others in Scottish society. This Christian heritage was also movingly exemplified when the very private, yet simultaneously public, religious devotion of the late Celtic player, manager and coach, Tommy Burns, resonated with Celtic fans worldwide and – for a short while during a time of united mourning – gave permission for many openly to express their faith or revive their often suppressed Catholic allegiances. It was further evidenced in the language used in tributes to Burns – written, spoken and sung.

Hailed as a 'true Celt', Tommy Burns will forever be upheld as a Celtic role model, who embodied the club's historic identity in action and word, and whose Catholic faith was appreciated (if not always properly understood) as being central to both. The well-rehearsed journalistic demands for Celtic to repudiate any openly religious ties on the grounds of bigotry, sectarianism or broader 'cultural appropriateness' were exposed for what they were during this sad but incredibly symbolic episode in the club's recent history. Burns' faith and Celtic identity were inextricably linked and the positive contribution that this had made – and will continue to make – to the club, its history and identity, could not at that highly charged moment be easily denied or criticised, lest bigotry and prejudice be blatantly exposed for all to see.

In less exalted terms, Celtic supporters who regularly attend matches – domestic and European, home and away – often comment on their awareness of a unique 'spirit' that they claim unites them with fellow Celtic fans, and which contributes to a distinctive Celtic 'ethos'. This ethos, it is argued, is built on an understanding of shared values, steeped in the language and registers of a Catholic tradition. Articulating it has, on occasion, proven to be problematic, owing to the frequently hostile responses from those rejecting the concept. Those more confident in explaining and exploring it with 'nonbelievers' often rely on anecdotal evidence to support their claims. Accounts, for example, of an expansive, worldwide fanbase being drawn together in a small Spanish city for a UEFA Cup Final in 2003, and policing themselves to ensure that their fellow man (or woman) was safe, well and adhering to the unspoken but understood 'Celtic code of conduct', have been well-documented.

Compared with similar major sporting events, involving other

> Tommy Burns will forever be upheld as a Celtic role model, who embodied the club's historic identity in action and word, and whose Catholic faith was appreciated as being central to both

clubs from the English Premiership or SPL, the behaviour of the Celtic support stands out – it is, in fact, distinctive. While isolated incidents and individual behaviour will always make the headlines, and at times deserve wholesale reproach, the overwhelmingly positive and community-orientated dimension to the Celtic support (which is often ignored by the Scottish media) is arguably the continued legacy of a club that, from the time of its foundations, has had its values steeped in a religious tradition and world-view. Indeed, it is often from out of this same values-set that just condemnation of transgressors derives its moral force. Cynical attempts within the media to reject, ignore or dilute this fact have never been fully successful, owing to the unequiv-ocal belief of the majority of the Celtic support that this identity is something of lasting significance and an experience of which to be proud. The constant barrage of press accusations that the club's affiliations with the Catholic faith are nothing other than sectarian, coupled with the reaction that assertions of a religious affinity routinely excite in a febrile and uncertain secular culture, continue to raise questions about the authenticity of the supposed pluralism and inclusivity that contemporary Scotland is striving to achieve.

the overwhelmingly positive and community-orientated dimension to the Celtic support is arguably the continued legacy of a club that, from the time of its foundations, has had its values steeped in a religious tradition and world-view

Although the SFA is constantly defending its actions and responses – and its unswerving commitment to ensuring a just and tolerant Scotland in which to play football – Celtic fans might join with their spiritual forebear, Liam Shakespeare, in noting that, in this particular instance, perhaps 'the lady doth protest too much'. Ultimately, the considerable stretches of time separat-ing us from Shakespeare, compounded by the culture of suspicion and secrecy within which much of his work was crafted, makes it difficult for us to pronounce with any certainty on his sporting and religious loyalties. As this essay suggests, however, debating the question is less about providing definitive answers and more about allowing its presentation to create a space where previously occluded continuities between football, faith and cultural and religious identity can be openly affirmed and examined free of prejudicial prior assumptions. Only then can a complex society such as late modern Scotland justly proclaim itself as a multiple, heterogeneous polity that wants sincerely to welcome everybody.

'Sectarianism' and Catholic Schools

Joseph M Bradley

Sectarianism is an intensely disputed and often sensationalised matter in Scotland. This chapter explores an aspect of 'sectarianism' as it is frequently represented within Scottish society. There is little if any direct reference to Celtic or Celtic supporters included. Nonetheless, the Catholic religious and/or cultural identities of the vast majority of Celtic supporters and Irish immigrants in Scotland over the past 150 years is intrinsic to understanding ethnic and religious cleavage in Scotland. Amongst the topics that can be sub-headed as part of popular discourses about sectarianism is the subject of Catholic schools. This chapter reflects on facets of the debate concerning these schools.

In Scotland over the past thirty years or so, many people have learned to perceive and represent 'sectarianism' as an aberrant mentality based on outmoded religious prejudices. In its Scottish context sectarianism has been utilised as a concept to explain areas of Scottish life that in reality remain obscure, misrepresented, poorly understood, as well as intentionally and unintentionally disguised and concealed. Further, the dominant construction and perception of sectarianism largely derives from, and is a reflection of, many of the inherent related issues. In reality, as is often the case where and when prejudice is concerned, its currency in Scotland is connected to issues of social and cultural power as well as powerlessness. The way the term is commonly used, who is using it and in what context, and the manner it is popularly addressed, has arguably, purposely and inadvertently, often confirmed the lack of knowledge and understanding as well as prejudice, intolerance, narrow-mindedness and bigotry of numerous organisations, associations and individuals throughout Scottish society.

When talking about sectarianism it is uncomplicated and unproblematic for commentators to concentrate on football, a few songs not to the taste of various people, and street demonstrations and marches. Although these can partly say something about the subject, an overstated focus on them means that understanding the range of aspects that are part of Scotland's ethno-religious cleavage are largely superficial and fraudulent, as well occasionally as intrinsically prejudiced. In addition, this analytical narrowness does nothing to address the relative substantive issues that have in the past and does in the present affect society to its detriment.

In Scotland the term sectarianism has powerful connotations in terms of behaviour, beliefs and identities. The dominant language of sectarianism has, in much of the public mindset, helped establish tribes of bigotry on the opposite sides of a wall of ignorance: tribes that simply reflect each other's sectarianism as defined by their religious identity – often merely by the football team they support. The prevailing use of the word 'sectarianism' in Scotland is erroneous, essentially because it is catch-all and evasive and offers little towards understanding what is actually being described; varying degrees of ignorance, bias, prejudice, racism, discrimination, hate and intolerance. Apart from being a uniformed perspective, such an approach involves a privileged narrative that distorts much of the reality of these. The indolent overuse of the term sectarianism avoids penetration of the subject: including its historical origins, its manifestations, its consequences and its currency today. It also allows the ignorance, bias, prejudice, racism, discrimination, hate and intolerance of people and groups in Scotland to avoid being identified. The way the concept is currently used and its existing popular understandings can act to conspire in favour of dominant ideologies and identities that can in turn be laced with or characterised by the very same social and cultural attributes.

Since the 1970s media commentators have largely shaped

considerations and discourses of sectarianism. This divulges something about how the subject has evolved, how it has been popularly represented and reported, and how it is generally understood in society. Various people in the media in Scotland have largely defined sectarianism for public consumption: they have become the main source for learning what it is and what it means – and who is responsible for 'it'. This also informs us about that industry's role and focus in the current debate, considering that until around thirty years ago it had not shown any interest in addressing the topic while it was itself popularly known – at least among a section of the population – as a 'sectarian' and racist employer from where Catholics of Irish descent were largely excluded.[1]

Other commentators, political or otherwise, might be seen as having colluded in the media's inadequate and prejudiced definitions. This means that in the popular mind-set the true nature of anti-Irishness and anti-Catholicism will remain hidden in the face of something that purports to be the story of 'sectarianism' in Scotland. Socially and culturally its consequences will continue to disable and disempower individuals, families and communities, at the same time distorting enquiries, research and narratives, that in turn can never truly recover or reveal the what, why, where and when of the past (and their consequences for the present and future) in terms of ethnic and religious prejudice, bigotry and racism – in particular, in relation to how this has affected the minority Catholic community of Irish descent in Scotland.

As currently used the term sectarianism is an inaccurate and evasive expression. How it is perceived and comprehended depends on experience, knowledge, insight, and understanding. In turn, one's national, class, ethnic, religious roots and identities can affect these.

Likewise, the 'two sides of the same coin' argument rarely holds in relation to any conflict – for example, those that have a minority-majority context or that have an economic basis – and often this typology is in actual fact a reflection of a lack of knowledge about an issue, a way to avoid analysis and of course, a way to avoid accepting or apportioning much of the respons-

1 See Hugh MacDonald's chapter in Celtic Minded (2004) and also references to former Herald editor English-born Arnold Kemp. In a Guardian newspaper obituary the writer told how Kemp 'never forgave his Herald employers for furtively testing him for 'reliable' Protestantism', 15/9/02

ibility for the conflict concerned. Because the 'two sides' argument is seen as the standard diplomatic way to address and report sectarianism does not mean that it is the most trustworthy or accurate. Indeed, with regards a number of conflicts, it might be argued that this line of discourse is generally often propagated by those primarily responsible for the conflict concerned.

It is not surprising that the 'two sides' argument is powerful in Scotland. The superiority and domination involved in ethno-religious prejudice has long been a feature of Scotland: many people have either actively or passively conspired or colluded in, or accepted it, and it has been normalised. Others have accepted its normalisation because they were forced to: they kept their heads down, they didn't (or don't) know any better and what they knew was considered routine and typical. Power and powerlessness are crucial to understanding sectarianism. This power comes from events and ideologies whose consequences are embedded in the banal experiences of the everyday things that dominate and affect our inner and outer beings, as individuals and as part of the various communities people inhabit.

As an important sporting, social and cultural institution in society where understanding ethnicity and religious faith are intrinsic to history and identity, it is not difficult to see that as currently understood and used, the term sectarian is one that frequently intrudes or is imposed, when and where matters involving Celtic Football Club or its support are concerned. Few reports, documentaries or remarks that purport to explore or explain Celtic, especially those that anticipate attracting a significant number of viewers, listeners or readers, fail to use the term in a way that contrasts with what is customary stereotypical, conventional and sensational. In addition, few can achieve this without a stirring reference to Celtic's great city rivals Glasgow Rangers – and thus the 'two sides of the same coin' discourse is endorsed and advanced. When asked to comment on a newspaper story or take part in a television documentary, numerous contributors to this volume of essays have in the past become exhausted in trying to explore and explain ethnic and religious cleavage in Scotland employing a more challenging use of language, ideas and concepts that for them at least, more accurately and sincerely help address the issues at stake.

When I was asked to contribute to a BBC Scotland radio programme on 'sectarianism' several years ago, after twenty minutes of discussion the researcher admitted that the subject was actually much more complicated than she had first imagined. She added that the presenter, whom she was carrying out the research for, 'knew nothing about this subject anyway and just does what he is good at – presenting'. The main lines of enquiry from the researcher revolved around the familiar topics of football fans singing, flags, football hooliganism, disruption caused by contentious public parades and 'separate' schools. Although a limited medium that is essentially commercially driven, such programmes again essentially replicate dominant understandings and perceptions. In this light it becomes difficult to challenge prevailing beliefs, patterns of discernment and ignorant, racist or bigoted identities.

This chapter looks at ONE area of Scottish life where the term 'sectarian' is used ubiquitously. The first section reflects on those individuals or groups that traditionally and contempor-aneously share a particular understanding of the meaning of the term in the context of Catholic schools. The final part engages with a body of thought and some of the rationale for these schools that in fact opposes anything that purports to create or sustain the human constructions known as racism, bigotry, prejudice and 'sectarianism'.

The constant threat: perceptions of Catholic education

The Education Act (Scotland) of 1918 was passed while the country was pre-occupied with the outcome of World War I, and this may have prevented an immediate backlash occurring. It is also relevant that it was introduced by Robert Munro of the then declining Liberal party and passed into law by a coalition government. This meant that although Labour supported the Act, and thus consolidated or increased its support among Catholics, militant Protestants did not see the Party as being overly supportive of the Catholic community.

Nonetheless, with Catholics of Irish descent frequently being scapegoats for the harsh social and economic conditions occurring at the time in Scotland, for one commentator, 'the schools question breathed life into the No Popery movement to an alarming degree in the two subsequent decades'.[2] The issue was to become symptomatic of the hostility towards Catholics in Scotland, the vast majority of whom were either born in Ireland or who were second and third generation Irish. In 1935, the Glasgow Herald reported a Church of Scotland minister as saying:

> The indignant opposition to the provision of Section 18 of the Education (Scotland) Act, 1918, is that public money is being expended in educating an increasing section of the population, in the main Free Staters or their offspring, in a faith and a loyalty hostile to the tradition and religion accepted by the vast majority of the Scottish nation. . . Why should we feed, clothe, and educate these people who everywhere plot and plan for the downfall of Great Britain.[3]

Gallagher believes that this minister; 'was only expressing what a large number of ministers and their congregations elsewhere shared, if in a somewhat modified form'.[4] Certainly, the almost non-existent hostility towards the Episcopalian Church whose voluntary schools were also transferred under the 1918 Act seems to bear out the argument that it was Catholics who remained the target.

One of the most prominent manifestations of general anti-Catholicism at the time, but primarily of the feelings against Catholic schools, was to be found in Alexander Ratcliffe's 'Scottish Protestant League' of the 1920s and 1930s. The popular Ratcliffe and his thousands of supporters saw Catholic schools as 'sectarian' and his Party gained much political success at the time.[5] In Edinburgh, anti-Catholic demonstrations and violence reached a highpoint during the mid to late 1930s. Although not specifically concentrating on Catholic schooling, such ideas were inevitably included in John Cormack's Protestant Action progr-amme given that it was to call for the expulsion of Catholics from Scotland. The political successes gained by Cormack's Party were based upon both working and middle-class support.[6] In addition, the 1930s also witnessed some of the founders of the

2 Gallagher T, 1987, p. 104

3 Glasgow Herald, 8/5/35

4 Gallagher, 1987, pp. 138-139

5 For Ratcliffe, see ibid chapter 4

6 For Cormack, see Gallagher, Edinburgh Divided, Polygon, 1987

Scottish National Party express similar antagonism towards the 1918 Act.[7]

According to the Rev Andrew Douglas a member of the Church of Scotland's General Assembly Education Committee in the 1970s:

With the passage of time, and the graver concerns of World War II, controversy died down. It became an almost annual habit for the highest court of the Kirk to agree that 'the time was not opportune' to raise the question of the separation of children of school age simply on the grounds of the religious preferences of their parents.

Nonetheless, Douglas had the matter re-opened when he proposed that the Kirk declare:

itself opposed to segregation in schools, and in favour of a national integrated system without respect to denominational interests. The motion, accepted by the Committee, was submitted to the General Assembly and approved.[8]

For Douglas, and presumably for many of his adherents, 'only educational factors ought to determine the nature of the provision to be made'.[9] Ironically, Douglas argued 'sectarianism in schools is not the cause of division' and pointedly stated that, 'religious bigotry has a longer history in Scotland than the situation created by the Education Act of 1918'.[10]

The Free Church of Scotland and the Free Presbyterian Church are both against Catholic schooling, though both also fear secularisation.[11] The Orange Order in Scotland has opposition to Catholic schools at the top of its social and political agenda. Like other protagonists engaged in the argument, the Orange Institution views Catholic schools as sectarian and divisive, whilst it favours 'integrated education'. It argues that it wishes to end Catholic schooling for the benefit of Scottish society: so that young people would come together in toleration and together-ness. Thus, 'Rome on the Rates' and 'Religious Apartheid' have become amongst the most penetrating of cries for the Orange community.

The contentiousness of the schools issue returned to the

7 Finley, 1991, pp. 46-67

8 Douglas A M, Church and School in Scotland, The Saint Andrew Press, Edinburgh, 1985, p. 94-95

9 Ibid, p. 95

10 Ibid, pp. 95-97

11 In 1967, the Free Church's General Assembly stated that education cannot be utterly secular

fore in 1970 when Glasgow City Labour Party passed a resolution that: 'segregation of schools on religious grounds be terminated but that provision for religious instruction be continued in accordance with individual belief'.[12] Nonetheless, in as much as the people who want them support Catholic schools, and despite official Labour policy to phase them out, as with the Scottish Conservative Party, Scottish Labour accepts the reality of their existence. The Green party oppose Catholic schools, while in 1993, the Scottish Liberal Democratic Party conference voted against them, though it agreed that Catholic schools could only end after the widest public debate.[13] Liberal Lord David Steel stated:

> The stark evidence is that in large parts of Scotland they do [perpetuate the 'sectarian' divide], and the Catholic Church buries its head in the sand if it pretends otherwise.[14]

Steel did not produce any relevant evidence to support his argument while a similar discourse on the part of former Labour Education Minister Sam Galbraith emerged in 2007. Galbraith stated that:

> Religious schools entrench a divide in society in young minds, which carries on in later life and leads to divisions and sectarianism. **It is the root cause.**[15]

Galbraith's beliefs were dismantled by Professor Robert Davis who pointed out that such people must obviously be:

> In possession of information of which both Her Majesty's Inspectorate of Education and the international educational research community are unaware. . . Catholic schools flourish from New York to New Zealand, and are acclaimed globally for their contribution to social inclusion, economic mobility and intercommunal cohesion.[16]

Peter Kearney of the Catholic Media Office supported Davis arguing:

> It is time to tell those who attack faith schools they are wrong and the historical divisions that still leave us tainted with sectarian bigotry pre-date the existence of such schools, so it cannot have been created by them.[17]

12 Glasgow Herald, 10/3/70

13 The Herald, 27/3/93

14 Orange Torch, February 2007

15 Scottish Catholic Observer, 5/1/07, p.3

16 The Times Educational Supplement, 12/1/07, p.18

17 SCO, 5/107, p.3

Although there is significant hostility within the membership of the SNP towards Catholic schools, in recent years positive statements and supportive commitments with regards the schools on the part of leader and Scottish Government First Minister, Alex Salmond, have been amongst the strongest from anyone similarly positioned in society.

> All faith-based schools play a significant role in helping to shape, inspire and strengthen our young people to learn. It's time to celebrate their contribution to Scottish education.[18]

Against this affirmative view a motion passed in 1979 by the Educational Institute of Scotland (EIS), the schoolteachers' main trade union, displaying opposition to Catholic schooling, resulted in a large proportion of its Catholic membership threatening to leave the union. In a speech in 1985, the retiring president of the EIS also criticised Catholic schools stating:

> The segregation of children only five years old on religious grounds is wrong, grossly so. . . In this matter the law is not merely an ass but an assassin. . . The results. . . the tribalism of broken heads at Hampden and the broken hearts of couples whose plans to marry in good faith have been defeated by prejudice, are unacceptable to the majority of the Scottish people.[19]

In 1999 the EIS attempted to set up a campaign through the new Scottish Parliament for the abolition of denominational schools. This was narrowly defeated (164 votes to 153) and the motion was amended. The EIS resolved to 'formulate a policy on campaigning for denominational schools' abolition – subject to the consent of churches and parents'.[20]

The media is an opinion former but it also reflects public attitudes and identities. Since the 1990s in particular the (Glasgow) Herald newspaper letters columns have reflected the heated nature of the schools debate, with correspondence on a regular basis. The letters originate from people from a wide range of social and political strata in Scottish society. Many repeat the themes of those of the past that remonstrated against Catholic schools. These arguments are evidence of how the schools issue is ideologically connected to matters in contemporary society

18 Sunday Herald, 3/2/08, p.7

19 Times Higher Education Supplement for Scotland, 14/6/85

20 The Herald, 12/6/99

that may otherwise seem unrelated, even with regards football in Scotland.

> Why should there be such antagonism to our interdenominational system of education system having as its aim integration rather than separation, combined with a purposeful unification of all factions? In perpetuating the ghastly system of apartheid it is obvious what is feared most by the Roman Catholic hierarchy is losing the tenacious grip that is invaluable for indoctrination during the child's tender years. Such a loss would spell a major blow to Roman Catholicism.[21]

> I do believe that the religious prejudice which still exists in some quarters, and in many ways is peculiar to the west of Scotland, will disappear altogether within a generation if separate schools are removed from our educational system.[22]

> Religion should be left to parents and the church. . . it is certainly not the business of teachers.[23]

> Why can't those who advocate the retention of the dual education system admit that they are both bigoted and hypocritical? They want to maintain their segregationist policies while living under a facade of Christianity. The only contribution the system makes to the Scottish Nation, and to the West of Scotland in particular, is to provide us with a breeding ground of superstition and mistrust. The sooner the children come together, the sooner they will stop growing up to perpetuate their parents hatred.[24]

> The answer is simple. The Roman Catholic Church should be given two options; their schools remain within the State system and appointments are made by the education authority; or Roman Catholic schools opt out of the system and are funded by the Church. . . The situation as it stands is unacceptable.[25]

> . . . Scotland's very own 'apartheid' – separate schools with children divided by religion. . . In an increasingly secular society, why should religion, any form of religion, be taught in state schools? Religion is divisive.[26]

> . . . referring to the last Old Firm match at Ibrox, and the continuation of segregated schools. . . If we are serious about eradicating the hatred which is vented in the name of sport. . . the only solution is for a full integration of our schools.[27]

Perhaps a popular source for some of the greatest arguments exerted against Catholic school identity originates from within,

21 The Herald, 10/5/91

22 Ibid, 24/4/91

23 Ibid, 14/12/90

24 Ibid.

25 Ibid, 5/11/90

26 Ibid, 14/9/90

27 Ibid, 18/11/87

and is reflected by, the media in Scotland. Such reporting in the Daily Record periodically proclaims 'Barred, Kids caught in the storm over Catholic schools', 'We Are United' (a headline repeated on occasion), and 'It's Pupil Power: Walkout kids in schools protest'. One article stated:

> They swim together. . . they play football together. . . and last night David became old enough to join his pal in the Beavers. But there is an Act of Parliament that says Douglas, six, and five year-old David could be kept apart during the day — because one is a Protestant and the other is a Catholic.[28]

In 1998, the Daily Record, promoted as the 'Voice of Scotland', described two schools in Lanarkshire as, 'side by side, but the children who play together outside are kept apart when they go through the gates'.[29] Numerous feature writers for the Daily Record and its sister newspaper the Sunday Mail have over the years also opposed Catholic schools.[30]

The terminology and arguments used by antagonists of Catholic schools, letter writers, some Churches, newspapers and TV presenters, as well as many members of the wider public — are thematically comparable over the period of these schools entering the state system. In his Edinburgh Festival lecture in 1999, James MacMillan referred to The Herald newspaper and some of its feature writers as providing a dimension of the hostility served on Catholic schools. Other Catholics share this perception.[31] During June 1999, a Sunday Herald editorial stated:

> some might conclude that it is time we moved on towards ending separate state-funded education based on religious selection. . . We have to ask if we want our children to be educated to be 'separate' and to grow up feeling alienated from their neighbours in 21st century Scotland.[32]

The Herald's use of 'it is time we moved on', 'separate' and 'feeling alienated' reflected some of the terminology used in many of the letters and comments from other groups and individuals. An implication of The Herald's comment is that Scotland is backward in relation to this matter, conjuring images of a time when some writers believe that Catholic Irish immigrants lived in self-imposed religious and ethnic ghettos. Catholics like

28 Daily Record, 17/5/88, 18/5/88 and 13/1/89

29 Daily Record, 13/2/98

30 See for example Scottish comedian Elaine C Smith's column over several years until 2009 in the Sunday Mail. Smith's opposition to Catholic schools was expressed via comments such as 'sectarianism — getting rid of separate schools would top my list but the Executive won't tackle it. Too many votes at stake', 5/2/06, p.17

31 See T M Devine (edt), 1995, pp. 83-121

32 Sunday Herald, 6/6/99

MacMillan oppose this view believing that their schools can be socially and morally beneficial to the rest of Scottish society. The popular arguments of a hostile Scottish media also mislead in the sense that Catholic schools exist in many countries in the world, in North America, South America and all over Europe, and generally they do not attract any antagonism at all. In 2009 the St Mungo Museum of Religious Life and Art in Glasgow included in its education display a piece on Catholic schools that reiterated a dominant viewpoint of Catholic schools as separate:

> Some Scottish parents, because of their religious beliefs, send their children to separate denominational schools for their particular religion. Other parents send their children to non-denominational schools where there may be children from various religious backgrounds.

In 2009 a student attending an introductory group discussion at his degree course at the University of Glasgow to become a primary school teacher introduced himself to a fellow student. The young student asked him if he was 'here for the Catholic schools or normal schools'.[33] In such discourses it is clear that the Catholic perspective is being excluded, not accepted, not tolerated, disapprovingly rendered 'separate' and 'abnormal', and the schools are being re-branded in a way not conceptualised by their adherents. Such attitudes can even be seen to permeate some of the bodies that work in the 'anti-sectarian' industry, including 'Nil by Mouth' and 'Sense over Sectarianism' though neither sees fit to take a public stance on the issue, partly it is argued by some, in case their funding is negatively affected. Nevertheless on several occasions representatives from these bodies have either raised questions over the existence of Catholic schools or have said they are contributors to sectarianism in Scotland.[34]

Amidst the dominant discourses utilised whenever 'sectarianism' is mentioned in relation to football in Scotland, a number of sports/football journalists and commentators also demonstrate their enmity towards Catholic schools and state their belief that they are significant contributors to, or are the actual cause of, 'sectarianism'. For example, a considerable influence in BBC Radio Scotland sport and the Daily Record sports feature writer billed

33 As told by student, 10/9/09

34 Witnessed 3/4/05 Conference attended by representatives from Nil by Mouth and Sense over Sectarianism, Glasgow Religious Museum. Also expressed in workshop attended by same

as the 'Voice of Authority' in that newspaper opined:

> If the Executive – who have so far provided £100,000 to fund school projects across the religious divide – can set up partnerships in areas such as sport field trips and dramas, can someone remind me why our kids don't sit in the same classroom? If it is considered beneficial to play together and join various activities, why wouldn't it help if they all learned together? Please just explain that to me one more time. [35]

Other football figures in Scotland have also occasionally let it be known their opposition to Catholic Schools and how they see them as a contributory factor or even as root cause of what they term 'sectarianism'. Laurence Macintyre, a former Commander at Strathclyde Police and subsequently Head of Security at Glasgow Rangers, authored the Ibrox club's submission to a consultation on sectarianism for the 'Gorrie Bill' during 2002. Macintyre wrote that:

> I am disappointed personally that the Bill is not intended to affect the contentious issue of denominational schools. . . many believe this is where sectarianism and religious hatred begin.

In its submission to the same consultation process Motherwell Football Club expressed a similar opinion over why Catholic schools were omitted from the bill's remit.[36]

There are a number of distinct but often related categories that the anti-Catholic schools lobby falls into, in terms of education, secularism, politics, community relations, economics, religion, ethnicity, culture, law and order, and football. On many occasions these cross over and sometimes antagonism is characterised by several or all of these simultaneously. As is evidenced, hostility towards Catholic schools can often be expressed vehemently by parties, organisations and individuals, as well as through a number of public channels and forums. Many of the ideological arguments have been in place at least since Catholics ceased (via the 1918 Act) specifically funding their own schools in addition to state – in effect Protestant – ones. Most schools in Scotland, whether Catholic or non/multi denominational, now operate under the auspices of Scottish local authorities and today Catholics, Protestants, other denominational as well as non-religious people together pay taxes to fund

35 Jim Traynor, Daily Record, 18/12/06, p.24

36 Scotland on Sunday, 10/2/02, p.19

all state schools whether non/multi-denominational or faith based.

Catholic perspectives are of course offered that support Catholic schools – and their defence includes several high profile sources that are not Catholic. Cameron Harrison, a former chief executive of the Scottish Consultative Council on the Curriculum, consultant and advisor to governments on education policy, and an ordained minister of the Church of Scotland said in 2007:

> For a long time I've been convinced that the debate in Scotland about sectarianism and faith schools has been over-simplistic and ill-thought-through. . . the evidence is that, on average, Catholic schools are better, and that's the blunt truth. And, judging by the queues of non-Catholic middle class parents enrolling their children at my local Catholic primary, you won't want for support. . . Rather than exacerbating the problem of sectarianism in our society, it seems to me that Christian schools have the potential to be part of the solution.[37]

However, minority Catholic communities in Scotland make up only 15% of the population and this means their viewpoints often struggle to be heard or represented – unless by acquiring a sensational headline. With such a welter of antagonism against them this can also mean that the anti-Catholic schools lobby more readily finds favour in public forums, whilst support and defence of the schools is marginalised. Supporting Catholic perspectives similarly resonate with matters educational, historical, political, in terms of community relations, economics, religion, ethnicity, culture, law and order, and football. Nonetheless, although Catholic supporters of Catholic schools can and do respond in such terms, and although defence is characterised by a rejection of the argument that such schools contribute to ethnic or religious cleavage in society, for such Catholics the most important factor determining their support relates at core to spiritual matters, values, practices, attitudes and ultimately, to the perceived purpose and meaning of life itself.

The remaining part of this chapter will reflect upon the faith, religious and spiritual thesis and rationale for the existence of Catholic schools, not solely in Scotland, but generally in any society they are to be found, and one that is commonly omitted or lost amidst other arguments.

37 The Herald, 15/1/07, p.15

The faith ethos

Christ came to engage people to make a choice between right and wrong: a choice characterised or not by actions of peace, service and love. He knew that as well as bringing people together such choices would also create distinctions between those on the side of 'right' and those choosing 'wrong': between seeds that fall on fertile ground and seeds that wither amongst the rocks and weeds. For most supporters of Catholic schools, the idea of taking sides, of opting for a body of beliefs that promote and give life to the teachings of Christ through attitude and action is to be found at the heart of the rationale for Catholic schools.

In his 1999 Edinburgh lecture, James MacMillan asserted his belief that where the Catholic faith is practised with humility, honesty and holiness, society is improved and role models and examples are created for others. He implied that the ultimate role model is Christ whom Catholics and other Christians aim to follow. For MacMillan and others like him, the Catholic school is an essential social avenue in shaping the kind of people he views as offering stability in an unstable and often morally ambivalent society. In this light, the Catholic school setting also helps provide a critique of prevailing values and an alternative set of ideas in the face of challenges from an accelerating secular and material-istic age.

In a letter to a broadsheet newspaper in late 1999, a minister of the United Free Church of Scotland, asserted that this alternative set of beliefs, considered to be 'in step with Jesus Christ', as opposed to the ways and beliefs of modern Scotland, was the most fertile set of ideas to draw upon. The minister concluded that:

> It is certainly the case that Jesus was often out of step with the political correctness of his own day. I suppose he was something of a revolutionary. He insisted that God's will always took precedence over man's will. Never a popular notion when God's will doesn't coincide with our own. Which is why he warned that in this world his disciples would face tribulation, ie they would be under pressure from the society in which they lived. Society and Christians have frequently been at odds.[38]

Another commentator opined that in contrast to an education

38 The Herald, Saturday Essay, Professor John Haldane, 6/11/99

system that merely exists to serve society by equipping it with an appropriately trained workforce oriented to the values and practices of contemporary western capitalist cultures, Catholic education has a different rationale, one rooted in a philosophy of human nature and society.[39]

Many faiths believe that everyday living cannot be divorced from religion. In this context, for practising and conscientious Catholics, faith has a role in every thought and deed governing human life. It provides and sustains the motivation for what is good while helping to provide a counter to that viewed negatively. Here we can also find the rationale for Catholics seeing faith as something that cannot be compartmentalised. It is intrinsic in a way that conflicts with the idea that faith can be taught in school at a particular time of day. Faith is intended as a resource drawn upon in every moment of life. It is a referral for all thought and action. It goes beyond overt and simple religious observance. The Catholic vision is one characterised by an ennobling conception of the human condition, a conception that recognises that all humans are created in the image and likeness of God. This philosophy is intended to determine Catholic ideas concerning matters economic, political, social and cultural.

Catholic educationalists and their supporters believe that Catholic schools contribute towards and encourage positive human conduct and endeavour that benefits all of society. An intention of Catholic schooling is to assist in the creation of a radically different version of the human experience from that which dominates: one based on Gospel rather than upon other human created values. Catholics are compelled by their faith to show that there is an alternative set of beliefs and life styles to those that dominate: this alternative is assisted in its formation through the work of the Catholic family, Catholic parish and Catholic school. Such an alternative may also be viewed as striving to create difference and distinctiveness, to shape individuals and society in a fundamentally different way from that governed by other moral, cultural, social and economic forces. To this end, Catholic schools aim to assist in the formation of individuals and a community set apart by its actions, beliefs and attitudes. For many conscientious and practising Catholics in Scotland (although

39 Rev David Cartledge, letter to The Herald, 12/11/99

their presence will be of little consequence to some Catholics), a Catholic school can make a significant contribution to the formation of a follower of Christ – and in turn assist in the creation of a enhanced and more just society.

For Catholics, if people are infused with the teachings of Christ, society is morally improved. The best way to change society is not by advancing materially, or simply by looking at the world in a politically right or left wing fashion, although these might also be important. The principal way for Catholics and Christians is to be Christ-like in thought and deed. Catholics believe this assists them formulate a plan for life that is advanced and promoted in the setting of a Catholic school: a space that in turn helps prepares its youth for 'the ways of the world'. The Christian calling is not an easy one. For Timothy, in the face of the temptations around us we cannot sit still, 'you must aim to be saintly and religious' (1 Timothy 6:11).[40] The Catholic educational idea is that Christ's community is built up as the journey of life proceeds. This idea provokes the image of a 'pilgrim people' that is continually growing and developing. In this thinking can also be discerned the Catholic argument that the three important institutional dimensions to this growth and development are expressed in the family, the parish and the Catholic school.

Freedom is at the heart of Christ's teachings. True freedom for Christians is discovered through the enlightening path of Christ. Many of these themes lie at the core of the Catholic rationale for Catholic schools.

> So Jesus said to those who believed in him, 'If you obey my teaching, you are really my disciples; you will know the truth and the truth will set you free. . . everyone who sins is a slave of sin. . . If the Son sets you free then you will be really free.'
> (John 8:31-36).

The contribution teachers can make to a young person's life is supported by a Government Department of Education leaflet produced in the 1990s. Advertising the general teaching profession the document states:

> You can't overestimate a teacher's contribution to a child's development. School helps to shape future adults. Not simply in

40 Catholic Church/ Mass literature 1999, undated

terms of careers but in less obvious ways too. Attitudes, outlook and self-confidence, for example, are all affected by a teacher's skills.

Catholic educationalists agree and further believe it is important to have Catholics guiding a school in a direction commensurate with values that link with Christ's teachings. They are also of the opinion that the atmosphere and ethos of a school is governed and shaped by those same teachings. This is viewed as essential to the Catholic School in being a distinctive setting, although simultaneously being fully integrated with the rest of society.

Although formal religious observance is viewed as part of the life of the Catholic community, is an important aspect of the faith formation of pupils and an important adjunct to religious education, as with every school the formal educational dimension of Catholic schools is always to the fore. The school's role remains specifically 'educational'. Nevertheless, Christian and Catholic examples, role models, precepts and ideas are expected to be integral aspects of the Catholic school. The idea is propounded that it is better to be a disciple of Christ than to have all the knowledge, power, wealth, fame and worldly success that man creates. If these are not used in the interests of building God's Kingdom, then it becomes like the work described by John when discussing Christ as the 'Bread of Life':

> Do not work for food that goes bad; instead, work for the food
> that lasts for eternal life.   (John, 6:27)

Mark's gospel (16:15) states: 'Go out to the whole world: proclaim the Good News to all creation'. The 'Good News' leads to faith and for Catholics, as well as those of other religions, faith needs nurturing. Although parents are expected to be the first teachers in all instances, especially in matters of faith, Catholics also rely on the support and co-operation of the school environment.

In addition, contrary to some popular beliefs and in a less insular fashion than in the past, Catholic schools also teach an appreciation of other world faiths through an appropriate knowledge of their principal beliefs, spiritual values and traditions. Supporters of Catholic schools believe that Catholic religious education has the capacity to assist pupils to develop an understanding of not only their own faith but also an understanding of and respect for those who adhere to other Christian traditions, other world religions as well as those of a secular identity. Likewise, a Catholic school is expected to be sensitive to and help to promulgate appeals for peace, justice, freedom, progress for all peoples and assistance for countries in need.

In a Catholic school (as with a Catholic home), pupils ought to be encountering an environment illuminated by the light of Christ. The spirit of the Gospel should be evident in a Christian way of thought as well as the life that permeates all facets of the educational climate. Daily witness is important to those Catholics conscious of where their children learn and who teaches them. If this is not present, for Catholics, there is little that distinguishes the school as being Catholic apart from the routine, ceremonial and ritual. For conscientious Catholics, Catholic schools have a significant role in a secular society. Catholic schools are intended to assist in the development of young people with attitudes, opinions and lifestyles that challenge those which often seem to dominate throughout much of society. This does not equate with exclusion or isolation, but on the whole is seen as one of many influences in society, and for Catholics and Christians generally, an influence for the better. As with other Christian denominations, this is considered a belief born of faith and the need to bear witness to that faith.

The idea of a Christian lifestyle means that morals are crucial. Religious education necessarily entails the cultivation of a production of knowledge as shared activity of a learning community, as well as the skills to make a reasonable moral decision and to act upon it. In a Catholic school, moral education is not solely the remit of formal religious educators, but the concept of a moral community or of being a moral person, is to be transmitted through example and precept and through the relationships that exist within the whole school. If Christianity is to be a determining factor in life choices, supporters of Catholic schools say it must therefore be integrated into the everyday, in terms of community and lifestyle. Indeed, Catholic educationalists argue that despite their school's failings, this helps Catholics make a positive contribution to Scottish society.

In 1999, a lecturer at St Andrews University argued that by copying a model taken from the USA, children in Scottish schools could engage in 'marriage lessons' to equip partners 'with well-developed relationship skills'.[41] Although this argument was opposed by some teaching unions and politicians the idea that schooling in Scotland should partly be about future wider life experiences and relevant preparations, rather than solely concerned with formal education, links with the rationale for Catholic schools. Formal education is recognised as important, but a universal education grounded in Gospel values is viewed as having the capacity to equip children to deal better with many of their life experiences. From a Catholic perspective, life experiences and relevant preparation for them cannot be adequately dealt with without faith formation. Ultimately, Catholics will and do choose their 'lifestyle'. Where the example of Christ is missing, viewed as an historical or educational nicety, or is seen as an intrusion to the formation of personality and character, many practising Catholics (indeed many practising Christians) perceive life itself as losing meaning and value.

Like other members of the wider population many Catholics clearly value formal education, recognising its general advantages, its requirement for rewarding employment and its capacity for creating a better society. However, supporters of Catholic schools believe that a Christian lifestyle and the nature of a person and the community have a fundamentally more significant role to play in creating a better society than that which is based purely on educational attainment. A Catholic school should reflect God as seeing everyone equally, as we should all see each other. If it does not matter to God whether we are black, brown or white, fat, thin or tall, blind or deaf, He is also not interested in how many school passes, degrees or post-graduate qualifications we have or how much money we make. Indeed, if this were not the case, such restrictions would diminish a God who is concerned about how we use what we have, rather than what we have. Luke's Gospel supports the view that a list of worldly virtues, important in context, does not provide guidance for a spiritual life that is the essential requirement above and beyond that which man finds important. Luke's Gospel states, 'Man cannot live on bread alone' (4:4) and Christ's apostle Paul re-affirms this teaching in his letter to the Corinthians: a letter frequently used for Catholic marriage ceremonies.

> I may be able to speak the languages of men and even of angels, but if I have no love, my speech is no more than a noisy gong or a clanging bell. I may have the gift of inspired preaching; I may have all knowledge and understand all secrets; I may have all the faith needed to move mountains – but if I have no love, I am nothing. . . (1:13)

This is similar to that explained in Paul's first letter to the Corinthians (15:1-4), in which he stresses that 'believing anything else will not lead to anything'. In this sense Cathiolic schools can be seen as environments that legitimise experiences often 'marginal' to the interests of the 'secular' schools.

For those who advocate Catholic schools and a Catholic/Christian lifestyle, the way to live is to go beyond oneself, to consider the other as much if not more than the self, to be less selfish and more giving and to serve: 'To love your neighbour as you love yourself'. (Matthew 22:39) In a letter from Pope Paul VI to Cardinal Conway in 1973, he said:

> The law of Christian maturity demands that we lose ourselves in concern for others. One must not wait until all problems at home are solved before beginning to address oneself to those of the neighbour. In fact an awareness of the immensity of the tasks and problems of progress which face humanity as a whole can stir individuals to work more seriously for progress in their own society.

A lay commentator has given voice to this line of thinking: 'Our neighbour is more than our immediate circle. Who is my neighbour? My neighbour is all mankind.' This author believes this to be one of the most revolutionary, radical, subversive sentiments in the entire history of mankind. 'It means no stereotyping, no categorisation of Jew and Gentile, Irish and English, Catholic and Protestant, man and woman, old age and youth.'[42] In these sentiments also lie moral lessons against secular values. In the context of accepting the continued presence of human frailties and imperfections, for Catholic educationalists, this also means that ideas of equality, toleration, understanding and generosity of spirit are at the heart of Catholic education.

Hope is an aspect of faith and this also exists in abundance amid the negativity. Like the Church itself, as well as the people who consciously comprise it, for adhering Catholics, a Catholic school aims to retain its mission to show the real face of Christ – however well it performs at achieving this. It aims to equip its pupils with the make-up and character that enables them to live lives fully human and fully holy and to share this with the rest of society.

The reality is that like all of humanity, the Church and Catholics are touched by 'sin'. Nonetheless, amidst considered social confusion, moral ambiguity and 'inhuman' ideologies, for Catholic supporters of Catholic schools, their educational institutions remain conduits for the advancement of Christian lifestyles. Whether this is important or has any real meaning for the wider population seems certain to remain a matter of continuing debate. Likewise, whether this can be understood, accepted or tolerated by their antagonists or/and those who ubiquitously use the term 'sectarian' when discussing ethnic or religious matters in Scotland, can be another question entirely.

42 Professor Joe Lee, University of Cork. Quoted in Michael Commins, 'Don't let traditions get left behind', Irish Post, 29/8/99

Christ, the Catholic world vision, Brother Walfrid and Celtic: 'Come follow me'

Aidan Donaldson

The Gospel writer Mark tells us that soon after his baptism by John the Baptist in the River Jordan Jesus walked by the Sea of Galilee – about to start his mission. He met two brothers, Simon and Andrew, who were catching fish with their nets. Jesus invites them to come and follow him – 'and I will make you fishers of men'. [Mk. 1:17] Later, passing the same lake Jesus issued a similar invitation to the brothers, James and John. Immediately, we are told, 'they left their father, Zebedee, and the hired men, and followed Jesus'. [Mk. 1:20]

Despite the simplicity and brevity of this story, and the direct way in which Mark tells it, there is something remarkable and fundamentally rich and complex about this episode. The invitation to 'Come, follow me' requires an unpacking, analysis, exploration and examination beyond the (apparently) clear and uncomplicated three word instruction – as does the astonishing immediate and total response of the first disciples. To see it simply as an attempt by a new and young rabbi to attract followers and the apparently almost foolhardy and naive decision on the part of simple fishermen to abandon the security of their livelihood for the possibility of 'something better' – as yet unknown – misses the point entirely. 'Come, follow me' is both an invitation and a challenge. It is simultaneously an invitation and a challenge to posit and to enter a new world – a world which is shaped by a new order which is beyond and, in many ways, hostile to the accepted reality and ways of thinking. Old certitudes, comforts and established means of dealing with 'the real world' are abandoned and left behind by the very thinking of new ways of seeing and responding to the world. It is to leave the 'comfort zone' of life as it is, precisely what Eamonn Bredin wrote about in his definitive work on discipleship, 'Disturbing the Peace'[1]

Bredin points out that to accept the radical challenge to become a disciple of Christ involves moving out of the familiar, releasing the comfortable reins of control and safety and accepting the path of discipleship wherever that might lead. According to Bredin 'accepting [the call of discipleship] means being willing to set out and continue a journey which leads us onwards, upwards and inwards. . . being constantly coaxed and lured forward by the newness of what God and his Christ wish to achieve in us and through us.'[2] For the first disciples the invitation to 'Come, follow me' – as it does for all followers of Christ – involves a new (although often unacknowledged) world as it might be. At the crucial juncture in the first chapter of Mark when the fishermen leave everything to follow Jesus they cease to be the people they were and become **new** people. For them, the world they knew and in which they lived has, through their action, been radically changed and transformed. The world as it was now has become a world as it might become, be made. All of this is marked by a radical newness and a step into a world as how it might be imagined and how it might become.

A new world?

The world that Jesus invited his disciples into is certainly different from the world almost all of us live in today. Our world is a most peculiar, contradictory and confusing place. Fabulously rich yet incredibly poor; technologically advanced and knowledgeable on the one hand yet committing environmental suicide on the other; able to transport millions of holiday-makers to far off destinations and hedonistic 'paradises' every day while unable (read 'unwilling') to send some of the surplus food in the affluent Western World

[1] Bredin E 1985
[2] Ibid. pp. 10–11

to feed those who are starving in the so-called Developing World. Oh, and by the way, if you need to impose a war on people in some far off country – don't panic. It seems that in today's world there is no shortage of materials to use in conflict. After all, the arms industry today is the single biggest industry in the world (the sex and the sport industries come not far behind) with over 1,000 billion US dollars being spent on weapons annually. Let us consider a few other statistics to see what kind of world we live in:

- The six richest people in the world own more than the six hundred million poorest.

- The three hundred richest people in the world own more of the world's wealth than half of humanity.

- We spend 30 times more on military expenditure than on international development.

- One million tons of food is thrown out each year in Europe alone.

- In the US they spend 5 times more on cosmetics than on helping the world's poor.

- 30,000 African children will die today from starvation.

For me this last statistic illustrates just how inhuman and detached from human suffering our society has become. As you read this there are 30,000 African children who are alive right now who will be dead by tomorrow – from '**starvation**'-related causes. There is nothing unusual or even remarkable about this since each and every single day some 30,000 children in Africa die. Let us put this statistic into context: 30,000 deaths roughly equates to the following:

- Almost 10 times the number of those who died in the recent conflict in relation to the north of Ireland that lasted some three decades.

- The number of people who die in the conflict in Iraq every 10 months

- The same number of those (approximately 900,000) who perished in the 1994 '100 Day Genocide' in Rwanda dying each month

- The equivalent of the Holocaust committed by the Nazis repeated every 7 months.

- Half the attendance at the next Celtic match against Rangers at Celtic Park

'Never again would such crimes against humanity be allowed to happen again' – so universally stated the voice of world opinion after the Holocaust of the Second World War. Yet life continues to be cheap in Africa and much of the rest of the world. The communications revolution of the past two decades – as evidenced by the omnipresence (and all-pervasive influence) of 24-hour satellite television channels, the internet and mobile phones – means that we can no longer claim that we do not know what is happening in the world. Indeed, we frequently know about – indeed, we accept or are indifferent, apathetic and even collude via our own ignorance and lifestyles with – what is going on. For many people, especially in the Developed World, it is not a case of not knowing; rather it is simply a case of not caring or at the very least feeling so disempowered or detached from what is happening that making a difference seems not to be an option.

Not that one should be surprised at this. After all, we live in a world bombarded by, saturated with, and, ultimately, moulded by a repressive, intellectual narrowing and suppressive form of ideological control based on a diet of reality television, pornography, advertising and consumerism: the selfish 'me' age, so to speak. The staggering degree to which modern humankind has embraced and shaped its own powerlessness can be illustrated by the fact that not only do more people tune into Big Brother every day than watch the news – often more people vote on who they wish to be evicted from the Big Brother House (something which they actually have to pay for) than exercise their franchise in voting in party political elections. With such inverted values, disconnection and a distorted world vision, it is little wonder that the plight of those dying in such vast numbers throughout the so-called Developing World does not significantly appear on the Western World's radar of concern. Those who live in the margins also appear to exist only in the margins of the consciousness and conscience of the world.

The world that Jesus sought to bring about – the Kingdom – is this aforementioned world turned upside down, revolved, revolutionised. It is a world in which the dignity of each person – and especially the marginalised, downtrodden and oppressed victims of poverty and/or injustice – is recognised, affirmed and celebrated. At the time of Jesus – as it is today – the poor, the marginalised, the sick, the mentally and physically disabled, and any other social group that did not belong to the dominant, affluent and respectable – were shunned, despised and ignored. They were (and are) non-persons whose existence was (and is) an embarrassment and an affront. They were (and are) an unwelcome and uncomfortable reminder of the fact that society at the time of Jesus – like that of today – treated those who need help, love, support and, above all, justice, shamefully. So what did 'respectable society' do with this challenge? It negated it by making the victims of injustice the authors of their own conditions.

According to the society in which Jesus lived, the poor, the sick, sinners and the rest of those who were outside of the realms of respectability were guilty of their own conditions and outside of God's and, therefore, society's favour. They were to be excluded, their human dignity denied, their very existence despised. For them there was no cry 'We are the People!' All injustice is a denial of human dignity – both in the Developing World and here in our own societies. In Scotland, Ireland and much of the Developed World, travellers, the homeless, drug abusers, the alienated etc. are no less victims of structural injustice and neglect than those suffering from the effects of famine and other victims of poverty in the Developing World. They all share one thing in common: to those in or with power they do not matter. They are not important enough to matter. Yet it was precisely these whom Jesus sought out and whose dignity he affirmed both through his actions by associating with them and through his teachings – especially the Sermon on the Mount.

And what message did the young firebrand rabbi, standing on a hillside (like Moses when delivering the Ten Commandments) and addressing the marginalised and oppressed, give them? He spoke just outside the Walls of Jerusalem above which was the magnificence of the Temple from which many of them would have been excluded due to their lack of wealth and lowly social status. That '**theirs** is the Kingdom of God. . . that **they** shall be comforted. . . that **they** shall inherit the earth. . . that **they** shall be satisfied. . . that **they** shall be called sons of God. . . that **they** shall see God'. (Mt. 5:1–12; my bold) If ever there was a world turned upside down then Jesus had just proclaimed it! Little wonder did he, himself, become marginalised to the extent that the two most powerful groups in Palestine at that time – the Jewish religious leaders and the Roman authorities – came together to rid society of such a dangerous figure.

Viewing the world differently

Andrew Kerins would have looked in much the same way at those Irish Catholic, huddled and impoverished masses crammed into the hovels of the East End of Glasgow and shunned and rejected by many in Scottish society as Jesus would have looked at the poor that surrounded him. Born in 1840 in Ballymote, Co. Sligo he witnessed at first hand the appalling suffering of so many of his fellow people and members of his immediate family and community during the Great Hunger and its aftermath. He would have witnessed many villages being emptied as the survivors of Ireland's holocaust sought refuge and survival through emigration. He would have met with many of these fellow countrymen and women in Bridgeton and the Calton in the 1870s when he moved to Glasgow. As a teacher in St. Mary's School and Headmaster of Sacred Heart in the East End he would have recognised their children as his community. It may seem only natural therefore, that Andrew Kerins would have felt an empathy towards and compassion for his fellow Irish Catholics.

Yet there was another dimension to Andrew Kerins that would have led him beyond empathy based on common cultural identity and simple compassion for those in need. Andrew Kerins was no simple emigré: as Brother Walfrid he was a member of a religious order, the Marists, and would, therefore, have been shaped and formed by a Catholic world outlook and would look at the world through untypical eyes. The Catholic world vision is an alternative (from those visions based on greed, avarice, selfishness and the accumulation of material and financial wealth) way of viewing the world and the purpose of humanity. Reflecting the teachings of Christ, it not only involves an alternative way of looking at the world but also invites, provokes and, in fact, necessitates critical action aimed at transforming the world we encounter in order to bring about a society based upon love, solidarity, the common good, truth and justice. The obligation to commit oneself to the service of others is not an 'add-on' or choice which one may or may not take. For Christians it is an inescapable and unconditional moral imperative and obligation that lies at the very heart of the gospel message and Christian world-view. Matthew 25 instructs us on this.

In the 'Parable of the Sheep and the Goats' it is made clear that our lives are judged on how we lived them **'for others'** – especially the marginalised, poor, down-trodden and oppressed. In the parable those who ask 'Lord, when did we see you hungry and feed you, thirsty and gave you to drink, naked and clothed you, a stranger and made you welcome, in prison and visited you?' are told that 'when you did this to the least of my people, you did that to me'. [see Mt. 25: 31–46] The corollary is also true, for we are similarly told, to neglect the poor, marginalised, hungry, thirsty etc. is to ignore the God-given dignity of each person and to betray one's vocation as a person for others. The answer to the question posed by Cain in Genesis 'am I my brother's guardian?' must be an unequivocal 'yes'. And who is my neighbour? Perhaps the greatest challenge to all religious and other world visions is defining who this other-directedness extends to. For some – including some fundamentalist Christian denominations – one's duty extends only to members of one's own tradition, class, nation or creed.[3] Yet the 'Parable of the Good Samaritan' demonstrates a most challenging sense of inclusiveness and clearly informs us that our duty to our neighbour extends to all – including those who are from other, and sometimes, hostile traditions and backgrounds.[4]

This fundamental command to address the needs of **all** others – especially those in situations of inhuman suffering and oppression – occupies a central position in Catholic social teaching. The great Catholic theologian, and Church leader, Archbishop Oscar Romero, who was assassinated by right-wing government-sponsored killers in 1980 for his courageous and unswerving opposition to the oppression of the Salvadoran people, clearly identified the Church's primary duty to side with the poor, the 'option for the poor' adopted by the Latin American Church at the celebrated Medellin Conference in 1968. Romero proclaims the following:

> The poor have shown the Church the true way to go. A Church that does not join the poor, in order to speak out from the side of the poor against the injustices committed against them, is not the true Church of Jesus Christ.[5]

For Romero and many within the Church in Latin America and elsewhere it is the fundamental duty of the Church to speak out and act on behalf of the poor, especially in situations of injustice, oppression and marginalisation. At Medellin, for example, the bishops speak of 'a deafening cry. . . from the throats of millions asking their pastors for a liberation that reaches them from nowhere else'.[6] For Romero and the other radical theologians of the Latin American Church, this 'option for the poor' was a necessary outcome of viewing the poor (along with everyone else) as fully alive images of Christ. In his Lenten Reflections Romero urges us to see Christ not in the commercialised Christmas crib form but alive and living on the margins of society – an image with which Brother Walfrid would have concurred when he observed the children of the Irish Catholic immigrants when teaching in the East End of Glasgow. According to Romero:

> We must not seek the child Jesus in the pretty figures of our Christmas cribs. We must seek him among the undernourished children who have gone to bed tonight with nothing to eat,

[3] This can be true of Christian denominations based on the theology of John Calvin and his follower John Knox.

[4] Luke 10: 20–37

[5] Oscar Romero, 'Lenten Reflections', Number 1, February 17th 1980. These 'sermons' are redactions of various passages from the homilies of Archbishop Oscar Romero, arranged as if the were commentaries on the seven Works of Justice and Peace, which is the mission statement of the Oklahoma City Catholic Worker House. For these, and more of Archbishop Romero's homilies, see James R. Brockman, SJ, (ed.) 1988

[6] The Latin American Bishops Conference (CELAM) 1968

among the poor newsboys who will sleep covered with
newspapers in doorways.[7]

Nor is the obligation to commit to the side of the poor and
to the service of others only to be found among the more radical
and, indeed, revolutionary elements of the Church, as found in
the liberation theology of the Latin American Church or the
actions of the missionary orders who are active throughout the
Third World, often acting as the 'voice of the voiceless' in
situations of extreme danger. Radical social Catholicism has been
propounded by the papacy for more than a century. Leo XIII's
famous encyclical **De Rerum Novarum** (1891) – largely based
on the teachings of the medieval theologian Thomas Aquinas –
supported workers' rights and condemned 'the misery and
wretchedness of workers under economic liberalism', and has
given a direction for social Catholic thought and action from
which it has not deviated. At the centre of this thinking is the
fundamental importance of the dignity of the human person.
Typical of this radical message is Pope John XXIII's encyclical
Pacem in Terris (1963) and the documents of the Second Vatican
Council (to which Pope Benedict XIV was a key adviser and
reader), notably **Gaudium et Spes** adopted in 1965. The latter
declaration calls for a continuing and deepening dialogue between
the Church and the world, denounces economic inequality and
disparities between rich and poor nations, and bases human
freedom and interdependence in the quest for justice and love,
especially regarding the marginalised and needy. Strikingly, the
declaration also contains a strong invitation to others – including
non-Christians and even those of no faith – to participate in the
transformation of the present and the creation of a new society.
The moral imperative aims at all of humanity and does not belong
to an exclusive group or sect. The Vatican Council declares that
'all men, believers and unbelievers alike, ought to work for the
rightful betterment of this world in which all alive live.'[8]

Some critics have suggested that this trend was halted or
even reversed during the papacy of John Paul II. They are
incorrect. Despite his difficulties with aspects of liberation
theology and some of its more radical proponents, John Paul
made a very significant contribution to this area of Church

[7] Oscar Romero, 'Lenten Reflections' Number 1, (24th December 1979)

[8] The Documents of the Second Vatican Council, Gaudium et Spes, (Rome, 1965–1968) para. 21

teaching, notably in his 1988 encyclical **Sollicitudo Rei Socialis**. In it he singled out 'the option or love of preference for the poor', applying it to world poverty and recalling the principle of Christian social doctrine of 'the goods of this world originally [being] meant for all'.[9] The encyclical concludes with the observation that since the Second Vatican Council:

> a new way of confronting poverty and underdevelopment has spread in some areas of the world, especially in Latin America. This approach makes liberation the fundamental category and the first principle of action. . . The aspiration for freedom from all forms of slavery affecting the individual and society is something noble and legitimate.[10]

John Paul II also reiterates throughout his encyclical the universal and inescapable duty of all to reach out and to live for others based on a universal sense of solidarity that incorporates charity and love and he roots this firmly in a distinctive Catholic view of each human person – including even our enemies – as nothing less than a living reflection of God. In clear and unequivocal language John Paul II issues the challenge thus:

> Solidarity is undoubtedly a Christian virtue. In what has been said so far it has been possible to identify many points of contact between solidarity and charity, which is the distinguishing mark of Christ's disciples (cf. Jn 13:35). In the light of faith, solidarity seeks to go beyond itself, to take on the specifically Christian dimension of total gratuity, forgiveness and reconciliation. One's neighbour is then not only a human being with his or her own rights and a fundamental equality with everyone else, but becomes the living image of God the Father, redeemed by the blood of Jesus Christ and placed under the permanent action of the Holy Spirit. One's neighbour must therefore be loved, even if an enemy, with the same love with which the Lord loves him or her; and for that person's sake one must be ready for sacrifice, even the ultimate one: to lay down one's life for the brethren (cf. 1 Jn 3:16).[11]

[9] Pope John Paul II, Sollicitudo Rei Socialis, Rome, 1988) para. 41

[10] Ibid., para. 46

[11] Ibid., para. 40

In the light of such words and the holiness that many Christians aspire to in their lives, it might be argued that a person wearing a top sporting the image of John Paul rather than wearing a multi-national or global company logo, pop star or celebrity branded t-shirt, deserves credit and recognition for showing an integrity and social and political awareness that reflects an admiration for John Paul II, challenges the greed of global capitalism and confronts the blindness and hate of Scottish anti-Catholic prejudice and bigotry.[12]

Ireland and the Third World

Perhaps unsurprisingly – given its long and difficult experience of colonialism and oppression – missionaries from Ireland (and 'of' Ireland when we include people of Irish descent) both religious and lay, have taken this vocational and visionary sense of life to considerable lengths in playing an extraordinary role in attempting to alleviate poverty and hunger and opposing injustice in the Third World. The work of Trocaire – the Irish development agency (similar to CAFOD Catholic Agency for Overseas Development and SCIAF Scottish Catholic International Aid Fund) – established by the Irish Bishops Commission in 1973 – is exemplary in this respect with volunteers from all over Ireland working in at least 60 countries throughout the Third World involving more than 8,000 development or aid projects. The reasons for this extraordinary commitment to the support of others requires exploration and explanation, especially as it is continuing at a time when Ireland has achieved a recent level of prosperity previously unimaginable due to the performance of the economy, often referred to as the 'Celtic Tiger'. While working with the Christian Brothers in Nairobi a couple of years ago it was suggested to me by Father Kevin McGarry, a missionary priest from Belfast with the Société de Missionairies d'Africe, that one of the primary reasons for Irish people's remarkable commitment to the Developing World lies in a deep collective consciousness of their own past disasters, especially the Great Famine or an Gorta Mor of the mid-nineteenth century.

Like many societies that have undergone such a radical transformation in a relatively short period of time, Irish society too has had to face the challenge of increased materialism, consumerism, individualism and secularism that seems to accompany relevant economic development. A certain tension or struggle between two mutually suspicious if not downright

[12] See chapter by Gerard Gough in this volume for Scottish reactions to Celtic's Artur Boruc wearing an image of John Paul II on a t-shirt

hostile value systems has emerged in Ireland over the past two decades with some who would favour Ireland modelling itself on the pseudo-liberal consumerist tendencies that characterise much of modern Europe and the USA while others question the direction this would lead Irish society. Unsurprisingly, those who favour the former view the role which the Catholic Church plays in the everyday life of Irish society as a major bulwark against the creation of a secular materialist Ireland and have, throughout recent years, launched an incessant, energetic and, some would say, unjustifiably hostile campaign against the Church's right to participate in public life. In particular, it is the Catholic Church's role in the educative sphere and its right to express its voice in the ethical realm that is most questioned by those who wish to remodel Irish society on the modern capitalist model.

'The global market and the price of your soul'

Of course, it would be a serious error to claim that Catholicism is the only faith or value system that views the world in such a fashion. Numerous people from the widest variety of faith backgrounds strive ceaselessly and selflessly to achieve this type of transformation based on an inspirational world vision. It is also equally obvious and true that not all Catholics look at the world with Catholic eyes. Globalisation, along with the rise in secularism, consumerism and individualism, provides a powerful alternative and, for many, attractive world outlook through which some, especially in the West, view the world and live their lives accordingly. The American writer George Ritzier identified the trend towards a One World Order based on defining one's life through product identification in his excellent work The MacDonaldization of Society.[13]

Ritzner points towards the increasing homogeneity of society, with its accompanying mid-Atlantic culture and accepted set of values, morals and world outlook. In today's modern society the power of the media – often in the hands of individuals such as Silvio Berlusconi, Rupert Murdoch and the late Kerry Packer – has greatly increased this sense of the imposition of a single way of looking at the world. The twenty-four hour diet of satellite

[13] G. Ritzer 1996

television, non-stop music channels and an endless subjection to advertising now shapes how many perceive the world and accordingly, act in relation to one's self and others. For many the primary reference point for moral discussion and opinion formation is not the family, community, churches, educational establishments, philosophies or documentaries (even if some are misinformed or one-sided). Increasingly it is the soap opera and Hollywood films that inform and shape moral debate and opinion. Attitudes towards a wide of range of issues including relationships, sexuality, suicide, abortion, poverty, euthanasia, racism, immigration etc are presented to the unsuspecting audiences of Coronation Street, Brookside, East Enders, Emergency Room, Desperate Housewives, Sex and the City, Friends, Footballers' Wives, etc, with all the presumed authority of a moral theologian, sociological expert or leading psychiatrist. The effects and intervention of such exposure on the formation of moral and social attitudes as well as identity cannot be underestimated.

At a very simple level this can be illustrated by looking at the effects of mass advertising and marketing of replica football shirts. Many parents know that the onset of the 'latest' football shirt at the start of a new season will be accompanied/preceded by a demand of a son or daughter to get – in the most affirmative terms – the new, and indeed, **real** shirt. And none of us are immune from this. As Celtic supporters we are fortunate to follow a team that wears a unique football shirt of green and white hoops – recognisable the football world over. Perhaps only the likes of Barcelona, Juventus, AC Milan and a few other clubs carry the distinctive colours of their club without need of identification or explanation. Yet, the introduction of sponsors of teams over the past number of years would appear to have affected the simplicity of supporter/club identification. As in the case of every football club (and many aspects of social life) the love of the hooped shirt – for many – is no longer sufficient nor fulfilled unless the latest sponsors' logo emblazons it. It is a matter for ongoing debate amongst conscientious supporters whether we are supporting Celtic Football Club and what that means and entails or, are we supporting the latest sponsor (and whatever that may entail)? And if things are difficult enough, with increasing commercialist interests threatening to influence club traditions identities and symbolism,[14] perhaps a greater danger to the identity, values and ethos that have given birth and defined and sustained a club such as Celtic, and through which a love for the club has been passed on from one generation to the next, is the question of these qualities being sacrificed or seriously modified to satisfy commercial or perceived 'politically correct' interests.

One might question the re-branding, re-invention and re-definition of some football clubs today as they seek to access the financial resources deemed necessary to succeed at the top level in the modern game. Success on the football field (perceived?) is, of course, important – but at what price? If this entails selling fundamental aspects of one's history, traditions and, crucially, breaking the connection with one's own supporter base then, many would argue, the price is simply not worth it. Something else will have surreptitiously been created in place of that which once existed.

The influx of huge amounts of private capital – some from individuals whose prior connection with a club may be non-existent, whose sources of income somewhat questionable, whose power and control over their new acquisition is disproportionate to the wealth they have invested, and whose long-term aim for and stewardship of a particular club is unclear, or, in some cases, all too clear in that they see it purely as a financial venture – has exacerbated the dangers for a number of high profile clubs. One wonders how traditional (in terms of longevity, family and community connections, knowledge and awareness of history and traditions) supporters of clubs such as Chelsea and Hearts, owned by Abramovic and Romanov respectively, view their new situation and the ethics of global capitalism in the way their beloved clubs have been taken over. Perhaps, so long as results are going well and their team is making 'progress' on a large stage, some supporters might ignore the moral questions that lie at the heart of such developments? For some the price of a football club's soul may well be winning the English Premier League or, in the case of Hearts, striving to match Celtic and Glasgow Rangers. Even on the pragmatic level, however, one should be considering the wisdom of entering such a one-sided

[14] The decision by Celtic Football Club to adopt a new design of shirt which did not have continuous hoops in 2001 marked, for some, a potentially dangerous move away from history and tradition. Many fans – and former players – made their dissatisfaction known and the 'breaking of the hoops' was resolved with the unbroken version of the hoops restored in due course.'

relationship. If, one day, such financial backers decide to re-locate their capital elsewhere some clubs might discover exacerbated difficulties. Until then they might ponder what their club actually means or stands for.

There are numerous examples of clubs succumbing to outside pressures and reconstructing themselves as something else.[15] This is not a recent phenomenon although the mechanisms and rationales for changing might be variable. Hibernian Football Club is a clear example of how a club can move from its traditional and historical character and develop an identity altogether different from its original – and, in so doing, become a different entity from that which its founders and first generations of supporters intended. Hibernian, like Celtic, was founded by and for Irish immigrants who had settled in the Edinburgh area. For more than a decade after its foundation Hibernian saw itself in Scotland as the Irish Catholic club par excellence.

However, it is clear that Hibs have over the years abandoned its cultural and historical identity. The club formed in 1875 by Irish-born football enthusiasts, the most prominent being Canon Edward Joseph Hannan and Michael Whelahan, is far removed from the modern Hibernian Football Club: gone even are the green nets and the harp and shamrocks that adorned the ground. Hibs have become not a hybrid Irish club that has become a Scottish institution, but a Scottish club that has historical Irish origins and which are safely tucked away only to be brought to the surface for nostalgic or marketing reasons from time to time. The modern Hibernian can be safe in the knowledge that the rest of Scottish society will not be too scornful of their Irish 'roots' so long as they maintain a contemporary Scottish identity. Some might also argue that this is close to the version of Celtic that some (eg, those particularly associated with the Fergus McCann era) aspire to. Yet others, including this writer, would contend that the interplay of cultural, social and economic forces in Scotland – alongside a unique and distinctive world vision which formed, shaped and sustains Celtic – has ensured that it remains something much more than a football club, but a vehicle through which an immigrant community identity is sustained, nurtured and expressed. In addition, Celtic, as intended by its

[15] The decision by Wimbledon Football Club in 2003 to re-locate 70 miles away in Milton Keynes to form the MK Dons is one of the most extreme examples of how a club can be, literally, changed.

various Irish founders, also became a means by which the human dignity of a Catholic community excluded from social recognition and affirmation came to be proclaimed. In light of contemporary anti-Catholicism and anti-Irishness in Scotland it is not too difficult to see that the club retains a totemic symbolism for many of the offspring of the Irish in Scotland.

Brother Walfrid,
the Irish Community and Celtic Football Club

The way Catholics are expected to learn about or should be taught to approach the world, involves a specific vision based upon an invitation or vocation to embrace and, hence, transform it. It involves a unique conception of humankind based on universality, inclusivity, openness and a distinctive sense of duty to the care of others guided by the gospel values of human dignity and justice. This vision is underpinned by an acceptance of the sacramentality of reality – both physical and social – a view of the sacred and the secular in which there is no division or separation. Indeed, for Catholics there can be no 'God-slot' – a sacred or private religious domain that does not impact upon or lead one into the secular world. Catholicity and Christianity cannot be left at home or outside at the door of whatever building or environment one enters.

As a Marist religious Brother, Walfrid would have recognised the sacred worth of each person, especially the marginalised and those oppressed by poverty and injustice. While looking on the faces of fellow Irish immigrants in the East End of Glasgow he would have been struck by how their conditions conflicted with their God-given dignity. Like many other Catholic leaders Brother Walfrid would have, in the words of the Vatican II document **Gaudium et Spes**, read 'the signs of the times' and responded to the call appropriately. In this sense, Celtic Football Club is a Catholic and Christian response to the conditions of the poor. Celtic is an answer to cultural, social, political and religious oppression, domination, racism, bigotry and exclusion. These are the reasons and rationale as to why Brother Walfrid, John Glass, Pat Welsh, John O'Hara, Thomas Flood, William McKillop, Hugh and Arthur Murphy and Dr. John Conway – gave birth to a unique and special Irish community focus in the shape of a football club.

The vision that Brother Walfrid and the other founders of Celtic possessed went far beyond forming a simple football club or even a straightforward charity organisation. As well as having a political, social and cultural aspect to its identity, as pointed out by numerous contributors to the Celtic Minded series,[16] the club not only had and has these political, social and cultural aspects to its character, but Celtic has also had an ethos which is significantly shaped by the religious and moral outlook of the community which gave it birth and which sustains it. This is not to say that Celtic is a 'Catholic' club in any confessional, exclusive, specific or institutional sense. Indeed, to be such would be a betrayal of the very principles its founding Irish Catholics applied when they formed it. It would also be anathema for such an association or establishment that was significantly influenced by Catholic thinking, social mores and identity, to exclude anyone on the basis of ethnic origin, or religious or national identity.

Walfrid saw the needs of the poor and acted in precisely the same fashion as organisations such as St. Vincent de Paul and the Credit Union Movement that reach out to those in need: likewise, any other Catholic or Christian body that has political, social or economic goals at its heart. It is unfortunate, as well as 'disappointing', that some, with a different vision and agenda, would seek to portray it otherwise. The entire effort and vision of Brother Walfrid, as well as a number of his compatriots, is centred on an other-directed, fully altruistic and universal view of the world and sense of duty.

To that extent it is both humanistic (in that it aims at the realisation of the fundamental dignity of each person) and incarnational (in that is sees each and every person as a fundamentally precious fellow brother and sister). He looked at the world differently because he was called to make the world different. The contradistinction between the humanistic and incarnational way of embracing the world, on the one hand, and the dehumanised means by which modern society seeks to dominate the world, on the other, is clearly expressed by the former leader of the Jesuits, Pedro Arrupe:

[16] J M Bradley, Celtic Minded and Celtic Minded 2, 2004 & 2006

What is it to humanise the world if not to put it at the service of mankind? But the egoist does not humanise the material creation, he dehumanises people themselves. He changes people into things by dominating them, exploiting them, and taking to himself the fruits of their labour. The tragedy of it all is that by doing this the egoist dehumanises himself. He surrenders himself to the possessions he covets; he becomes their slave – no longer a person, self-possessed but an un-person, a thing driven by his blind desires and their objects.[17]

As the main founder of Celtic Football Club Brother Walfrid clearly shared this vision. He did not solely set out to set up a successful sporting club that would simply be a means of delivering charitable goals such as providing meals and education for those in need – although he also succeeded in doing both. He set out, however, to recognise the God-given human dignity of each person and, as a religious person, he would have viewed his actions in helping to found Celtic in line with a vision beyond the secular. Looking at those oppressed by poverty and social exclusion in the latter decades of the nineteenth century in the East End of Glasgow, Brother Walfrid may well have reflected on 'The Sermon on the Mount' for inspiration and guidance:

Seeing the crowds, he went up on the mountain, and when he sat down his disciples came to him. And he opened his mouth and taught them, saying:
'Blessed are the poor in spirit,
for theirs is the kingdom of heaven.
Blessed are those who mourn, for they shall be comforted.
Blessed are the meek, for they shall inherit the earth.
Blessed are those who hunger and thirst for righteousness,
for they shall be satisfied.
Blessed are the merciful, for they shall obtain mercy.
Blessed are the pure in heart, for they shall see God.
Blessed are the peacemakers,
for they shall be called sons of God.
Blessed are those who are persecuted for righteousness' sake,
for theirs is the kingdom of heaven.
Blessed are you when men revile you and persecute you and
utter all kinds of evil against you falsely on my account.
Rejoice and be glad, for your reward is great in heaven, for so
men persecuted the prophets who were before you.'
(Mt.5: 1-12)

[17] P. Arrupe, 1973, p. 12

To many of those listening to Jesus at the Sermon on the Mount he must have appeared as a most utopian and radical of thinkers. A young firebrand rabbi, standing on a hillside addressing the marginalised and oppressed, just outside the Walls of Jerusalem above the magnificence of the Temple, a place from which many of them would have been excluded due to their lack of wealth and lowly social status. What message did he give them? That: **theirs** is the Kingdom of God. . . that **they** shall be comforted. . . that **they** shall inherit the earth. . . that **they** shall be satisfied. . . that **they** shall be called sons of God. . . that **they** shall see God. (my bold)

If ever there was a world turned upside down then Jesus had just proclaimed it!

The people who live on the margins feel abandoned precisely because they have been abandoned. Homeless people, travellers, drug abusers, the unemployed, immigrants and the other groups of non-persons in the affluent world, the slum dwellers in the Third World and victims of climate change: all of these people are the conscious and unconscious victims of a social order that not only doesn't care about them, but they are necessary victims of an economic order that needs them to be sacrificed so that the rich and powerful continue to be rich and powerful. It was exactly the same at the time of Jesus. Hence, he proclaimed a Kingdom that was based on the very opposite to what our kingdom, based on greed, individualism, inequality, exclusion and injustice, is about. The Kingdom Jesus outlined at the Sermon on the Mount and throughout his teachings and affirmed through his actions is based on absolute respect for the dignity of others – and especially the poor – and a commitment towards ensuring that the needs of all are met, even if this means (which it does) that the material abundance of the West will have to be given up in order to meet the needs of others. If we are sincere about abolishing poverty then we will have to be prepared to abolish our affluent Western lifestyles.

Like every effective minister of Christianity Walfrid recognised that the Christian ministry has to be contextualised and placed in its historical, concrete situation. The context then was the East End of Glasgow at the close of the nineteenth century. As a result of much of the thinking behind Celtic, the Club and many within its community of supporters have continuously reached out to those in need. O'Hagan notes that the social justice tradition and ethos of the founders of Celtic has continued. Despite the pressures of developing into a thriving professional football club he cites the forming of the 'Celtic Charity Fund' in 1995 as a conscious revitalisation of the Club's official charitable traditions and recognition of its 'responsibility of being a major social institution promoting health, well-being and social integration'.[18] Beyond the club though, it has essentially been many of the supporters that Celtic was founded for that have maintained the ethos of charity and living in service of others as an inherent, meaningful and distinguishing feature of the club's character. Mirroring the club's meaning and essence, it is the moral actions and social and political consciousness of the core Celtic support that helps make Celtic more than a football club.

[18] Bradley 2004, p. 99

Celtic through and through

Tommy Burns*

In 1989 I wrote three dedications in my book 'Twists and Turns, The Tommy Burns Story'. One was for my wife Rosemary and another was for the Celtic supporters who I thanked for accepting me: 'You'll Never Walk Alone'. The final one was to Christ's Mother.

> To Our Blessed Lady. My thanks for carrying me through all the hard times and keeping my feet on the ground on the many great times – your servant

Some people seem embarrassed to talk about their faith. However, for me it's never been a problem. It's at the very core of who and what I am. Ironically, my father worked away a lot so it was my mother that was the one who put a lot into raising us in the faith, making sure we got to Mass, despite the fact that she was a Protestant and didn't convert to Catholicism until the early 1990s when she was probably about 70. My mother didn't really have much knowledge of our faith during these times but probably felt it was right and the best thing to do. For many years I have done my best to attend Mass and receive Holy Communion every day. I also regularly visit a Chapel just to spend ten minutes in silence with God.

When I attended St Mary's Primary School in the east end of Glasgow, only ten minutes walk from Celtic Park, we learned a lot about our faith from Marist Brothers like Jerome and Kazimiarz. The Marists are of course important to the chronicle of Celtic and its following and Jerome used to fill me with great

* Tommy Burns composed this chapter the year before he died on 15th May 2008. It is dedicated to his wife Rosemary, their children and grandchildren. Our Lady pray for them.

stories about Celtic. At school there was a strong ethos of daily prayer and therefore a small seed was being planted regarding this side of our lives. I also prayed that I would one day play for Celtic.

I took my faith seriously from a young age and was always conscious about doing right and wrong. I lived in an area that was blighted by a lot of wrong-doing and although in amongst it I was never that comfortable with it all. Football in that sense was very much a saving grace for me. It helped take us off the street, offered a lot of fun and also allowed us to meet some good people who in turn were a positive influence all around. There were others too that weren't such good role models and we often heard older lads talking about things they shouldn't have been doing, what gangs they were running with and things like that. There were a lot of dangers there too of course and parts of Glasgow where people like me came from were very territorial and could be dangerous for young teenage boys. However, I was always very aware of being a Catholic and having a conscience that informed me about what was right and what was wrong though in that climate it wasn't easy. I had my mind set on being a footballer but a lot of friends and acquaintances around me were finding other things to do and making such activities seem attractive. Then it was alcohol whereas now this has been added to with drugs of course.

There comes a time though when you have to make a mature and responsible decision and with regards to becoming a footballer, I had to break away from the things that were beginning to dominate in my area. I had games to prepare for and going out on Friday evenings and such like just wasn't on if I was serious about my football – and I was. I went out with my friends on a Saturday night but by Sunday I was back to preparing for the week ahead. So even from a young age I was conscious of looking after myself and preparing for football and I think my faith reinforced the idea of my being able to discipline and restrain myself. I suppose the further I was progressing in football the more I felt that God was guiding me and allowing me this opportunity. Even when I was down sometimes I would say a wee prayer and face whatever was ahead with a new confidence.

Life is full of challenges and God has always been there to help me.

Passing my faith on to my children has also been very important to me. Getting them going to Mass regularly while they would also of course get an input from their Catholic schools: these were and are important. However, maybe it's by showing an example that it all comes down to in the end, how to treat people whether they are Catholic, Protestant, Hindu, whatever they are. I generally think that there are many good people out there with no faith who are still outstanding: they are nice human beings. Nonetheless, the fact that Catholics have faith is something that is worth hanging on to. Maybe being a Catholic doesn't make us any better than anyone else but I do think that it's our relationship with God that counts most. It's partly about how many times, as well as when, you communicate with God: and not just when things are going against you.

A lot of people might just live away as they please and suit themselves and only turn to God when things go wrong. Maybe that's part of God's plan that different people have different ways of looking at it. I talk to God often, tell him how much I love Him, thank Him or whatever. I am inspired by God's presence. Faith helps make me a less self-centred person, it makes me appreciate that I can't do it all myself. We're only passing through this life, regardless of how many years we are given. I think we are put here for a reason – to develop our souls. I think we are supposed to live on this earth but also remain detached from overly focusing on worldly things. It's about what we can do, what we can achieve, about how many people we can help in the day and lift their spirits and generally try to be part of something that's uplifting.

Faith is good, it's focused, its true. It also assists us deal with people that might be hostile towards us, like maybe those connected to other football teams with a history against us. We can see beyond that and see them as human first and foremost – as important in God's eyes. That's always the number one ingredient before we think of them as supporters of 'the other' team. We should not allow ourselves to hate just because someone hates us or belongs to something different from us. As life goes by we are faced with many temptations, but our conscience, that voice inside, keeps pulling us back on track. When God looks at us on our death-beds it is to be hoped that He finds the person He wants to.

When I came to Celtic there ware a significant number of people who were conscientious practising Catholics. Celtic did have, and always has had players and supporters who were Protestant or of no faith, but we have always been a club where Catholics were not inhibited the way they might have been elsewhere. The Catholic faith was something people here were comfortable with and no one felt a need to hide or disguise it.

This is one of the reasons why I had a lot of difficulty with Fergus McCann's Boys Against Bigotry campaign. I had been here a long time and as far as I was concerned our club had no problem with bigotry. We were at ease with Catholics, Catholicism was a part of our roots and heritage, but I never sensed anything untoward against people at our club or elsewhere who were not from the Catholic faith. That wouldn't have been Catholic in the first place and would have been against what being Catholic was about.

Something happened at the club around Fergus's time – whether it was someone in PR or something I don't know – but they seemed to want to embark on a sort of crusade: to change aspects of the club. I told Fergus that we don't have bigotry here. We certainly have supporters who were idiots who hated Rangers or that hated Protestants because that is what they had learned and they had not learned anything different. Some of the obscene things I've heard at times I wonder where or earth these people could have come from: sometimes the numbers are small but they are vociferous, daft and often the most drunken of people: it's an ignorance really. It's probably the case that those kinds of people harbour prejudice and bigotries that Celtic and most of its real supporters want nothing to do with. It's difficult to deal with this and I disagree entirely with these kinds of people.

Nonetheless, I always felt that the Boys Against Bigotry campaign was not really addressing these people and a whole lot of other things were being thrown in or invented. Certainly as a club I never experienced any bigotry within or towards anyone else. That would be against our ethos. Some of greatest players, and some that I have played with like Kenny Dalglish and Danny McGrain are of course Protestants. There was never so much as a whisper about that from anyone at this club. It didn't matter. So long as they wanted to play for Celtic that's all that mattered. The club has always stood in a way that said all were equal at Celtic. Then all of a sudden I was pulled into this campaign.

Obviously Rangers have been different about all these kinds of things but I think in recent times that club has made an effort to deal with its past. I heard rumours whereby some people were saying that it almost became difficult for a Catholic to get a job during Fergus McCann's time here. However, looking back on it from the perspective of twenty years later, I think I understand it better than that now. I think Fergus simply didn't want to have anyone too close to him that was driven by a strong emotional attachment to the club, which I think was a contradiction of the Celtic ethos. Fergus didn't want anyone telling him what the fans wanted, how they saw the club and what it meant to them. He surrounded himself with a lot of people who had good business acumen but weren't into the ethos of the club. Even in terms of the club's charity giving as opposed to the supporters I could never quite get my head around a charity function where a seat cost £50 or more a head. Sure that might raise a lot of money but how many people were being excluded from even attending the event in the first place because of the extortionate cost: even the idea of signing the back of a £20 note for a raffle and the auctions and things like that? I have always maintained that the club needs to back up its founding fathers and history by genuine charity giving and don't rely on the supporters to do this all the time.

Fergus McCann came in with a total business plan and nothing else mattered. Where he did pay heed to the emotional side of course was when it came to making him money: and so it proved. It was unbelievable at the time the amount of money Celtic supporters put into their own club. He knew that money was out there and he had his plan in place and wouldn't be deflected from it in any shape or form. He knew he had to pay a lot of money for salaries, for transfers and things like that but he was quite happy for the club to drift along while Celtic-driven people were looking across the city where Rangers were winning six and seven in a row. He never appreciated what Celtic had achieved when the club won nine-in-a-row and he never recognised what this meant to the support. Although how important it really is anyway I don't know.

When you're at Celtic as manager and also a supporter then you are part of all the emotions, but Fergus had his five-year plan and he carried that through. The most important thing for Fergus was not success on the pitch but getting his business plan through. At the end of the day for a businessman to come to Celtic and do what he did then he has to be considered a success in those terms. In an odd way I admire the way he went about it for the simple reason that he did what he said he would.

Fergus didn't listen to any tittle-tattle from small-minded people at the club. There's always been people attached to Celtic, even seeing themselves as Celtic minded, that I think didn't do our ethos justice: people with their own agendas and who ducked and dived here and there. Fergus could see through them: he was good at that. He wasn't a football man but he was driven by business and as such he can be considered a successful businessman, through I think the five years that he spent here at the club probably took its toll on his well-being.

When I was a youngster coming into Celtic I looked at players like Kenny Dalglish as the number one. Danny McGrain also of course was someone to look up to and he became a great friend. Others that said something significant about Celtic in terms of the ethos and identity of the club, how they thought about the club and what it meant to them were Jim Steele the club masseur who I first met when I was fifteen years old. I had a lot of contact with him then through cleaning the dressing rooms, tidying strips, cleaning boots etc. He was always here and he was also with Scotland when I played with them too of course. The one thing I could do for him was when we won the Scottish Cup in 1995 in my first season as manager, he led the team out at Hampden.

He loved that moment and really appreciated it. He was one of the nicest and most selfless human beings I ever met: he always gave of himself. He was a good Celtic man who worked for this club for many years for nothing and ended up with something like a fifty years association with the club.

Another of that type was John Fitzsimmons who was the doctor here for years and his faith meant much to him too. Whenever Celtic travelled away in Europe it was John that would go and find the nearest Chapel for Mass. Whereas John was quiet and reserved, in many ways Steely was everything else – he was the ambience, the character, the lot.

Paul McStay was another good example of what good Celtic people should be like: brought up in a good family and was always a big Celtic fan. Good-living people and Paul recognised the example people like him had to give as Celtic people. He stayed here during some very tough times. He knew the importance of Celtic and tried to set a good example. It's important that the people at this club can pass on what has been and what remains valuable from our past.

These things need to be passed onto the youth that are coming through at the club. It is imperative that the kids coming though at Celtic don't just get a good football education but also an education that informs them about how unique this club is, its value and what it means. Try to make them not only good footballers but also good people. That's why we are very careful about who we appoint. The club should mean something to these sorts of people so that they themselves can pass this on: good football coaches but also exceptional people.

People like Gordon Strachan have learned much more about this club from being here and I think he definitely sees us as more than just a football club now. If it's true that it's the religious, social, political or whatever that makes a club different from the vast majority of other clubs then I'm sure also that players who come to Celtic from outside of Scotland eventually grasp not only how big this club is, but also the glory of being part of this great club's history: they leave with a feeling that this club is something special. You don't need to come from a Catholic or

Irish background to become part of this club, special though these things may be to our history and to many of the support. This club prides itself on its openness to people from all sorts of backgrounds. This club is about us and not about what or who we are against. There's a lot to football rivalries but this club is much more than the sum total of that kind of thinking. This club is about so much that is positive. This is Celtic where people never walk alone.

heriot-watt & edinburgh universities celtic supporters club presents for one last time

The Tommy Burns Supper

DISORGANISED FLAME-HAIRED DEVOTION SINCE 1987

Teviot Row House Student Union
Edinburgh University

Friday 30 October 2009
7pm until very late

Tickets: £30 each

A night of commemoration and celebration

Guest of Honour:
Mrs Rosemary Burns

And many other special guests

TommyBurns 10
SKIN CANCER TRUST

Casa Alianza
Opening Doors for Homeless Youth

All proceeds to the Tommy Burns Skin Cancer Trust and Casa Alianza

Contributors

Dr Joseph M Bradley, is editor of the collection of 'Celtic Minded' essays. He is also the author of Ethnic and Religious Identity in Modern Scotland (Avebury 1995), The Gaelic Athletic Association and Irishness in Scotland (Argyll, 2007) and joint author of Sport Worlds: a sociological perspective (Human Kinetics 2002). The latter book was translated for China in 2009. Dr Bradley has published in edited books, journals and newspapers on sporting matters in relation to religion, ethnicity, diaspora and politics. His publications in journals in Britain, USA, France and Ireland include works on Orangeism in Scotland, Scotland's international support, politics in Scottish football and the Irish diaspora in Scotland. He is senior lecturer in Sports Studies at the University of Stirling.

Tommy Burns (1956-2008) signed professional for Celtic in 1973. He made his debut in early 1975 and played his final game in November 1989, playing over 500 times for the club. Tommy returned as manager from 1994 to 1997. He again returned in early 2000 to assist Kenny Dalglish in his short-lived managerial role. With the arrival of Martin O'Neill, Tommy took charge of youth development at Celtic and was instrumental in instigating the new academy at Lennoxtown.

Dr Roisín Coll is BEd Programme Leader at the University of Glasgow and lectures in Religious Education within the Faculty of Education. Her research interests include the Religious Education curriculum in Scotland, Catholic education and Irish influences in Scottish culture. She has a range of publications and has recently co-authored a book, 'All Together: creative prayer with children'.

Gerry Coyle is a freelance writer and journalist. He was born and lives in Glasgow, although part of his formative years were spent in Ireland, where he attended St. Fintan's Christian Brothers School in Dublin. His work has appeared in a variety of publications in Britain and Ireland including the Irish Times.

Robert A. Davis is Professor of Religious and Cultural Education, and Deputy Dean of the Faculty of Education in the University of Glasgow. He has written widely on religion and education, childhood studies, folklore and myth, and literary criticism. His recent publications include 'Futures of Faith Schools', in S. McKinney (Ed), Faith Schools in the 21st Century, Edinburgh: Dunedin Academic Press, 2008; and 'Escaping Through Flames: Halloween as a Christian Festival' in M. Foley and H. O'Donnell (Eds), Trick or Treat: Halloween in a Globalising World, Newcastle: CSP, 2009.

Colin Deeny was born in Glasgow in 1970 and brought up in Toryglen. He is now married with children and lives in Inishowen, County Donegal. He is a pharmacist by profession. His father is from County Derry and his mother is from Glasgow, but of Lithuanian parentage. Is maith é an bád a dhéanann amach an caladh a d'fhág sé.

Dr. Aidan Donaldson is Assistant Head of Religious Education at St. Mary's Christian Brothers' Grammar School, Belfast. He has acted as education spokesperson for the Catholic Church on various forums and in the media on numerous occasions and has published widely on the subject of Catholic education. His most recent work on Catholic schooling in Northern Ireland was used to front the European section of the highly regarded International Handbook of Catholic Education (Gerald Grace and Joseph O'Keefe, SJ, (eds., Dordrecht: Springer, 2007). As co-ordinator of the radical Christian Brothers justice organisation, Project Zambia, he has visited Africa on numerous occasions helping to establish and develop links with projects in the missions among the victims of poverty and injustice. He is also currently working in support of the Edmund Rice International in Geneva on the issue of advocacy for the marginalised and dispossessed. His personal account of his experiences in Africa, entitled Discovering God in the Margins: Reflections of a Justice volunteer, is due to be published in the Spring of 2010.

Stephen Ferrie is a communications professional working in the financial services industry in Scotland. He is married with two children and lives in Coatbridge where his love of Celtic has been carefully nurtured since the 1960s. This is his third contribution to the Celtic Minded collection.

Jackie Fitzpatrick teaches Irish in a Belfast Secondary school. After working for twenty years in a variety of unskilled/semi-skilled occupations he graduated as a mature student, with an honours degree in Celtic and Italian from Queen's University Belfast in 1992. After completing the Post Graduate Certificate in Education he started teaching in his current employment. He recently completed a MA in Irish Translation Studies (QUB). As a result of anti-Catholic pogroms in 1920s Belfast, his grandmother sought refuge among relatives on the Garngad Road in Glasgow, where his mother was born in June 1922.

Gerard Gough is Chief Sub-Editor and Reporter for the Scottish Catholic Observer. In 2006, along with editor Harry Conroy, he took the 'Blessing yourself is not a crime' petition to the relevant committee of the Scottish Parliament. He has also written for the Irish World, Celtic View and is a published poet.

Professor Mary Hickman is Director of the Institute for the Study of European

Transformations at London Metropolitan University. She established the Irish Studies Centre at the University in the 1980s and has been a Visiting Professor at: New York University, Columbia University, the New School for Social Research and Victoria University in Melbourne. Recent publications include: 'Census ethnic categories and second generation identities', Journal of Ethnic and Migration Studies (forthcoming 2010); 'Migration, Postindustrialism and the Globalised Nation State: social capital and social cohesion re-examined' Ethnic and Racial Studies (with Helen Crowley) 2008 and 'Monocultural (Re)Imaginings in Ireland and Britain' Translocations: The Irish Migration, Race and Social Transformation Review, 2007.

Professor Christine Kinealy is a graduate of Trinity College, Dublin. She has written extensively on nineteenth-century Irish history. Her publications include, Repeal and Rebellion – 1848 in Ireland (Manchester University Press, 2009), The Forgotten Famine – Hunger and Poverty in Belfast 1840-50 (with Gerard MacAtasney, Pluto Press, 2000), and This Great Calamity – The Irish Famine 1845-52 (Gill and Macmillan, Dublin, 1994; republished in 2006). She is currently Professor of Arts and Letters at Drew University in the United States.

Gerard McDade is a broadcaster, writer and stand-up comedian

from Greenock. He has worked extensively with Celtic FC, club channel CelticTV as well as BBC Scotland and commercial radio. He has just written his first book, Celtic – The Supersonic '70s.

Dr James MacMillan is a composer whose music is played all over the world. He studied as an undergraduate in music at the University of Edinburgh, and completed his doctoral studies at the University of Durham. He has numerous honorary doctorates and fellowships from various British universities and colleges. He was awarded a CBE in 2004. His Edinburgh Festival speech 'Scotlands Shame: anti-Catholicism as a barrier to genuine pluralism', was delivered in 1999 provoking a bout of national soul-searching. While alienating him from many of the Scottish commentariat, it has attracted much more objective and thoughtful reflection elsewhere. He composed the music, Walfrid at the Gates of Paradise for the unveiling ceremony of the commemorative sculpture of Brother Walfrid at Celtic Park in 2005.

Willy Maley is Professor of English Literature at the University of Glasgow and Visiting Professor in Irish Studies at the University of Sunderland. He is editor of Representing Ireland: Literature and the Origins of Conflict, 1534-1660 (Cambridge, 1993) and Edmund Spenser's View of the State of Ireland (Oxford, 1997). Together with Ian Auld, Bertie's brother, he wrote The Lions of Lisbon (1992), a play celebrating the silver anniversary of Celtic's European Cup victory. Willy also contributed essays to Celtic Minded volumes 1 and 2. This completes his hat-trick.

Tom Minogue is a retired businessman who has lived in Rosyth and Dunfermline all his life. He served a craft apprenticeship in Rosyth Dockyard and joined the merchant navy before returning home to marry and work in the construction industry. At its peak in 1987 his firm employed over 200 skilled craftsmen. Since retirement Tom has been active in civic issues.

Dr Sarah Morgan is a civil servant based in London who retains an interest in Irish diaspora studies and particularly the Irish in Britain. She was formerly based at the Irish Studies Centre, University of North London (now London Metropolitan University). Sarah worked on a number of research projects, most recently the Irish 2 Project. She has published in numerous academic journals and contributed to the study for the Irish government's Taskforce on Policy Regarding Emigrants.

Professor Patrick Reilly was educated at the University of Glasgow and the University of Oxford where he completed his research degree on Jonathan Swift. He was Head of the Department of English at the University of Glasgow before retiring as Emiritus Professor in 1997. A journalist and broadcaster, he has published seven books on literary criticism including studies of Swift, Orwell, Golding, Fielding, Conrad and Joyce. He lives in Glasgow.

Bronwen Walter is Professor of Irish Diaspora Studies at Anglia Ruskin University. She has published widely on Irish migration to Britain and Irish women in the diaspora. She is co-author of the Commission for Racial Equality Report Discrimination and the Irish Community in Britain (1997) and her book Outsiders inside: whiteness, place and Irish women was published by Routledge in 2001. Her current research explores multi-generational Irish identities in Britain, New Zealand and Newfoundland.

Lewis Waugh recently retired as a Support for Learning teacher in Edinburgh and divides his time between painting, photography, family life, mountaineering and supporting Celtic. He graduated from Edinburgh College of Art and holds an M.Ed. in Special Educational Needs. He has worked in the on-shore oil industry; taught art in Edinburgh; and held the post of Assistant Director of a psycho-therapeutic community in Surrey.

Bibliography

Allison L. The Politics of Sport, Manchester University Press, 1986

Ahmed, B., P. Nicolson and C. Spenser 'The Social Construction of Racism: The Case of Second Generation Bangladeshis', Journal of Community and Applied Social Psychology 10: 33–48, 2000

Anderson B. Imagined Communities: Reflections on the Origins and Spread of Nationalisms, Verso, London, 1991

Andrews D L (Ed) Manchester United: A Thematic Study, Routledge, London, 2004

Anthias, Floya & Yuval-Davis, Nira Racialized Boundaries: Race, Nation, Gender, Colour and Class and the Anti-racist Struggle, London: Routledge, 1992

Archer I. & Royle T. (Eds) We'll Support You Evermore: The Impertinent Saga of Scottish 'Fitba', London: Souvenir Press, 1976

Armstrong G. and Giulionotti R. (Eds) Entering the Field: New Perspectives in World Football, Oxford: Berg, 1997

Armstrong, G and Giulionotti, R. (Eds), Fear and Loathing in World Football, Oxford, Berg, 2001

Arrowsmith, A. 'Plastic Paddy: Negotiating Identity in Second Generation "Irish-English" Writing', Irish Studies Review 8(1): 35–43, 2000

Arrupe P. Men for Others, International Centre for Jesuit Education, Rome, 1973

Audrey S. Multiculturalism in Practice: Irish, Jewish, Italian and Pakistani migration to Scotland, Ashgate, Aldershot, 2000

Bairner A. 'Football and the idea of Scotland' in G Jarvie and G Walker (Eds), Scottish Sport in the Making of the Nation, Leicester: Leicester University Press, 9-26, 1994

Beresford D. Ten Men Dead, Grafton Books, London, 1987

Billig M. Banal Nationalism, London: Sage, 1995

Billig M, 'Humour and hatred: the racist jokes of the Ku Klux Klan' in Discourse and Society, 12, 3, pp.267-289, 2001

Black I. Tales of the Tartan Army, Edinburgh: Mainstream Publishing 1997

Blain N. and Boyle R. Battling along the boundaries: The marking of Scottish identity in sports journalism, in G. Jarvie and G. Walker (Eds) 'Scottish Sport in the Making of the Nation' Leicester: Leicester University Press, 125-141, 1994

Bloch J & Fitzgerald P, British Intelligence and Covert Action, Brandon, 1983

Bonnett, A. White Identities, Historical and International Perspectives, Harlow: Prentice Hall, 2000

Boyle M. 'Edifying the rebellious Gael: uses of memories of Ireland's troubled past among the west of Scotland's Irish catholic diaspora' in D. Harvey, R. Jones, N. McInroy and C. Milligan Celtic Geographies: old cultures, new times, London: Routledge, 2002

Boyle R. and Haynes R. 'The Grand old game: football, media and identity in Scotland', in Media, Culture and Society Vol.18, No.4, pp.549-564, 1996

Boyle R. and Haynes R. Power Play: Sport, the Media and Popular Culture, London, Longman, 2000

Bradley J M. Celtic Minded: essays on religion, politics, society, identity and football, Argyll Publishing, Argyll Scotland, 2004

Bradley J M. Celtic Minded 2: Essays on Celtic Football Culture and Identity, Argyll Publishing, Argyll Scotland, 2006

Bradley J.M. Ethnic and Religious Identity in Scotland: Politics, Culture and Football, Aldershot: Avebury, 1995

Bradley J.M. 'Facets of the Irish Diaspora: "Irishness" in 20th Century Scotland' in Irish Journal of Sociology Vol.6, 1996

Bradley J M. 'Gaelic Sport, Soccer and Irishness in Scotland' in Sport in Society, Vol 10, No 3, pp.439-456, 2007

Bradley J.M. 'Identity, Politics and Culture: Orangeism in Scotland' in Scottish Affairs No 16, Summer, pp.104-128, 1996

Bradley J.M. 'Images of Scottishness and Otherness in International Football' Social Identities: Journal for the Study of Race, Nation and Culture, 9, 1, pp.7-23, 2003

Bradley J.M. 'Imagining Scotland: nationality, cultural identities, football and discourses of Scottishness' Stirling Research Papers in Sports Studies, University of Stirling, 2001

Bradley J.M. 'Intermarriage, Education, and Discrimination' in T. M. Devine (ed) St Mary's Hamilton: A Social History 1846-1996, John Donald, Edinburgh, pp.83-94, 1995

Bradley J M. The Patriot Game, International Journal for the Sociology of Sport, vol 37, no 2, pp. 177-197, 2002

Bradley J.M. 'Profile of a Roman Catholic Parish in Scotland' in Scottish Affairs No 14, Winter, pp.123-139, 1996

Bradley J.M. The Gaelic Athletic Association and Irishness in Scotland, Argyll Publishing, 2007

Bradley J.M. 'We Shall Not Be Moved! Mere Sport, Mere Songs?: a tale of Scottish Football' in Fanatics, London: Routledge, pp.203-218, 1998

Bradley J M, 'Wearing the green: a history of nationalist demonstrations among the diaspora in Scotland' in The Irish Parading Tradition: Following the Drum, Ed T G Fraser, pp 111-128. Macmillan Press, 2000

Bradley J.M., Maguire J., Jarvie, Mansfield L. 'Sport Worlds: A sociological perspective' Human Kinetics, USA, 2002

Brah A. Cartographies of Diaspora. London: Routledge, 1996

Brah A., Hickman M.J., and Mac an Ghaill M. Thinking Identities: Ethnicity, Racism and Culture, London: MacMillan Press, 1999

Bredin E, Disturbing the Peace: the Way of Disciples, Blackrock, Co. Dublin, 1985

Brown A. (Ed) Fanatics: Power, Identity and Fandom in Football, London: Routledge, 1998

Brown A., McCrone D., Paterson L., and Surridge P. The Scottish Electorate: The 1997 General Election and Beyond, London: Macmillan Press, 1999

Brown S.J. 'Outside the Covenant: The Scottish Presbyterian Churches and Irish Immigration 1922-1938', The Innes Review, Vol.XLII, No.1, Spring pp.19-45 1991

Brockman, J R, SJ, (ed.), The Violence of Love, Harper & Row, New York, 1988

Brown C. The Social History of Religion in Scotland Since 1730 Methuen, London, 1987

Brown C. 'Did Urbanisation Secularize Britain' Urban History Yearbook 1988

Brown C. Religion and Society in Scotland since 1707, Edinburgh: Edinburgh University Press, 1997

Brown S.J. 'Outside the Covenant: The Scottish Presbyterian Churches and Irish Immigration 1922-1938' in The Innes Review, Vol.XLII, No.1, Spring pp.19-45, 1991

Brubaker, R. 'Cognitive Perspectives', Symposium on Ethnicity,'Ethnicities 1(1): 15–17, 2001

Brubaker R. 'The return of assimilation? Changing perspectives on immigration and its sequels in France, Germany, and the United States' in Ethnic and Racial Studies, 24, 4, pp.531-548, 2001

Bruce S. 'No Pope Of Rome: Anti-Catholicism In Modern Scotland' Mainstream Publishing, Edinburgh, 1985

Bruce S. 'Out of the ghetto: the ironies of acceptance' The Innes Review, Vol.XLIII, No.2, pp.145-154, 1992

Bruce S. 'Comparing Scotland and Northern Ireland' in Scotland's Shame: Bigotry and sectarianism in modern Scotland, Mainstream, Edinburgh pp.135-142, 2000

Bruce S. 'Catholic Schools in Scotland: a rejoinder to Conroy' in Oxford Review of Education, vol 29, no 2, pp.269-277, 2003

Buckley M. 'Sitting on your politics: the Irish amongst the British and the women among the Irish' in J. McLaughlin (ed) Location and Dislocation in Contemporary Irish Society, Cork University Press, Cork, pp.94-132, 1997

Burdsey D, ' "One of the Lads"? Dual Ethnicity and Assimilated Ethnicities in the Careers of British Asian Professional Footballers.' Ethnic and Racial Studies 27, no. 5, 757-779, 2004

Burdsey D and Chappell R, ' "And If You Know Your History. . ." An Examination of the formation of football clubs in Scotland and their role in the construction of social identity' in The Sports Historian, No.21, pp.94-106, 2001

Burdsey D & Chappell R. Soldiers, sashes and shamrocks: Football and social identity in Scotland and Northern Ireland, Sociology of Sport Online (SOSOL), School of Physical Education, vol 6, 1, 2003.

Campbell, S. 'Race of Angels: The Critical Reception of Second-generation Irish Musicians', Irish Studies Review 6(2): 165–74, 1998

Campbell, S. 'Beyond "Plastic Paddy": A Re-Examination of the Second generation Irish in England', Immigrants and Minorities 18 (2 & 3): 266–88, 1999

Campbell, S. 'Britpop: The Importance of being Irish – The Relevance of Ethnicity for Understanding Second Generation Irish Musicians in England', in T. Mitchell and P. Doyle (Eds) Changing Sounds: New Directions and Configurations in Popular Music, Sydney: University of Technology, 2000

Campbell, S. 'Sounding Out the Margins: Ethnicity and Popular Music in British Cultural Studies', in G. Smyth and G. Norquay (Eds) Across the Margins: Cultural Identities and Change in the Atlantic Archipelago, Manchester: Manchester University Press, 2002

Campbell T. and Woods P. The Glory and The Dream, The History of Celtic FC, 1887-1986, Mainstream Publishing, 1986

Canning Rev B.J. Padraig H Pearse and Scotland, published by Padraig Pearse Centenary Commemoration Committee, Glasgow, 1979

Cassidy L. 'Faded Pictures from Irish Town' in Causeway, pp.34-38, Autumn, 1996

Castro-Ramos E, 'Loyalties, commodity and fandom: Real Madrid, Barca and Athletic fans versus 'La Furia Roja' during the World Cup', Sport in Society, vol 11, no 6, pp.696-710, 2008

Cathcart R. The most contrary region: the BBC in Northern Ireland 1924-1984, Belfast: Blackstaff Press, 1984

Cherwell District Council. North Oxfordshire: the Cherwell Valley, Banbury: Cherwell District Council, (undated)

Clifford, J. 'Diasporas', Cultural Anthropology 9:302-338, 1994

Coakley J.J. Sport in Society: Issues and Controversies, Mosby, Colerado, 1990

Coakley J.J. 'Sport in Society: Issues and Controversies' USA, Irwin, McGraw-Hill, 1998

Cohen, P. 'The Perversions of Inheritance: Studies in the Making of Multiracist Britain', in P. Cohen and H. Bains (Eds) Multi-racist Britain, London: Macmillan, 1988

Cohen, P. 'Through a Glass Darkly: Intellectuals on Race', in P. Cohen (ed.) New Ethnicities, Old Racisms, London: Zed Books, 1999

Cooney J. Scotland and the Papacy, Paul Harris, Edinburgh, 1982

Conroy J. ' "Yet I Live Here. . ." A Reply to Bruce on Catholic Education in Scotland' Oxford Review of Education Vol.29, No.3, Sept pp.403-412, 2003

Crabbe T, 'England fans – A New Club for a New England? Social Inclusion, Authenticity and the Performance of Englishness at "Home" and "Away", Leisure Studies, vol 23, no 1, pp63-78, Jan 2004

Crawford M. E. (Ed) The Hungry Stream: Essays on Emigration and Famine, published by Institute of Irish Studies Queens University Belfast & Centre for Emigration Studies Ulster-American Folk Park, 1995

Curtice, J and Seawright, D. 'The Decline of the Scottish Conservatives and Unionist Party 1950-1992: Religion, Ideology or Economics?' Journal of Contemporary History, 2, 2, 319-342, 1995

Curtis L. Ireland The Propaganda War, Pluto Press, 1984

Curtis L. Nothing But The Same Old Story: The roots of Anti-Irish Racism, published by Information on Ireland, 5th edition, 1988

Davis G. The Irish In Britain 1815-1914, Gill and Macmillan, 1991

Della Porta D & M Diani, Social Movements: An Introduction, Oxford, Blackwell, 1999

Devine T.M. (ed) 'Irish Immigrants and Scottish Society in the Nineteenth and Twentieth Centuries, Proceedings of the Scottish Historical Studies Seminar: University of Strathclyde, 1989/90', John Donald Publishers Ltd, 1991

Devine T.M. Scotland's Shame: Bigotry and Sectarianism in Modern Scotland, Edinburgh: Mainstream, 2000

Devine T.M. (ed) St Mary's Hamilton: A Social History, 1846-1996, John Donald, Edinburgh, 1995

Devine T.M. & Mitchison R. People and Society in Scotland: Vol.1, 1760-1830, John Donald, Edinburgh, 1988

Dickson T. (Ed) Capital and Class in Scotland, John Donald Publishers 1982

Docherty D. The Celtic Football Companion, John Donald, Edinburgh 1986

Donovan R. 'Voices of Distrust: The Expression of Anti-Catholic Feeling in Scotland 1778-1781', in The Innes Review Vol.XXIX, 2, pp.111-139, 1978

Doyle A. 'Ethnocentrism and History Textbooks: representation of the Irish Famine 1845-49 in history textbooks in English secondary schools' Intercultural Education, Vol.13, No.3, 2002

Dunning E. Sport Matters: sociological studies of sport, violence and civilization, London, Routledge pp.130-158, 1999

Eitzen D. Stanley and Sage, George H. Sociology of North American Sport, 5th ed. Dubuque I.A., Brown and Benchmark, 1993

Esplin, R. Down the Copland Road, Argyll: Argyll Publishing, 2000

Esplin R & Walker G (Eds) It's Rangers For Me, Fort Publishing, Ayr, Scotland, 2007

Feehan J.M. Bobby Sands and the Tragedy of Northern Ireland, Mercier Press, Dublin and Cork, 1984

Finley R.J. 'Nationalism, Race, Religion and The Irish Question in Inter-War Scotland' in The Innes Review, Vol.XLII, No.1, Spring, pp.46-67, 1991

Finn, G.P.T. 'Racism, Religion and Social Prejudice: Irish Catholic Clubs, Soccer and Scottish Society – I The Historical Roots of Prejudice' in The International Journal of the History of Sport, 8, 1, pp.72-95, 1991

Finn G.P.T. 'Racism, Religion and Social Prejudice: Irish Catholic Clubs, Soccer and Scottish Society - II Social Identities and Conspiracy Theories' in The International Journal of the History of Sport 8, 3, pp.370-397, 1991

Finn G.P.T. 'Faith, Hope and Bigotry: Case Studies of Anti-Catholic Prejudice in Scottish Soccer and Society' in Scottish Sport in the Making of the Nation: Ninety-Minute Patriots, Leicester University Press, 1994

Finn G.P.T. 'Sporting Symbols, Sporting Identities: Soccer and Intergroup Conflict in Scotland and Northern Ireland' pp.33-55 in Scotland and Ulster, I.S. Wood (ed), Mercat Press, Edinburgh, 1994

Finn G.P.T. Series of papers lodged with Jordanhill Library, Strathclyde University on the role of conspiracy in anti-Catholicism in Scotland and Northern Ireland, 1990-1994

Forgacs D. The Antonio Gramsci Reader, Lawrence and Wishart, London, 1999

Forsyth R. in Linklater M. and Denniston R. (Eds) Anatomy of Scotland: how Scotland works, Edinburgh: Chambers, pp.334-353, 1992

Fraser T.G. (ed) The Irish Parading Tradition: Following the Drum, Macmillan Press, London, 2000

Free, M. ' "Angels" with Drunken Faces? Travelling Republic of Ireland Supporters and the Construction of Irish Migrant Identity in England', in A. Brown (ed.) Fanatics! Power, Identity and Fandom in Football, London: Routledge, 1998

Gallagher D.J. 'Neutrality as a Moral Standpoint, Conceptual Confusion and the Full Inclusion Debate' Disability & Society Vol.16, No.5, pp637-654, 2001

Gallagher T. Glasgow The Uneasy Peace, Manchester University Press,1987

Gallagher T. 'The Catholic Irish in Scotland: In Search of Identity' in T.M.Devine (Ed) Irish Immigrants and Scottish Society in the Nineteenth and Twentieth Centuries, John Donald Publishers Limited, 1991

Garrett P. M 'Responding to Irish "invisibility": anti-discriminatory social work practice and the placement of Irish children in Britain', Adoption and Fostering 24.1:23-33, 2000

Gilley S. and Swift R.(Eds) The Irish in the Victorian City, Croom Helm, London, 1985

Giulianotti R. 'Scoring away from Home: A Statistical Study of Scotland Football Fans at International Matches in Romania and Sweden' International Review for Sociology of Sport 29/2, pp.172-200, 1994

Giulianotti R. 'Football and the Politics of Carnival: An Ethnographic Study of Scottish Fans in Sweden' in International Review for Sociology of Sport 30/ 2 1995, pp.191-223, 1995

Giulianotti, R. 'Taking Liberties: Hibs casuals and Scottish law' pp.229-261, in Football, Violence and Social Identity, R. Giulianotti, N. Bonney & M. Hepworth (eds), London, Routledge, 1994

Giulianotti, R. Game Without Frontiers: Football, Identity and Modernity, Aldershot, Arena Ashgate, 1994

Giulianotti R. 'Built by the Two Varelas: The Rise and Fall of Football Culture and National Identity in Uruguay' in Finn G.P.T. and Giulianotti R. Football Culture: Local Contests, Global Visions, Frank Cass, London (originally from Galeano E. (1997) 'Football: in Sun and Shadow' London p.42, 2000

Giulianotti R & Gerrard M, 'Cruel Britannia? Glasgow Rangers, Scotland and "Hot" Football Rivalries', in Armstrong, G and Giulionotti, R. (Eds), Fear and Loathing in World Football, Berg, Oxford, pp.23-42, 2001

Goulbourne, H. Race Relations in Britain since 1945, Basingstoke: Macmillan, 1998

Gramsci A. Selections from prison notebooks of Antonio Gramsci, New York, International Publishers, 1971

Greely A.M. McCready 'Does Ethnicity Matter' in Ethnicity Vol.1, No.1, April, pp.91-108, 1974

Gruneau R. & Whitson D. Hockey Night in Canada, Toronto, Canada, Garamond Press, 1993

Hall, S. 'The Question of Cultural Identity' in Hall S & Hubert D (Eds),
Modernity: An Introduction to Modern Societies, Blackwell, London,
pp.595-634, 1996

Handley J.E. The Irish in Scotland, John S Burns & Sons, Glasgow (this book
incorporates both 'The Irish in Scotland 1798-1845' and 'The Irish in
Modern Scotland' 1943 & 1947, Cork University Press, 1964

Handley J.E. The Celtic Story, Stanley Paul, London, 1960

Harding, S. and R. Balarajan 'Patterns of Mortality in Second Generation Irish
living in England and Wales: Longitudinal Study', British Medical Journal
312: 1389–92, 1996

Hargreaves J. Sport, Power and Culture – A Social and Historical Analysis of
Popular Sports in Britain, Cambridge, Polity Press, 1986

Hargreaves J. (Ed) Sport, Culture and Ideology, Routledge, pp.30-61, 1982

Hargreaves J. & McDonald I. 'Cultural Studies and the Sociology of Sport' in J.
Coakley & E. Dunning, Handbook of Sports Studies, Sage, pp.49-60,
2000

Harte, L. ' "Somewhere beyond England and Ireland": Narratives of "Home"
in Second-generation Irish Autobiography', Irish Studies Review 11(3):
293–305, 2003

Henderson, A. 'Political Constructions of National Identity in Scotland and
Quebec', Scottish Affairs, 29, 121-138, 1999

Hickman, M.J. 'A Study of Incorporation of the Irish in Britain with Special
reference to Catholic State Education: Involving a Comparison of the
Attitudes of Pupils and Teachers in Selected Secondary Schools in London
and Liverpool', Ph.D. thesis, University of London Institute of Education,
London, 1990

Hickman, M 'Integration or segregation? The education of the Irish in Britain
in Roman Catholic voluntary-aided schools' British Journal of Sociology of
education 14.3:285-301, 1993

Hickman, M.J. Religion, Class and Identity, Aldershot: Avebury,1995

Hickman M.J. 'Incorporating and denationalizing the Irish in England: the role
of the Catholic church' in P. O'Sullivan (Ed) The Irish Worldwide Volume5
Religion and identity, Leicester: University of Leicester Press, 1996

Hickman, M.J. 'Reconstructing Deconstructing "Race": British Political
Discourses about the Irish in Britain', Ethnic and Racial Studies 21(2):
288–307, 1998a

Hickman, M.J. 'Secularisation amongst Irish Catholic Emigrants and their
Descendants in Britain', in P. Brennan (Ed.) La Sécularisation en Irelande,
Caen: Presses Universitaires de Caen, 1998b

Hickman, M.J. 'The Religio-Ethnic Identities of Teenagers of Irish Descent', in
M. Hornsby-Smith (Ed.) Catholics in England 1950–2000, London:
Cassell, 1999

Hickman M.J, Morgan S. and Walter B. The second-generation Irish: a
demographic, socio-economic and health profile, London : University of
North London, 2001

Hickman, M.J. ' "Locating" the Irish Diaspora', Irish Journal of Sociology
11(1): 8–26, 2002

Hickman, M.J. 'Ruling Empire, Governing the Multi-National State: the impact of Britain's historical legacy on the contemporary ethno-racial regime', in G. Loury, T. Modood and S. Teles (eds) Ethnicity and Public Policy in the US and UK, Cambridge: Cambridge University Press (forthcoming)

Hickman, M.J and B. Walter Discrimination and the Irish Community in Britain, London: Commission for Racial Equality, 1997

Hickman, M.J, S. Morgan and B. Walter Second-Generation Irish People in Britain: A Demographic, Socio-Economic and Health Profile, London: Irish Studies Centre, University of North London, 2001

Hillyard P. Suspect community: people's experience of the prevention of Terrorism Acts in Britain, London: Pluto Press, 1993

Hoberman J. Sport and Political Ideology, Heinemann, London,1984

Hobsbawm E. Nations and Nationalism Since 1780: Programme, Myth, Reality, Cambridge: Cambridge University Press, 1990

Holmes M. 'Symbols of National Identity: The Case of the Irish National Football Team' in Irish Political Studies 9, pp.81-98, 1994

Holt R. 'Sport and History: The State of the Subject in Britain' in Twentieth Century British History Vol.7, No.2, pp.231-252, 1996

Horne J. 'Racism, Sectarianism and Football in Scotland' in Scottish Affairs 12, pp.27-51, 1995

Horne J, Tomlinson A, Whannel G. Understanding Sport, London, E&FN Spon, 1999

Inglis J 'The Irish In Britain: A Question Of Identity' in Irish Studies in Britain No.3, Spring/Summer 1982

Isajiw W. W. 'Definitions of Ethnicity' in Ethnicity Vol.1, No.2, July, pp.111-124, 1974

Jarvie G. & Maguire J. Sport and Leisure in Social Thought, London, Routledge, 1994

Jarvie G. & Reid I. 'Sport, Nationalism and Culture in Scotland' in The Sports Historian, 19, 1, pp.97-124, 1999

Jarvie G. Walker G. (eds) Scottish Sport in the Making of the Nation: Ninety Minute Patriots, Leicester University Press, 1994

Jenkins R. The Thistle and the Grail, MacDonald & Co, Glasgow, 1983

Johnson, N. 'Nation-building, language and education: the geography of teacher recruitment in Ireland, 1925-55', Political Geography 11:170-189, 1992

Kelly E. 'Challenging Sectarianism in Scotland: The Prism of Racism' in Scottish Affairs, No.42, Winter, pp.32-56, 2003

Kelly R, Celtic, Hay, Nisbet & Miller Ltd, Glasgow, 1971

Kendrick S. 'Scotland, Social Change and Politics' in The Making of Scotland: Nation, Culture and Social Change, D. McCrone, D. Kendrick & P. Straw (eds), Edinburgh University Press, 1989

Kennedy W. & Hills L. Sport, Media and Society, Berg, New York, 2009

King C.R., Staurowsky E.J., Davis L.R., Pewewardy C. 'Of Polls And Race Prejudice: Sports Illustrated Errant Indian Wars' in Vol.26, No.4, pp.381-402 2002 Journal of Sports and Social Issues

Kircaldy J. 'Irish Jokes: No Cause For Laughter' Irish Studies in Britain, No.2, Autumn/Winter 1981

Kinealy C. This Great Calamity: The Irish Famine 1845-52, Gill & Macmillan Ltd, 1994

Latin American Bishops Conference (CELAM), Medellin Documents, 1968

Law, S. 'Near and far: banal national identity and the press, Scotland', Media, Culture & Society, vol 23, pp.299-317, 2001

Lennon, M., M. McAdam and O'Brien, J. Across the Water: Irish Women's Lives in Britain, London: Virago, 1988

Lewis, G. Forming Nation, Forming Welfare, London: Routledge with the Open University Press, 1998

Logue P. (ed) Being Irish: Personal reflections of being Irish today, Oak Tree Press, Dublin, 2000

Lugton, A. The Making of Hibernian, John Donald, Edinburgh, 1999

McCaffrey J. 'Roman Catholics in Scotland in the nineteenth and twentieth centuries', Records of the Scottish Church History Society, 21, 2, 1983

McCrone D. The Sociology of Nationalism, London: Routledge, 1998

McCrone D. Rosie M. 'Left and Liberal: Catholics in modern Scotland' in Boyle R. & Lynch P. (Eds) Out of the Ghetto: The Catholic Community in Modern Scotland, Edinburgh: John Donald, 67-94, 1998

McCrone D. Understanding Scotland: the sociology of a nation, 2nd edition, Routledge, London, 2001

McCrone D. 'Who do you say you are?' Ethnicities, 2, 3, pp.301-320, 2002

McDevitt R. A Life in the Tartan Army, Glasgow: Zipo Publishing 1999

MacDonald C.M.M. Unionist Scotland 1800-1997, Edinburgh: John Donald, 1998

McFarland E.W. Protestants First: Orangeism in 19th Century Scotland, Edinburgh University Press, 1990

Mac an Ghaill, M. and C. Haywood 'Young (Male) Irelanders: Postcolonial Ethnicities – Expanding the Nation and Irishness', European Journal of Cultural Studies 6(3): 386–403, 2003

McClancy J. Nationalism at Play: The Basques of Vizcaya and Athletic Bilbao, Sport, Identity and Ethnicity, J McClancy (Ed), Berg, Oxford pp.181-199, 1996

McKenna Y. 'Forgotten Migrants: Irish Women Religious in England, 1930s-1960s' International Journal of Population Geography, 9, pp.295-308, 2003

MacLaughlin J. 'Pestilence on their backs, famine in their stomachs: the racial construction of Irishness and the Irish in Victorian Britain' in Ireland and Cultural Theory, The Mechanics of Authenticity, C. Graham, R. Kirkland (eds), Macmillan

McPherson B.D., Curtis J.E. & Loy J.W. The Social Significance of Sport, Human Kinetics, Illinois, 1989

Magee P. Gangsters or Guerrillas? Representations of Irish Republicans in Troubles Fiction, Beyond the Pale, Ireland, 2001

Maguire, M. 'Missing links: working–class women of Irish descent', in P.

Mahony and C.Zmroczek (Eds). Class matters: 'working-class' women's perspectives on social class, London: Taylor and Francis, 1997

Maver I. 'The Catholic Community in Scotland in the 20th Century' in T.M. Devine & R.J. Finley (eds) Edinburgh University Press, Edinburgh, pp.269-284, 1996

Miller D. (Ed) Rethinking Northern Ireland, Culture, Ideology and Colonialism, Addison Wesley Longman, Essex, 1998

Min P.G. and Kim R. 'Formation of ethnic and racial identities: narratives by young Asian-American professionals', Ethnic and Racial Studies 23.4:735-760, 2000

Mitchell J. 'Religion and Politics in Scotland' unpublished paper presented to Seminar on Religion and Scottish politics, University of Edinburgh, 1992

Miles R. & Muirhead L. 'Racism in Scotland: a matter for further investigation?' in Scottish Government Yearbook, pp.108-136, 1986

Miles R. Racism, Routledge, London, 1989

Mitchell M.J. The Irish in the West of Scotland 1797-1848: Trade unions, strikes and political movements, John Donald, Edinburgh, 1998

Modood, T. 'The Changing Context of "Race" in Britain: A Symposium', Patterns of Prejudice 30(1): 3–13 and 36–42, 1996

Modood, T., R. Berthoud and J. Nazroo ' "Race", Racism and Ethnicity: A Response to Ken Smith', Sociology 36(2): 419–26, 2002

Moorhouse B. 'Professional Football and working class culture: English Theories and Scottish evidence' in Sociological Review, 32, 285-315, 1984

Moorhouse B. 'Scotland Against England: Football and Popular Culture' in International Journal of the History of Sport, 4, 189-202, 1987

Morley D. & Chen K.H. (eds) Stuart Hall: Critical dialogues in cultural studies, Routledge, London, 1996

Morrow S. The People's Game?: Football, Finance and Society, Palgrave Macmillan, Basingstoke 2003

Mosely, P A, Cashman R, O'Hara J & Weatherburn H, Sporting Immigrants, Walla Walla Press, Crows Nest, NSW, Australia, 1997

Muirhead Rev. I.A. 'Catholic Emancipation: Scottish Reactions in 1829' Innes Review, 24, 1, Spring 1973

Muirhead Rev. I.A. 'Catholic Emancipation in Scotland: the debate and the aftermath' Innes Review, 24, 2, Autumn 1973

Murphy B, The Origins and Organisation of British Propaganda in Ireland 1920, Aubane Historical Society & Spinwatch, 2006

Murray B. The Old Firm: Sectarianism, sport and society in Scotland, John Donald, Edinburgh, 1984

Murray B. Glasgow's Giants: 100 years of the Old Firm, Mainstream, Edinburgh, 1988

Murray B. Bhoys, Bears and Bigotry: The Old Firm in the New Age, Mainstream, Edinburgh, 2003

Nixon H.L. & Frey J.H. A Sociology of Sport, London, Wadsworth, 1996

Nora P. 'Between memory and history: les lieux de memoire' Representations 26: 7-25, 1989

O'Conner K. The Irish in Britain, Torc, Dublin, 1970

O'Hara B, Davitt, Mayo County Council in association with The Michael Davitt Association, 2006

O'Sullivan P. (Ed) 'The Meaning of Famine' in The Irish World Wide: History, Heritage, Identity, Vol Six, Leicester University Press, London, 1997

O Tuathaigh M.A.G. 'The Irish in Nineteenth Century Britain: Problems of Integration' pp.13-36, in Gilley and Swift, The Irish in the Victorian City, 1985

Parekh, B. Report of the Commission on the Future of Multi-Ethnic Britain. London, Runnymede Trust, 2000

Rattansi, A. 'On Being And Not Being Brown/Black-British: Racism, Class, Sexuality and Ethnicity in Post-imperial Britain', interventions 2(1): 118–34, 2000

Reid I. 'Nationalism, Sport and Scotland's Culture' in Scottish Centre Research Papers in Sport, Leisure and Society, Vol.2, 1997

Ricento, T. 'The discursive construction of Americanism' in Discourse and Society, vol 15 (5), pp.611-637, 2003

Ritzer G, The MacDonaldization of Society, Pine Forge Press, California, 1996

Rosie M. & McCrone D. 'The Past is History: Catholics in Modern Scotland' in Scotland's Shame: Bigotry and sectarianism in Modern Scotland, Mainstream, Edinburgh, pp199-217, 2000

Rowe D. & Wood N. (Eds) Editorial of Media, Culture and Society, Vol.18, No.4, 1996

Runnymede Trust, The future of multi-ethnic Britain – The Parekh Report, London: Profile Books, 2000

Schlesinger P. 'Media, the Political Order and National Identity' in Media, Culture and Society, Vol.13, No.3, pp.297-308, 1991

Silverstein, P. 'Realizing Myth. Berbers in France and Algeria', Middle East Report July–September: 11–15, 1996

Stone, C. 'The Role of Football in Everyday Life', Soccer & Society, vol 8, no 2/3, pp.169-184, 2007

Sugden J. & Bairner A. 'Northern Ireland; Sport in a Divided Society' in Allison L. The Politics Of Sport, pp.90-117, Manchester University Press, 1986

Sugden J. & Bairner A. Sport, Sectarianism and Society in a Divided Ireland, Leicester University Press, Leicester, 1993

Sugden J. & Tomlinson A. (Eds) Hosts and Champions: Soccer Cultures, National Identities and the USA World Cup, Aldershot: Arena, Ashgate, 1994

Sugden J & Tomlinson A. 'Sport, politics and identities: Football cultures in comparative perspective', in M Roche (ed), Sport, popular culture and identity, CSRC Edition 5, Aachen, Meyer & Meyer, pp.169-192, 1998

Ullah, P. 'Second Generation Irish Youth: Identity and Ethnicity', New Community 12(2): 310–20, 1985

Ullah, P. 'Rhetoric and Ideology in Social Identification: The Case of Second Generation Irish Youth', Discourse and Society 1(2): 167–85, 1990

Walker G. 'There's not a team like the Glasgow Rangers: football and religious identity in Scotland' in G. Walker & T. Gallagher (Eds) Sermons and Battle Hymns: Protestant Culture in Modern Scotland, Edinburgh: Edinburgh University Press, 1990

Walls P. & Williams R. 'Sectarianism at work: Accounts of employment discrimination against Irish Catholics in Scotland' in Ethnic and Racial Studies, Vol.26, No.4, pp.632-662, 2003

Walter, B. 'Challenging the Black/White Binary: The Need for an Irish Category in the 2001 Census', Patterns of Prejudice 32(2): 73–86, 1998

Walter, B. Outsiders Inside. Whiteness, Place and Irish Women, London: Routledge, 2001

Walter, B. ' "Shamrocks Growing out of their Mouths": Language and the Racialisation of the Irish in Britain', in Kershen, A. (Ed.) Language, Labour and Migration, Abingdon: Ashgate, 2000

Walter B. 'Time-space patterns of second wave Irish settlement in British towns', Transactions Institute of British Geographers, New Series 5:297-317, 1980

Walter, B., S. Morgan, M.J Hickman and J. Bradley 'Family Stories, Public Silence: Irish Identity Construction among the Second Generation in England', Scottish Geographical Journal 118(3): 201–17, 2002

Walvin J. The People's Game: The History of Football Revisited, Edinburgh, Mainstream, 1994

Warfield, D. & Daly, R. Celtic & Ireland in Song and Story, published in Ireland by authors, 2008

Wilson B. Celtic, A Century with Honour, Willow Books, William Collins Publications, Glasgow, 1988

Young, I.M. Justice and the Politics of Difference, Princeton, NJ: Princeton University Press, 1990

Younge, G. 'On Race and Englishness', in S. Chen and T. Wright (Eds) The English Question, London: Fabian Society, 2000

Yuval-Davis, N. 'Contemporary Agenda for the Study of Ethnicity', Symposium on Ethnicity, Ethnicities 1(1): 11–13, 2001